The Discerning Heart

# The Discerning Heart
## Discovering a Personal God

### Maureen Conroy, R.S.M.

Loyola Press

Chicago

Loyola Press
3441 North Ashland Avenue
Chicago, Illinois 60657

Cover and interior design by Nancy Gruenke

**Library of Congress Cataloging-in-Publication Data**
Conroy, Maureen, 1948–
    The discerning heart: discovering a personal God/
Maureen Conroy.
        p. cm.
    Includes the Rules for discernment from Ignatius of Loyola's
Spiritual exercises.
    Includes bibliographical references and index.
    ISBN 0-8294-0752-9
    1. Ignatius, of Loyola, Saint, 1491–1556. Exercitia spiritualia.
    2. Spiritual direction. I. Ignatius, of Loyola, Saint, 1491–1556.
Exercitia spiritualia. English. 1993. II. Title.
BX2179.L8C65 1993
248.2--dc20                                          93-12508
                                                     CIP


01  00  99  98  97           5  4  3  2  1

# Dedication

*This book is dedicated to all individuals whose personal relationship with God is like the air they breathe: their lives without God would be like life without air—they would soon wither and die.*

*It is also dedicated to all spiritual directors, whose deepest commitment is to help people grow in their relationship with God.*

# In Memoriam

*This book is written in memory of two "soul friends"—Patrick McCarthy and John Muthig—two priests who died at a very young age.*

Patrick and I were shuffleboard partners when I taught at Creighton University in the summer of 1986. The following year Patrick was in my course on the Rules for Discernment. We became good friends as we shared what meant most to us: our love for God and our desire to help people grow in a personal relationship with God. Patrick died a tragic death at age thirty-seven. In death we have remained "soul friends."

John came to me for spiritual direction for more than five years. I knew his heart and soul like no one else. His passionate love for God and desire to bring people closer to our all-loving God was an edification to me. John died suddenly at age forty-two. In death we also continue to be "soul friends."

Patrick and John were extremely gifted men. Both have been a gift to me and are a vital part of my Communion of Saints. I write this book in memory of and in gratitude to them for being such a special part of my life and spiritual journey.

# Contents

## Part IV: Education

# Foreword

In the past twenty-five years both spiritual direction and the individually directed retreat have enjoyed popularity as more and more Christians have felt the need to talk to someone about their prayer. Training programs for spiritual directors and for directors of retreats have proliferated. The language of the tradition has once again become somewhat current. Among the traditional spiritualities the one spawned by Ignatius of Loyola more than 450 years ago has had a featured place in this revival. We read and hear about the *Spiritual Exercises,* about "finding God in all things," about the First Week experience, and about discernment of spirits. Often enough these terms are bandied about as though they were coin of the realm, terms everyone understands. Often enough, too, they are discussed in theoretical or historical fashion, or both. The concrete meaning of these terms, that is, what experiences they refer to, is not often part of the discussion. Moreover, some of these terms, especially *discernment of spirits,* take on an aura of the arcane and the esoteric, something foreign to the ordinary experience of Christian people. *The Discerning Heart* aims to remedy that situation.

Maureen Conroy has, for many years, practiced the art of spiritual direction both in a retreat setting and in daily life. Also for many years she has been engaged in the work of training others as spiritual directors. In this timely and insightful book she brings to bear the experience and knowledge she has gained from hours of listening to others talk about their experiences and encounter with God. By focusing on experience she brings to life a work, Rules for Discernment, that was written almost five centuries ago. Initially she focuses on the experiences that led Ignatius to formulate these "rules." By a skillful use of his autobiography, she helps the reader to understand how the various rules emerged from Ignatius' own, often bitter, experience. Then, in a series of chapters, she describes the experiences of ordinary Christians of our day and, with great insight and sensitivity, demonstrates that the same principles that Ignatius discovered in his experience are at work in modern America. She uses conversations with spiritual directors to very good effect not only to demonstrate Ignatius' rules in action but also to illuminate the work of the spiritual director.

*The Discerning Heart* will be helpful not only to spiritual directors but also to Christians who want to develop their prayer life. The latter will find helpful hints about prayer and discernment and will also get a feel for how spiritual direction can be helpful to anyone seeking to develop a personal relationship with God.

I recommend the book highly.

William A. Barry, S.J.
Author, *Spiritual Direction*
Boston, Massachusetts
March 1993

# Preface

Developing a discerning heart is both an art and a skill. When we are in our artist mode, we pay attention to the mystery and beauty of God's personal love for us. We are able to be present with God in a receiving, open-ended, and contemplative way. We can listen with a free heart to the quiet whispers and the profound revelations of God's tender love. A beautiful tapestry of love is being woven in our hearts, and we become aware of the colorful, rich texture of who we are in God. We are like sponges, absorbing the refreshing living water of God's overflowing love.

When we are in our skillful stance, we sift through our reactions to God's outpouring of love. At times we allow God's loving presence to seep into our heart, spirit, mind, and body. At other times we resist God's loving touch because of the areas of darkness and brokenness within us. Most times we do not deliberately run from God. Our desire to be one with God persists, but unredeemed aspects of ourselves cause us spontaneously to move away. Even these movements away from God, however, are a result of God's loving actions: the light of God's permeating love is lighting up the darkness of our unredeemed self. We become aware of the loose threads on the other side of the tapestry that seem to have no rhyme or reason. We need to sift through these loose ends and see their connection with the beauty and mystery of God's powerful revelations of love.

Developing a discerning heart means being attentive to the movements and countermovements within, which are a result of God's intimate involvement with us. It is about discovering a personal God who embraces both our darkness and our light because in God's eyes "darkness and light are the same" (Ps. 139:12). It means striving to find God in all the realities of our life—the inner dimensions of our mind, heart, spirit, imagination, and memory and the outer aspects of our relationships, community, work, leisure, and world.

This book is about the development of a discerning heart by entering into an affective, lively relationship with God. It uses Ignatius of Loyola's Rules for Discernment as a framework. It concretely delves into the experience of interior movements: those moments of consolation or movement when we feel affectively in tune with God and, thus, interiorly free; and those experiences of desolation and countermovement when we feel distant from God, in darkness, and are caught in our unredeemed self. A basic tenet is that when we are discovering God in a personal way, we spontaneously experience movement toward and away from God. The development of a discerning heart is about sifting through these interior movements so that we can choose those movements that ultimately bring us to deeper union with God and reject those that draw us away from God's loving heart.

I pray that as you read these chapters and follow along with the prayer experiences at the end of each chapter you will experience the powerful art and develop the vigilant skill of a discerning heart. I pray too that you realize more deeply the beautiful colors, the rich textures, and nagging loose ends of your life with God.

# Introduction
# Our Experience of God

We all have stories to tell. Most of us focus on the outer details of our lives. A few delve into the deeper reality of feelings, hopes, and dreams. Our most intimate revelations are those that describe our interior experiences of joy, pain, desire, and hope. One of our most moving stories, and often the scariest to tell, is our experience of God. Some people's experience is secondary and is focused primarily on religious practices. Others' experience of God, which is rooted in deep feeling, strong desire, and lived experience, is the foundation of all stories. Their experience develops into a lively personal relationship with God that affects every part of their inner being and outer life. For them, life without a personal relationship with God is like life without air.

In my ministry of spiritual direction, God has given me the beautiful gift of listening to individual experiences of God. Again and again God offers me the profound privilege of entering into other people's most vulnerable struggles and helping them to discover God. Daily I am moved by the depth, the pain, the joy of their developing relationship. Each day a beautiful and colorful tapestry of lively religious experience unfolds before me. Truly, as I listen and enter into the profound ways that God loves each individual, I grow more deeply aware that together, in spiritual direction, we hold a treasure more precious than any other on earth.

Ignatius of Loyola, a spiritual director who has inspired many spiritual directors during the past four centuries, listened to innumerable stories of God. He helped individuals open themselves to experience God in a personal way. Then he helped them to recognize, understand, and respond to their experience and to see the differences in themselves as a result of God's touch. He did this so well for others because he did it so well within himself. Ignatius strove earnestly to find God in all things and to understand the interior process he underwent as he discovered this all-present and all-loving God. He told his own story of these inner discoveries in his autobiography. Ignatius recognized common dynamics in spiritual growth and discovered many ways to help people grow in an intimate and lively relationship with God and to understand the various interior movements that occurred within them as they experienced God. In the *Spiritual Exercises* and Rules for Discernment, he wrote down universal dynamics, suggestions for prayer, and ways to recognize, understand, and respond to interior movements.[1]

*The Discerning Heart* is about people's experiences of God and how the Rules for Discernment can help us deepen and understand our relationship with God. Although called *rules,* they are really *descriptions* of what happens to people as they relate to God in a personal way. They also serve as *guidelines* for understanding and sifting through spiritual experiences.[2] Beginning with Ignatius' experiences and then moving to experiences of contemporary people, this book describes stories of discovering a personal God—and the pain and joy that results—and explores the various interior movements that occur in relating affectively to God. Further, the book reflects on the approach spiritual directors take to help people experience God, to help them enjoy their experience, and to help them notice and understand subsequent interior movements and deep changes. Thus, three questions are explored:

1. What happens when people experience God and strive to grow in a personal relationship with God?

2. How do the Rules facilitate the understanding of the individual experience of God?

3. How does spiritual direction help foster the individual relationship with God, and how can the Rules and the Annotations assist spiritual directors?[3]

I consider these questions by:

1. Reflecting on Ignatius' experiences of God as described in his autobiography while exploring the relationships between these experiences and the Rules for Discernment;

2. Describing examples of contemporary people's experiences of God and reflecting on these experiences in light of the Rules;

3. Considering the approach of the spiritual director in relation to these Rules and the Annotations; and

4. Offering suggestions for prayer that can help people savor and explore their own experiences of God.

## Reasons for an Experiential Exploration

Both my spiritual journey and my ministry of spiritual direction have moved me to explore the Rules for Discernment experientially. In my own growing relationship with God, the Rules have helped me understand more clearly what is happening in my interior life. For example, more than twenty years ago, near the end of my thirty-day directed retreat, I experienced a dynamic that Ignatius refers to as "evil under the appearance of good."[4] At the time, I had little knowledge of the Rules, but my spiritual director briefly explored this dynamic with me in the context of my experience, which helped me understand the subtle ways in which I sometimes move away from God. Many times since then I have returned to this experience in light of Ignatius' explanation because that same tendency still exists within me. I continue to gain further insight into my own subtle, and sometimes unconscious, movement away from God.

Another example occurred when I experienced a strong temptation over a period of time, and God seemed absent as I struggled against it to remain faithful. Ignatius' description of desolation, the reasons for its existence, and what to do during desolate experiences provided me with helpful tools for self-understanding and offered guidelines to discern concrete actions.[5] In general, through using the Rules to reflect on my own experience I have become more keenly attentive to my own spontaneous movements toward and away from God and have discovered how consolation and desolation can reveal specific truths about God and about God's incarnate presence in me.

In offering ongoing spiritual direction, directed retreats, and supervision to spiritual directors, I have realized the great need for a more experiential approach to the Rules in order to help spiritual directors understand them more concretely and to use them more practically. First, much has been published about the foundational, theological, textual, and contextual dimensions of these Rules,[6] but little has been published in English regarding their pastoral, experiential, and practical aspects. Further, not much in the way of *actual experiences* of people as they undergo various interior movements in relation to the Rules has been published. Thus, I explore a key question: what do the dynamics of the Rules *look like* in individual experiences of God?

Second, the published literature on the practical use of the Rules has been confined mostly to applying them prayerfully in decision making.[7] Although this is essential, a need also exists to use them to recognize and understand interior movements *before* a decision is made as well as when no decisions are necessary. The Rules are *descriptive* of life with God and *foundational* for decisions affecting life circumstances. Therefore, I ask: how can the Rules help people *be attentive* to the inner movements of their life with God, and how can these inner movements result in differences in their interior lives and in their daily living?

Third, Ignatius formulated the Rules from his own lively experience of God and others.[8] Lively experience happened first; then came the attempt to understand experience. We need to explore and use the Rules in a similar fashion: to listen and observe our own—and others'—experiences of God; to reflect on the movements and patterns of these experiences in order to understand them more deeply; and to draw conclusions and guiding principles to help people grow in their relationship with God. Thus, I discuss what experientially happens when individuals relate to God; how the Rules address interior concerns; and specific ways that spiritual directors can use the Rules to help their directees *facilitate* and *understand* their experiences.

Fourth, in order for the Rules to be more meaningful for modern people, we must see them from a contemporary perspective. That is, we need to observe how they are operative in the lives and religious experience of twentieth-century people rather than from the cultural perspective of the sixteenth century. Ignatius derived these Rules from his experience of sixteenth-century Christians. Hence, I wonder: how can the Rules concretely relate to the spiritual lives of contemporary people?

Finally, experiential knowledge of the Rules can sensitize spiritual directors to pay attention to the inner motions of directees, can facilitate their understanding of the dynamics of growth in relationship with God, and can offer them principles that will help them use the Rules appropriately. To gain this experiential knowledge we need to observe the dynamics and use of the Rules in ongoing spiritual direction and directed retreats. Therefore, I ask: what should be the approach of the director while using the Rules practically in ongoing spiritual direction and during directed retreats?

In this book, I will explore my own ministry of spiritual direction as well as the experiences of other directors and will synthesize insights about these experiences in relation to the Rules for Discernment. I will delve into experiences, such as Consolation without Previous Cause,[9] with these questions in mind: how does Consolation without Previous Cause appear in a person's experience of God, and how do the Rules relate to this experience? Jesus says, "Come and see" (Jn. 1:39). In listening to others share their experience of God in spiritual direction and supervision sessions, I have observed various aspects of the Rules come alive. Through this observation, I have been better able to help people grow in their affective experience of and personal relationship with God.

## An Unfolding Process

The contents of this book unfolded over a period of seven years. In listening to and reflecting on people's experiences of the Rules, I have gained valuable insights. This unfolding process involved three steps:

1. On my own, and with other spiritual directors, I explored interior movements that occur in people's prayer when they relate to God in a personal way;

2. I examined these experiences with respect to the Rules for Discernment and the Annotations; and

3. I reflected on various writings about the Rules for Discernment in relation to these actual experiences.

The *exploratory approach* of this endeavor reflects the purpose and process of the Rules themselves. Ignatius begins his summation of the Rules with: "Rules for *understanding* to some extent the *different movements produced* in the soul and for *recognizing* those that are good to *admit* them, and those that are bad, to *reject* them . . ."[10] (my emphasis).

When Ignatius says "different movements produced," he assumes that something, even if it is minimal, is happening in our relationship with God. These different movements do not happen in isolation, but in a relationship. They do not take place unless we have experienced God in a personal way, even if it be the slightest of experiences.

My perspective is grounded in the same fundamental principle: In determining someone's readiness for spiritual direction, a spiritual director strives to determine that, at the very least, an individual has a *felt desire* to grow in a personal relationship with God, even if the desire initially is nebulous. Desire indicates that God is stirring within the person's heart, and the person is beginning to be aware of God's quiet stirrings.

The Rules help us to "recognize" and "understand" these different movements. The movements toward and away from God stirred by our relationship with God are already taking place. The Rules are intended to facilitate our awareness and understanding of them.

My approach reflects this purpose. I consider Ignatius' experience of God in light of the dynamics of the Rules for Discernment. I also observe various interior movements in people during spiritual direction sessions in order to better understand what happens when God acts in people and when they respond to God.

The reason for recognizing and understanding these different movements is to help directees "admit" those that will lead to greater spiritual growth and to "reject" those that will not. Directees, with the help of directors, can use these Rules to grow closer to God by moving with and moving against those interior motions that lead toward and away from God. Recognition and understanding lead to decision and action.

In the Annotations, Ignatius mentions ways that spiritual directors can apply the Rules. I explore the approach of the spiritual director and offer some practical ways that directors can use the Rules to facilitate a person's movement toward God.

The contents of this book, then, have a threefold thrust: the exploration of the individual experience of and relationship with God, including that of Ignatius himself as well as those of contemporary people; reflection on the role of spiritual direction in fostering growth in people's experience and relationship; and suggested ways for readers to pray with their own experiences of God.

## For Whom Is This Book Intended?

*The Discerning Heart* is for people who have varying types of interests. First, it is written for individuals who want to gain a greater understanding of what happens within themselves and others as they experience God and grow in a personal relationship with God. Second, it is for people who desire to enter into a more lively experience of God. Through reading other people's experiences of God, our own hearts can be stirred. Religious experience has a rippling effect: one person's growing relationship with God can inspire another's openness to and desire for a closer union with God. Third, it is written for people who want to grow in an experiential knowledge of the *Spiritual Exercises* and Rules for Discernment. Fourth, it is intended for spiritual directors who want to deepen their knowledge of the dynamics and use of the Rules for Discernment and the Annotations in spiritual direction.

The book is divided into four parts. The first three sections are of interest to a general audience. The last section, however, is intended primarily for spiritual directors. These practical learning tools can be particularly helpful for beginning spiritual directors who are developing their discernment skills.

Part I, Evolution, explores Ignatius' spiritual experiences in relation to the Rules for Discernment. It illustrates how various aspects of the Rules evolved from Ignatius' own experience and provides a focus for exploring contemporary people's experiences of God.

Part II, Environment, provides a backdrop for looking at the religious experience of contemporary people. First, it examines the various dynamics and dimensions of personal growth in our relationship with God and how these dynamics relate to the *Spiritual Exercises.* Second, it discusses how spiritual direction fosters our relationship with God.

Part III, Enfleshment, explores contemporary experiences of God by individuals in spiritual direction in relation to the Rules as well as the approach of their spiritual directors in light of both the Annotations and the Rules. The final chapter provides readers with prayer exercises to reflect on their spiritual journey and to enable them to write their own story of God.

Part IV, Education, offers practical learning tools for spiritual directors, both for individual and group learning; presents two case studies for further exploration into the dynamics of the Rules for Discernment; and discusses implications and raises questions related to the ministry of spiritual direction.

Suggestions for prayer that can help readers remember, relive, and explore their own experiences of God appear at the end of each chapter in Parts I, II, and III. These suggestions are followed by questions for reflection and discussion that can be used individually or discussed with others and questions and exercises for spiritual directors that can be pondered individually or explored with other spiritual directors.

## A Note on References

References to the *Spiritual Exercises,* the Rules for Discernment (paragraphs 313–336), and the Annotations (paragraphs 1–20) are made according to an internationally accepted method: references are to paragraphs rather than pages and appear in parentheses immediately following a given point rather than as a note. Except for chapters 4 and 5, in which I use two translations of the *Spiritual Exercises,* all other references to the *Spiritual Exercises* are from Louis J. Puhl's translation.

## Conclusion

My hope is that as you read you will discover not only the sacredness of other people's experiences but also the richness of your own. My desire is that you gain not only theoretical knowledge about the Rules for Discernment but also experiential knowledge of their various dynamics. My prayer is that the lively experiences described will inspire you to draw even closer to God and move you to savor even more deeply the sacred treasure—Jesus, our Lord—that lives within you.

# Part I

# Evolution

**Ignatius' Spiritual Experiences
in Light of the Rules for Discernment**

# 1

# Ignatius' Initial Experience of Interior Movements

Ignatius' spiritual journey is a vibrant one. In his autobiography, Ignatius focuses both on his life circumstances and on his interior experiences. However, his deeper purpose is to describe his experience of God. He shares various facts about the unfolding of his life, yet the richness and beauty of his story lies in the description of his interior movements. Ignatius' autobiography is primarily the story of his inner journey.

At the age of sixty-two, and after much encouragement from others, Ignatius feels a "great inclination and devotion . . . to make known all that had taken place in his soul up to that moment."[1] He decides to share his story with Luis González de Camara, who takes great care to write down verbatim Ignatius' words.[2] When Luis asked Ignatius how the *Spiritual Exercises* came into being, "he answered that the Exercises were not composed all at one time, but things that he had observed in his own soul and found useful and which he thought would be useful to others, he put into writing."[3] These writings took the form of the Rules for Discernment, which are a part of the *Spiritual Exercises*.

In his spiritual autobiography, Ignatius describes the various motions that arise within, the changes that take place in his heart, and the differences in his life and relationships with others—all resulting from a personal encounter with God. He shares the struggle, the pain, and the desolation as well as the joy, the energy, and the consolation that result from relating personally to God. With great clarity, Ignatius shares his spiritual experiences, remembering specific exterior facts of time, place, and circumstance as well as interior details of thought, feeling, and awareness (or lack of awareness)—differences he noticed as a result of these experiences. He reveals the development of a discerning heart; that is, the growth in his capacity to be open to God's self-communication, his ability to notice differences in his interior reactions to this self-communication, and his capacity to recognize the inner and outer effects resulting from God's touch. Ignatius' inner journey takes place in the pervasive environment of a discerning mind, heart, and spirit.

In chapters 1 through 3, I will focus on Ignatius' experience of God and interior movements. I will also explore various dimensions of Ignatius' spiritual experiences and examine them in light of the Rules for Discernment. These chapters enflesh the Rules and set the stage for the stories of contemporary people in Part III.

## Ignatius' Conversion Experience

Key elements in the *Spiritual Exercises* and the Rules for Discernment originate from Ignatius' conversion experience. Because Ignatius realized how essential this experience was to his spiritual development, he vividly describes key outer and inner facts.[4] He reflected on his conversion many times throughout his life and continued to learn from it.

Ignatius was born in 1491 to a wealthy family in Spain. He came from one of the twenty-four families of the Basque nobility in Guipúzcoa. The youngest in his Catholic family, he grew up with five sisters and seven brothers. The Catholic rulers, Ferdinand of Aragon and Isabella of Castile, governed Spain when Ignatius was born. One year after Ignatius' birth, in 1492, Christopher Columbus "discovered" America in the service of Queen Isabella.[5]

Ignatius lived during the era of kings and queens, princes and princesses, nobles and lords, knights and chivalry. Ignatius was drenched in the secular values of his time. His heart was focused on the glories of knighthood and furthering his ambition as a soldier. A competitive and strong-willed person, he was often involved in duels and fights. He devoted himself to women and, like any ambitious knight at the time, he fought battles for women of royalty with whom he was infatuated. His life was turned around, however, at the age of twenty-six.

When Ignatius was fighting a battle against the French, he suffered a serious leg injury. For months he stayed in bed recuperating. During that time he asked for books on the adventures of the knights, which he was accustomed to reading. However, since there were none available, he was given a life of Christ and the lives of the saints. As a result of his reading and pondering, a profound conversion took place.[6]

Ignatius told the story of his conversion thirty-six years after its occurrence, yet it was still alive in him. Luis González notes: "The Father's way of telling his story is what he uses in all things. It is done with such clearness that it makes the whole past present to the beholder."[7] Ignatius shares this and his other experiences clearly, concretely, and vibrantly. Although I have paraphrased Ignatius' story, I have used many of his words, particularly in his description of his inner experience (key words and phrases that relate to his affective experiences are highlighted in bold). Ignatius told his story in the third person; I retell it here from a first person perspective:

> By the frequent reading of these books, I **conceived some affection** for what I found there narrated. Pausing in my reading, I gave myself up to thinking over what I read. At other times I dwelt on things of the world which formerly had occupied my thoughts. One vain thought took such possession of my heart that without realizing it, **I spent two, three, four hours at a time thinking about it.**[8] I'd imagine myself being in the service of a certain lady of high nobility. I'd lie there for hours thinking of things I would say to her and promises I would make her. I'd imagine myself winning battles for her, and I'd make up all these poems to recite to her.

However, **our Lord came to my assistance** for **He saw that these thoughts were succeeded by others which sprang from the things I was reading.** I'd often pause and think: "Suppose that I should do what St. Francis did, what St. Dominic did?" I often thought of doing things difficult and important, saying to myself: "St. Dominic and St. Francis did these things, therefore I must do them." These thoughts would **last a good while**, then worldly thoughts would come back and **last for a long time.**

This **succession of diverse thoughts** was of long duration, either of worldly achievements or those of God. They **took hold of my imagination to such an extent** that **worn out with the struggle**, I turned my attention to other things.[9]

**There was, however, this difference.** When I was thinking of things of the world, I was **filled with delight**, but when I dismissed them from weariness I was **dry and dissatisfied.**

And when I thought of going barefoot to Jerusalem and of eating nothing but herbs and doing other disciplines the saints did, I was **consoled** not only when I entertained these thoughts, but even after dismissing them I **remained cheerful and satisfied.**

I paid no attention to this, nor did I stop to **weigh the difference**, until one day **my eyes were opened a little** and I began to **wonder at the difference and reflect on it. I learned from experience** that one kind of thought left me **sad** and the other **cheerful.** Thus, **step by step** I came to **recognize the difference** between these two interior movements, the one being from my own sinfulness and vanity and the other from God.

I gained **no little light** from this reading and began to think more seriously of my past life and the great need to do penance. It was during this reading that these **desires of imitating the saints** came to me but with no further thought of circumstances than of **promising to do with God's grace what they had done.** What I **desired** to do most of all, as soon as I was restored to health, was to go to Jerusalem, undertaking all the disciplines and abstinences that a generous soul on fire with the love of God desires.

The thoughts of the past were soon forgotten in the presence of these holy desires, which were confirmed by the following vision. One night, I saw clearly the likeness of our Lady with the holy child Jesus, of which I received most abundant consolation for a considerable interval of time. I felt so great a disgust with my past life, especially with its offenses of the flesh, that all such images that had formerly occupied my mind were wiped out. And from that hour until now as this is being written, **I never again consented to the least suggestion of the flesh.** This effect would seem to indicate that the vision was from God, although I never ventured to affirm it positively. But my brother and other members of the family easily recognized the **change** that had taken place in the **interior** of my soul from what they saw in my **outward manner.**

Without a care in the world I went on with my reading and good resolutions. All the time I spent with people in the house I devoted to God and spiritually they profited greatly. I took **great delight** in the books I was reading. I began to write passages very carefully in a book, the words of Christ in red ink and those of our Lady in blue. Part of my time I spent in writing and part of it in prayer. My **greatest consolation** was to gaze upon the heavens and the stars, which I did often for long stretches of time, because when doing so I felt within myself **a powerful urge to be serving our Lord.** I gave much time to thinking about this, desiring to be entirely well so I could begin.[10]

## Three Important Moments in Ignatius' Story

### First Moment: The Affective Experience Itself

The affective experience takes place in the environment of ordinary human experience, such as reading or remembering. Looking for something to do to pass the time, Ignatius asked for reading material. He read stories about people devoted to

God, and he remembered stories about people living in the world. The reading and remembering moved to a stage of prolonged pondering. He paused to think over what he read and, at other times, he dwelled on things of the world. His reflection engaged his imagination and heart. God drew Ignatius to spiritual realities through his feelings. He "conceived with affection" what he found narrated in the books.

However, his heart was absorbed in self-centered achievements. One vain worldly thought "took possession of his heart." A succession of diverse thoughts existed between two types of pondering—that of the world and that of God. Desire related to achievement is precipitated; initially this desire is rooted in vanity. His reaction was to become "worn out from the struggle," and he responded by turning his attention to other matters. Different affective reactions resulted. He had similar feelings while dwelling upon each set of thoughts—thinking of worldly things "fills him with delight," pondering things of God "consoles" him. However, a marked difference in his affectivity occurs after dwelling on each reality—reflecting on worldly achievements left him "dry and dissatisfied" but thinking of achievements for God left him "cheerful and satisfied."

### Second Moment: Noticing, Savoring, and Understanding the Affective Experience

All these feelings were felt, then inner awareness and insight took place. Ignatius' inner awareness had various dimensions. It also followed a logical progression: it was gradual (his "eyes were opened a little"); it involved savoring and thinking (he began "to wonder at the difference and reflect on it"). Ignatius gained insight from the experience ("learning from the experience . . ."). Further, he grew in understanding ("he came to recognize the difference") in his affective reactions of delight and dryness, satisfaction and dissatisfaction.

### Third Moment: The Results of the Experience

Not only did Ignatius experience differences in affective reactions—and gradually came to understand these differences—but also he experienced deeper affective changes of heart, desire, attitude, and behavior. The experience and understanding of these affective differences led him to a more serious examination of his past life and to the deeper realization of his great need to do penance. His desires became holy desires rooted in a love of God, rather than a vain desire to achieve. Through an explicit experience of God—his vision of Mary and Jesus—he experienced a deep affective movement and a great disgust for his past that eradicated all lustful images. He also underwent a deep inner change of attitude and desire—never again did he give consent to any desires of the flesh. He experienced interior freedom ("without a care in the world") and savored spiritual realities by writing out the words of Jesus and Mary. He spent hours contemplating the heavens and stars, which filled him with a powerful urge to serve God. He considered a specific life-style as a way of perpetual penance. Thus, Ignatius underwent a deepening of his experience of God that resulted in a deeper change of heart and outer changes in daily living and relationships with others. All this occurred from the inside out. God moving deep within him produced differences of affective responses, changes in deep-rooted attitudes, thoughts, and feelings, and a shift in behavior.

## Relationship to the Rules for Discernment

### Purpose of the Rules

Ignatius derived the purpose and use of the Rules for Discernment from his conversion experience. He begins:

> Rules for understanding to some extent the different movements produced in the soul and for recognizing those that are good to admit them, and those that are bad, to reject them.[11]

As the above quote makes clear, the purpose of the Rules for Discernment includes five key dynamics: (1) different movements; (2) God's action; (3) understanding; (4) recognizing; and (5) admitting and rejecting.

**Different movements**. Ignatius experienced various movements for a long period of time—days and weeks—before he noticed and understood their differences. Through the experience of consolations and desolations, God was freeing a deep-rooted disorder—Ignatius' vanity, which was manifesting itself in his desire to achieve. The more constant and pervasive the movements, the more weary Ignatius became because God was purifying his tendency toward vanity.

**God's action.** God's personal involvement caused interior reactions in Ignatius' heart and spirit. Through reading and pondering the life of Jesus and the lives of the saints, Ignatius realized that God was touching his inner world. Ignatius experienced consolation when his interior life was in tune with God's interior life. He experienced desolation when his imagination, thoughts, desires, and feelings were focused on worldly things.

**Understanding.** The Spanish word for understand, *sentir,* means to know by the senses, by feeling.[12] It means a "felt-knowledge," that is, an affective, intuitive knowledge possessed through the reaction of human feelings to exterior and interior experience.[13] Ignatius had an affective reaction in pondering the things of God and the world ("delighted," "consoled," "dry," "dissatisfied," "cheerful," "satisfied"), and he began to "wonder" and "reflect" on the difference. Ignatius' wondering was rooted in his affective reactions. A felt awareness was growing as he wondered and pondered.

**Recognizing.** Ignatius had a felt knowledge of the difference in his reactions and then moved to understand the difference with his mind (*cognoscer* means to learn from experience or recognize the difference). He felt and savored his interior reactions to God's movement, then understood, formed an opinion, and gained insight into his inner motions.

**Admit or reject.** Through God's personal involvement, undergoing affective reactions to God's presence, noticing these reactions, and understanding them, Ignatius consciously chose to receive those feelings that brought him closer to God and reject those that moved him away. For a long time, he experienced affective reactions in his pondering, felt a difference, and observed and understood more about the difference before the deeper effects were felt. These deeper effects included holy desires rooted in a love for God, lasting freedom from temptations of the flesh, and a change in his outward manner that flowed from his interior freedom. These choices to admit God-centered movements and reject flesh-centered reactions flowed naturally from experiencing and understanding differences in his interior motions. Although containing some degree of awareness, the choice Ignatius makes is more a natural and spontaneous one evolving from all that preceded it interiorly, a spontaneous choice that was confirmed through a vivid experience of God, that is, the vision of Mary and Jesus.

The Rules for Discernment, as in Ignatius' experience of God, suggests that movement toward God (admitting) and away from God (rejecting) must be deeply rooted in felt awareness and understanding. The more deeply interior movements are felt, savored, and understood, the clearer and freer is the choice to receive or reject certain inner motions. For instance, when Ignatius saw the likeness of Mary and the child Jesus (an experience of God) and "received more abundant consolation," he "felt so great a disgust with his past life, especially offenses of the flesh" (strong interior reactions), that "he thought all such images which formerly occupied his mind were wiped out" (immediate effect of interior freedom around an underlying disorder). And for the thirty-six years up to the moment his autobiography was written, "he never again consented to the least suggestion of the flesh" (his decision flowed from his experience of God, from his deep affective reactions, and from his deep inner freedom). His choices originated, then, not from willpower or self-control, but from a powerful experience of God. This vivid experience confirmed the holy desires that were growing within him.

Ignatius, then, derived the purpose of the Rules for Discernment from his own experience of God. He intended the Rules to be a way for people to understand, recognize, and receive—or reject—interior movements that are stirred through God's action.

## Two Fundamental Orientations

In Rules 314 and 315, Ignatius describes two basic stances, two fundamental orientations of heart, attitude, imagination, thought, feeling, and behavior.[14] These two orientations are not only different but also they are contrary. That is, they are diametrically opposed to each other. These two Rules are descriptions, statements of fact, about one's fundamental orientation. They are addressing the question: What is the overall thrust of one's heart and life at a given moment? Is this thrust congruent with God's ways or contrary to God's ways?

Rule 314 describes people whose deepest orientation at a given moment is away from God and toward sin. Their mind, heart, imagination, and behavior are being seriously tainted by one or more of the capital sins, such as vanity, pride, greed, or lust. Therefore, it is easy for the "enemy"—their sinful tendency—to "propose apparent pleasures" and to "fill their imagination with sensual delights and gratifications" in order to remain in darkness. God, the "good spirit," makes use of the "light of reason, rouses the sting of conscience, and fills them with remorse."

Rule 315 describes people whose fundamental orientation is congruent with God's ways. It focuses on those "who go on earnestly striving to cleanse their souls from sin and who seek to rise in the service of God our Lord to greater perfection." Sinful tendencies have opposite effects on these people. Contrary to those living a life of sin, those striving to respond to God's self-communication are disturbed by sin and darkness: "It is characteristic of the evil spirit to harass with anxiety, to afflict with sadness, to raise obstacles backed by fallacious reasonings that disturb the soul. Thus he seeks to prevent the soul from advancing."

Because their fundamental orientation is so closely connected to God, these individuals experience the realities of God as life-giving and life-freeing: "It is characteristic of the good spirit to give courage and strength, consolations, tears, inspirations, and peace. This He does by making all easy, by removing all obstacles so that the soul goes forward in doing good."

Though a religious person, Ignatius' deeper orientation—at age twenty-six—was affected by vanity and lust. His imagination and affectivity were filled with apparent pleasures and vain desires to please women of nobility. Up to the moment of his injury, his life included strong sexual temptations. However, reading stories of people devoted to a higher being allowed God to stir his reason, conscience, and emotions. His reason was enlightened: "He acquired no little light from his reading and he began to think seriously of his past life and the great need he had of doing penance for it." His conscience was aroused through interior movements, through growth in holiness, and through the "abundant consolation" derived from his vision of Jesus and Mary. This sting of conscience resulted in remorse—a "great disgust with his past life." All of this occurred because of God's stirrings, the "good spirit."

Through enlightened reason and the sting of conscience that resulted in great disgust and inner freedom, Ignatius' fundamental orientation changed. The direction of his life became the opposite of the life he was living. The holy thoughts and desires that God planted through his reading and pondering were manifested as lived experiences. Ignatius became one who "earnestly strives to cleanse his soul from sin." He tried to decipher which way of living—the Carthusian life or a path of self-denial—would enable him to live in perpetual penance. He experienced the spiritual life as easy with all obstacles removed. Without a care in the world he continued his reading and his good resolutions. Therefore, he went forward in doing good. He devoted conversation with members of his household to God. Shortly after leaving Loyola, he returned money he owed and gave his clothes to a poor man. He was filled with courage and strength and a powerful urge to serve God. He experienced consolations, tears, inspirations, and peace. He took "great delight" in reading his books, and "his greatest consolation" came when he contemplated the heavens and the stars.

## Consolation and Desolation: The Basis of Discernment

The experience of consolation and desolation is the foundation of discernment. Without consolation and desolation there are no inner movements to sift apart; therefore, no basis for discernment exists since discernment means to sift through, distinguish, separate, and divide interior movements that result from God's personal involvement.

Consolation and desolation are experienced in contrary ways. When our interior life is consonant with God's life, we experience consolation (316). When our inner life is dissonant with God, we experience desolation (317). God's personal self-communication precipitates either affective response.

Consolation and desolation are experienced when an "inordinate attachment" is being touched by God's grace. God moves in the heart and mind and brings to light areas of darkness that are not free. Inordinate attachments might be related to self-serving realities or one of the capital sins, such as vanity, pride, greed, gluttony, or lust. Or disordered attachments could be good realities in themselves, but they might not be congruent with God's specific desires. Different movements, then, occur around an area of sinfulness or an attitude of unfreedom concerning a choice or life situation. When affections are congruent with God's ways, then consolation is experienced. When affections are "inordinately attached" to something other than God's ways, desolation occurs.

In his conversion Ignatius experiences consolation and desolation at two junctures. First, consolation and desolation laid the groundwork for his growing desire to serve God, to begin to change the fundamental orientation of his life—that is, vanity and achievement for egotistical purposes. This groundwork of inner movements occurred even before he became aware of it. He was filled with delight that continued to give him satisfaction when pondering the stories of God. He experienced dryness and dissatisfaction when reflecting on the stories of the world. Both were touching into his disordered vanity, which was becoming a purified desire—achieving for God rather than for self.

Second, through undergoing the purifying experience of consolation and desolation, Ignatius grew freer from his self-centered desire to achieve. He experienced a pervasive movement of consolation for a long period of time, which had various manifestations. His desires were changed to God-centered desires. He felt a great disgust for his past life because of an abundant consolation. He took great delight in the books he was reading. Finally, his greatest consolation of gazing at the sky filled him with a powerful urge to serve God.

# Conclusion

Through the simple action of reading stories while sick in bed, Ignatius' heart was stirred, and his life began to change. A life journey focused on outer achievements changed to an inner journey focused on God. A person engaged in vibrant exterior actions in the world experienced lively inner movements in the atmosphere of the heart. Someone whose imagination, thoughts, feelings, and desires were permeated with worldly achievements became someone whose total humanness was affected by God-centered realities. A bound heart was being freed through the experience of different interior movements stirred by God's desire to draw Ignatius into a personal relationship.

# Experiencing God

God's touch, though taking place in a moment of time, lives on within us forever. When we experience God's love, God's self-giving, we are never the same. We may return to some of our old ways of being and acting, but deep down within we are not the same.

We can continue to let an experience of God bear fruit within us by going back to it and lingering over it. Through this remembering, lingering, and reliving process, we open ourselves to God—we allow God to move within us, to touch our hearts again so that our own experiences of God ripple deep within us and can continue to make a difference in our lives.

At the end of chapters 1 to 12, I suggest prayer exercises that can help open you to experiencing God anew through remembering and savoring your past experiences of God. I also offer several prayer exercises that have no connection to your past.

## Reliving a Significant Experience

In God's presence, remember a time that you underwent a very significant and, perhaps, life-changing event. Possibly a conversion experience, sudden or gradual, comes to your mind, a serious crisis, or something that brought about a major change in your outlook. Maybe you will recall an incident that led to the choice of your vocation. Sit with God, and let God help you bring to mind this important experience.

Remember the inner details and outer circumstances of the experience. Savor its richness, and relive it in your memory, feeling, imagination, heart, and mind. Notice God's presence.

✝ What were the circumstances of the experience, that is, were you by yourself, on a retreat, at a liturgy, in a group, or having a serious crisis in your life like Ignatius?

✝ What was God's presence like in the experience?

✝ What were some of your feelings, thoughts, and desires?

✝ What differences did you notice within yourself as a result of this experience? Did any change take place in your life?

✝ Do you notice anything new happening in you now as you remember and relive the experience?

Be attentive to God's presence. Share with God any feelings that arise, and listen to God's response.

## Exploring an Experience with Various Interior Reactions

Remember an event or a period of time when you experienced, like Ignatius, various interior reactions to something. For example, at times Ignatius felt consoled, cheerful, and satisfied, and these reactions lasted. At other times, he felt dry and dissatisfied.

✝ What were the circumstances?

✝ Did you notice God's presence at any point?

✝ What were some of your thoughts and feelings during the consoling part of the experience?

✝ What were some of your thoughts and feelings during the dissatisfying part of the experience? Were you struggling with unfreedom?

✝ Was your imagination involved?

✝ How did the desolation get resolved?

✝ Did any change take place in you as a result of this experience of consolation and desolation?

✝ What did you learn about yourself and God?

As you pray, be attentive to God's presence. Share with God your feelings. Listen to God's response.

## Questions for Reflection and Discussion

1. What touches you, moves you the most about Ignatius' conversion experience?

2. How would you describe God's presence? How did Ignatius' experience of God's presence differ at the end from the beginning?

3. How did Ignatius' prolonged pondering (two, three, and four hours at a time) add to his experience?

4. In what specific ways did Ignatius change as a result of his conversion experience? What did he learn about himself? What did he learn about God?

## For Spiritual Directors

### A Written Dialogue (individually)

Write out a spiritual direction conversation between Ignatius and yourself acting as his spiritual director.

✝ What in Ignatius' experience would you focus on?

✝ What questions might you ask him?

### Role Play (in a group)

Role play a spiritual direction session in which one person is Ignatius and another is his spiritual director.

✝ What in Ignatius' experience would you focus on?

✝ What questions might you ask Ignatius?

After the role play reflect, individually, on the experience, and then discuss the following questions:

1. What touches you about Ignatius' experience? Did any feeling or new insight come alive for you through the role playing?

2. What strikes you about the spiritual direction session and the spiritual director?

3. What did you learn? What, if anything, about spiritual direction was reinforced?

## Significant Insights

✝ What three significant insights about the Rules for Discernment did you gain or were reinforced through Ignatius' conversion experience?

# 2

# Ignatius' Deepening
# Discerning Heart

As our fundamental orientation becomes more deeply rooted in God, we continue to experience interior movements. These movements touch deeper areas in our person, and they lead us to a greater understanding of God's ways and a clearer knowledge of self. We experience desolating inner movements when a part of ourselves contrasts with God's life. On the other hand, we experience consoling motions when our desires and inner being are congruent with God. Both the desolating and consoling movements are essential to developing a discerning heart, growing in awareness of God's desires, cultivating a deeper understanding of ourselves, and becoming free.

After his initial conversion, Ignatius continued to experience different movements, which resulted in a deeper interior understanding and interior freedom to follow God more closely. In this chapter, I will describe Ignatius' growth in understanding interior movements, explore his intense struggle with desolation, and examine how Rules 318–327 affected his desolate experience.

## Experiencing Interior Movements
## without Understanding

Ignatius' interior changes continued to overflow into his life and actions. He lived a strict ascetic life. He collected money that was owed to him, distributing it to people to whom he felt an obligation, and used some of the proceeds toward refurbishing a statue of Mary. He was filled with a great desire to serve God and to perform great penances. However, his soul was still blind.[1] Although experiencing spiritual movements and the beginnings of awareness, his understanding was still lacking.

At this point in his spiritual journey, Ignatius' fundamental orientation toward God was influenced more by imitating the saints and achieving what they did rather than from a humble response to God's personal call. For instance, "when he remembered to do some penance which the saints had performed, he resolved to do the same and even more."[2] He says his "whole purpose was to perform these great, external works, for so had acted the saints for God's glory."[3] God continued to attract Ignatius' heart through his desire to achieve, as the saints did. His foundational conversion occurred, but his interior understanding still lagged behind: "he never took a spiritual view of anything, nor even knew the meaning of humility, or charity, or patience, or discretion as a rule and measure of these virtues."[4] Outer achievements for God, arising from a desire to imitate the saints rather than an inner desire to serve others, still prevailed in Ignatius' desires even though interior movements were simultaneously taking place.

Ignatius shares one particular story to show how he experienced interior movements without understanding them sufficiently to be able to make a decision with inner freedom. Ignatius and a Moor discussed Mary's virginity. The Moor argued that Mary, although a virgin before Jesus' birth, did not remain a virgin. After the Moor left, Ignatius pondered their conversation. An inner conflict took place. His "thoughts" gave rise to "emotions" that brought on a "feeling of discontent in his soul." Ignatius' desire to achieve great works like the saints was thwarted. He thought he had failed in his duty to defend Mary, which led to anger toward the Moor and a desire to give him "a taste of his dagger." He experienced a "battle of desires" that lasted for a long time and resulted in uncertainty about what he should do. Because he could not make a decision from an interior certainty, he depended on an exterior reality—in this case, a mule standing at a fork in the road. If the mule followed the road taken by the Moor, he would give the Moor a taste of his dagger. If the mule followed the other road, Ignatius would leave the Moor alone. He chose to follow the mule. Thus, although God was moving in him through his focus on achievements, his soul was still blind: though experiencing interior movement, he did not yet have the insight to make a decision from an inner clarity.[5]

## Growing Inner Strength from Consolation

Ignatius began to undergo different experiences of consolation, although he did not yet understand the difference between them. For a long time, Ignatius continued to experience a strong sense of consolation, but still with little interior understanding: "he continued in the same interior state of great and undisturbed joy, without any knowledge of the inner things of the soul."[6] However, he experienced another type of consolation. For days he found much comfort—because of its great beauty—in a serpent-like creature that appeared to him, although whether it was a dream or a vision was unclear. His delight and consolation were short-lived, however. When the vision disappeared, he was saddened, which precipitated a disturbing thought about the difficulty of his life: "How can you stand a life like this for the seventy years you have yet to live?"[7] Consolation results in encouraging thoughts; desolation causes discouraging thoughts: "For just as consolation is the opposite of desolation, so the thoughts that spring from consolation are the opposite of those that spring from desolation" (317).

Even so, growth was occurring because rather than depending on an outer reality—such as a mule—to resolve an inner conflict, Ignatius responded "interiorly with great strength."[8] His consolation helped him "to store up a supply of strength" to meet the desolation (323). He drew on the "sufficient grace offered him . . . and [found] strength in his Creator and Lord" (324). He "faces his temptation boldly, and does exactly the opposite of what it suggests" (325). Experiencing God's strength contrasted boldly with the doubts that haunted him about his ability to live a God-centered life for the next seventy years: "You poor creature! Can you promise me even one hour of life?"[9] Ignatius remained firm and constant in his growing resolution and in his decision to serve God for the rest of his life (318). By depending on the strength of God's grace and the experience of past consolation to counteract dark thoughts, Ignatius reexperienced consolation—he "remained at peace." Ignatius slowly learned the difference between true and false consolation: false consolation left him displeased and caused discouraging thoughts; true consolation brought him great joy, precipitated encouraging thoughts, and gave him inner strength to counteract temptation.

## Contrasting Movements around Spiritual Practices

Soon after the temptation of the serpent-like creature, Ignatius started to experience great changes in his soul. Desolation ("darkness of soul and turmoil of spirit"; 317) occurred. He felt great distaste and no relish in his prayers or in going to Mass. However, sometimes consolation occurred unexpectedly: "At other times everything was just the contrary, and so suddenly, that he seemed to have got rid of the sadness and desolation pretty much as one removes a cloak from the shoulders of another."[10] Possibly this strong alternation of consolation and desolation for no apparent reason resulted in Ignatius declaring in Rule 322:

> The third reason (for desolation) is because God wishes to give us a true knowledge and understanding of ourselves, so that we may have an intimate perception of the fact that it is not within our power to acquire and attain great devotion, intense love, tears, or any other spiritual consolation; but that all this is the gift and grace of God.

The consolation he had experienced in his usual spiritual exercises did not exist. There was only distaste. God helped him to realize that all is a gift, even consolation.

As Ignatius paid attention and savored the richness of his growing inner experience, "he began to marvel at these changes which he never before experienced, saying to himself: 'What new kind of life is this that we are now beginning?' "[11] Such attentiveness and appreciation eventually led to greater understanding.

During this time, an unidentified woman known for her many years of devotion to God challenged Ignatius. She said to him: "May our Lord Jesus Christ appear to you some day!"[12] Ignatius did not understand. Could the woman be encouraging Ignatius to allow God to reveal Self in a more personal way? Could she be challenging him to focus more on the person of God rather than on the achievements for God? The meaning of this statement would reveal itself in time.

## Desolation around a Deep Unfree Area

Through the experience of consolation and desolation, God not only purified deeper areas of unfreedom in Ignatius but also freed Ignatius' various "disordered attachments." God purified Ignatius on all levels: obvious areas of sinfulness, such as self-centeredness; vain desires to achieve; deep-rooted and pervasive attitudes. First, in his initial conversion experience, God freed Ignatius' inner being from lust and vain desires to achieve in the world. Second, God purified Ignatius' earnest desire to perform religious acts, that is, performing great penances as the saints did and wishing to attack the Moor for a religious reason. Now God focused on a deep-rooted unfree area—perfectionism as manifested in an intense struggle with scruples. God purified an even deeper disordered attachment, which resulted in great inner turmoil. Through this struggle, Ignatius acquired greater interior freedom and a deeper understanding of interior movements. He learned about how to handle desolation and developed an even deeper discerning heart. As with his conversion, I share the following story in first person, using the same words that Ignatius used to describe his inner experience but condensing some of the outer facts (as with the previous example in chapter 1, Ignatius' exact words appear in boldface):

I began to **suffer much from scruples**. Although the general confession I had made at Montserrat had been entirely written down, there still were some things I thought I had not confessed. This caused me a good deal of **worry**, for even though I confessed it, my mind was never at rest. I began, therefore, to look for some spiritual man who would cure me of my scruples, but without success. Finally a doctor of the Cathedral Church, a very spiritual man, told me in confession to write down all I could remember. I did so. But after confessing, my scruples returned, each time becoming more minute so that I became quite upset. Although I knew that these scruples were doing me much harm and that it would be good to be rid of them, I could not shake them off. Sometimes I thought the cure would be for the confessor to tell me in the name of Jesus Christ never to mention anything of the past, and I wished my confessor would so direct me, but I would not dare tell the confessor what to do.

However, my confessor finally did tell me not to confess anything of my past life unless it was something absolutely clear. But since I thought that everything was quite clear this direction was of no use, and the trouble continued. At this time, I was in a small room which the Dominicans had given me in their monastery, where I continued with my seven hours of prayer, on my knees, and performing other spiritual exercises. But none of these provided me with a cure for my scruples, although it was now some months that they had been afflicting me. One day when I was especially tormented, I began to pray and to call aloud to God, crying out fervently: "Help me, O Lord, since I find no help from people or from any creature. No trial would be too great for me to bear if I thought there was any hope of finding help. Please, Lord, show me where I can find it, and even though I should have to follow a little dog to find it, I would do so."

While these thoughts were tormenting me, I was frequently **seized with the temptation** to throw myself into the excavation close to my room and adjacent to the place where I prayed. But, knowing it was a sin to commit suicide, I cried again: "Lord, I will do nothing to offend you." I frequently repeated these words as I did with the prayer above. I thought of a saint who, to obtain from God something he much desired, went many days without eating. Giving a good deal of thought to this, I made up my mind to do the same.

I went a whole week without putting a morsel of food in my mouth. I omitted none of my ordinary spiritual exercises. But when I told my confessor the following week of my fast, he told me to give up this abstinence. **I obeyed my confessor** although I still felt strong, and for the next two days found myself free of my scruples. But on the third day, while I was praying, I began to recall my sins, thinking of my past sins, one after the other, as though one grew out of another, till I felt that it was my duty to confess them once again. As a sequel to these thoughts, **I was seized with a disgust of the life I was leading and a desire to be done with it. It was our Lord's way of awakening me as it were from sleep.** Since I now had some experience of the different spirits from the lessons I had received from God, I began to **look for the way in which that spirit had been able to take possession of me.** I therefore made up my mind, which had become very clear on the matter, never to confess my past sins again. From that day on I remained free of those scruples, holding it a certainty that our Lord in His mercy had liberated me.[13]

## Relationship to the Rules for Discernment

Ignatius' struggle with scruples was probably one of the most desolating experiences of his life. He experienced an intense "darkness of soul, turmoil of spirit, . . . restlessness rising from many disturbances and temptations" that led to a lack of faith, hope, and love. He felt "separated, as it were," from God (317). Through this horrible experience, his *awareness* grew. He learned the way the "enemy" operated (325–27) and developed concrete ways to deal with the desolation. In particular, he devised two types of counterattacks: *action counterattacks* (318–19) and *attitudinal counterattacks* (320–21).

### Awareness of Characteristics of the Enemy

Rules 325–27 describe three qualities of the "enemy," that is, how temptation can affect us around a disordered attachment or an area of unfreedom. Rule 325 discusses the strong and violent quality of temptation. The enemy "is a weakling before a show of strength, and a tyrant if he has his will":

> . . . the enemy becomes weak, loses courage, and turns to flight with his seductions as soon as one leading a spiritual life *faces his temptations boldly,* and *does exactly the opposite of what he suggests.* However, if one begins to be afraid and to lose courage in temptations, no wild animal on earth can be more fierce than the enemy of our human nature. (my emphasis)

Ignatius' struggle with scruples was deep, intense, and, at times, overwhelming. The scruples tormented him; the temptation to end his life was so strong that it could take over like a wild animal. However, Ignatius faced his temptation boldly at all levels of his being—thought, prayer, and behavior. The all-encompassing nature and strength of Ignatius' counterattack dissipated the tyrannical and fierce power of the temptations.

Rule 326 points to more subtle ways temptation takes place: "the enemy seeks to remain hidden and does not want to be discovered":

> . . . when the enemy of our human nature tempts a just soul with his wiles and seductions, he earnestly desires that they be *received secretly and kept secret.* But if one manifests them to a confessor, or to some other *spiritual person* who understands his deceits and malicious designs, the evil one is very much vexed. For he knows that he cannot succeed in his evil undertaking, *once his evident deceits have been revealed.* (my emphasis)

When the enemy fails through outright temptation to draw us away from God, then that enemy, that unfree area within us, will try secret and manipulative ways. A temptation will secretly creep into our mind, heart, and spirit to keep us distant from God and our true self. It will slowly and seductively try to move us away from God.

Ignatius' scruples would creep into his consciousness each time he confessed minute details of his past sins. He would think of one small sinful incident, then another and another until he was consumed with fear and guilt. Possibly what Ignatius needed to address with his confessor was not so much prior sins but rather the temptation to dwell on these sins. Possibly too he needed to focus on the disorder underlying them—guilt, fear, and an inability to forgive himself—and to accept God's forgiveness. Thus, repeatedly revealing his sins to his confessor proved counterproductive. It did not break the power of the temptation because that's precisely where the enemy was working—and moving him to confess again and again. He needed to do just the opposite: stop confessing his sins. The fact that Ignatius admitted his decision to fast to his confessor and his confessor's subsequent order that he end the fast helped Ignatius to be freed of his scruples for a few days.

Rule 327 explains that temptation will strike at our most vulnerable and weak areas, that is, those areas that are not yet in the light of God's grace:

> [the enemy] will attack at the *weakest point*. . . . the enemy of our human nature investigates from every side all our virtues, theological, cardinal, and moral. Where he finds *the defenses of eternal salvation weakest and most deficient,* there he attacks and tries to take us by storm. (my emphasis)

When Ignatius was recuperating from his illness, the areas of weakness where he experienced temptation most were those connected with his vanity and his lustful desires. As God moved into those weak areas, especially through a vision of Mary and the infant Jesus, Ignatius became stronger, and the temptations grew weaker. At this point, his weakness allied with a spiritual reality—the confession of sins. An important means of growing spiritually—confessing sins—became an obsession that needed to be freed. The beautiful virtue of sorrow for sin turned into a deadening enslavement. Ignatius needed God's grace to find liberation and to receive true sorrow rather than be overwhelmed by obsessive guilt.

## Action Counterattacks

Rule 318 states the principle of constancy of resolution and decision: "In time of desolation we should never make any change, but remain firm and constant in the resolution and decision which guided us the day before the desolation." Ignatius did not leave the Dominican monastery in which he was staying nor change his previous spiritual exercises. He remained firm in his decision to follow whatever his confessor said, even if he did not agree with him. For instance, he abandoned his week's fast at his confessor's request even though he was convinced that such fasting could relieve his scruples.

Rule 319 describes the spiritual exercises of counterattack:

> Though in desolation we must never change our former resolutions, it will be very advantageous to intensify our activity against the desolation. We can insist more upon *prayer*, upon *meditation*, and on *much examination of ourselves*. We can make an effort in a suitable way to do some *penance*. (my emphasis)

Not only must we remain firm, we must also fight the desolation in specific ways that are congruent with who we are as human beings. First, we must pray more (*oracion*) in an affective way, that is, involve our heart, feelings, and desires by telling God how we feel and by paying attention to God's response in our affectivity. Second, we must involve our minds and imaginations more through meditation. Third, we must involve our heart, mind, imagination, and memory through self-examination. Fourth, we must engage our behavior by taking concrete actions, such as fasting or other penances.

Ignatius earnestly prayed and begged God to help him. He counteracted the strong temptation to commit suicide by promising the opposite: "Lord, I will do nothing to offend you." Ignatius continued his exercises of prayer. He contemplated the lives of the saints and remembered how one of them fasted to obtain favors from God. He examined the dynamics of the scruples, how they were seeping in more and more minutely into his consciousness. He fasted and continued to obey his confessor. Ignatius engaged various aspects of his person to counterattack the strong hold the scruples had over him.

Ignatius became free of the scruples by opening himself to God's mercy through these action counterattacks. Although he wanted to continue to fast, he fought this desire and followed the order of his confessor to end the fast. This obedience helped him to be free for a few days. After experiencing a disgust for the life he was leading and an awareness that the Lord was awakening him from sleep (inner blindness), he began to look at the way that the enemy had taken possession of him (examination). Having learned many lessons from the experience of different movements, Ignatius arrived at his own decision: he made up his mind never to confess his past sins again. From that point on, he was free of the scruples and knew for certain it was God who liberated him.

## Attitudinal Counterattacks

Rule 320 describes the attitude of trust needed:

> He can resist with the help of God, which *always remains,* though he may not clearly perceive it. For though God has taken from him the abundance of fervor and overflowing love and the intensity of his favors, nevertheless, he has *sufficient grace* for eternal salvation. (my emphasis)

Though God's felt presence may be absent, and we might feel as if we are separated from God, God's grace always remains. We need to trust in *faith* that God's loving support is always with us, even when we feel the lack of it. Although the abundance of fervor was taken from Ignatius, he continued to trust God. Although he could not feel God's presence and could only feel torment, he steadfastly continued to call on God for help, believing God was with him.

Rule 321 suggests an attitude of patience and hope:

> When one is in desolation, he should strive to *persevere in patience.* This reacts against the vexations that have overtaken him. Let him consider, too, that *consolation will soon return . . .* (my emphasis)

The patience referred to here is an *active* and *energetic* patience, not passive and uninvolved. It is a specific patience in direct opposition to the precise nature of the struggle. For example, if we are struggling with fear, we need a *courageous patience* as we combat the fear with prayer, thought, and penance. If we are struggling with resentment in a given situation, we need an *accepting patience* as we continue to work toward changing the situation. This active patience helps us to see the desolation in perspective and keeps us confident that consolation will return in time. Ignatius actively persevered in patience as he contended with the desolation in concrete ways. His struggle with scruples was tempting him to give up all hope and end his life. The spirit of steadfast patience and hope prompted him to pray courageously for help and strength.

## Conclusion

The Rules for Discernment evolved from Ignatius' own experience of God. In this chapter, we saw how Ignatius grew in self-understanding through struggle, pain, desolation, and temptation. He discovered how temptation can affect him and how his weaknesses, untouched by God's grace, can keep him bound. Through several intense experiences of temptation, he learned what he could do to keep himself open to God's grace. Ignatius' ability to discern was growing deeper, clearer, and more practical as he continued on his longest journey—the journey of the heart.

## Experiencing God

### Asking God to Transform Your Blind Spots

Early in his autobiography, Ignatius frequently refers to his inner blindness, that is, "his soul was still blind." By this he means that there were things he was missing that God was trying to reveal to him, things he was not seeing with his inner eyes, and interior movements of which he was not yet aware.

In God's presence, sit with your own spiritual, inner vision as well as your inner blindness.

✝ What seems stronger—your ability to see or not to see through your spiritual eyes?

✞ Ask God to show you any blind spots about yourself, about God, about your relationship with God, about your life, about any important situations and relationships in which you are involved.

✞ Ask God to help you to see what God wants you to see about God, yourself, another person, or a specific situation.

✞ Ask God to give you the gift of spiritual insight in order to be able to discern and to follow God's ways in all circumstances of your life.

### A Vivid Sense of Jesus' Presence

A holy woman prayed for Ignatius: "May our Lord Jesus Christ appear to you some day!"

Remember a time when you saw Jesus with the inner eyes of your soul, when you experienced his presence in a vivid way, when he came alive for you in your prayer.

Remember the inner details and outer circumstances of the experience. Savor the richness of the experience and relive it in your memory, feeling, imagination, heart, and mind. Be attentive to God's presence.

✞ What were the circumstances of the experience, that is, were you by yourself, on a retreat, at a liturgy?

✞ How would you describe Jesus' presence in the experience?

✞ What were some of your feelings, thoughts, and desires?

✞ What differences did you notice within yourself as a result of this experience?

✞ Do you notice anything new happening in you now as you remember and relive the experience?

As you relive it, be attentive to God's presence. Share with God any feelings that arise, and listen to God's response. Ask God for the grace to notice Jesus more readily within yourself and within your life.

### Exploring an Intense Desolating Experience

In God's presence, remember a time you had a severe desolating experience, as Ignatius did.

☨ What were the circumstances?

☨ What did you notice about God's absence or presence before, during, and after the desolation?

☨ What were some of your thoughts and feelings during the experience? after the experience?

☨ Were you struggling with an area of unfreedom or sinfulness?

☨ How was this desolating experience resolved?

☨ Did any change take place as a result of this experience?

☨ What did you learn about yourself? about God?

As you pray with this experience, be attentive to God's presence. Share with God your feelings, and listen to God's response.

## Questions for Reflection and Discussion

1. What touches you, moves you most about Ignatius' intense desolating experience?

2. How would you describe God's presence in this experience? How was Ignatius' experience of God's presence different during and after this experience?

3. What specific things did Ignatius do to try to fight the desolation? What seemed to work? What did not seem to work?

4. If you were Ignatius' confessor, what would you suggest to Ignatius?

5. What did he learn about himself through this experience? What did he learn about God?

# For Spiritual Directors

## A Written Dialogue (individually)

Write out a spiritual direction conversation between Ignatius and yourself as his spiritual director.

✞ What and how would you focus on Ignatius' experience?

✞ What questions might you ask Ignatius?

✞ How would your approach be different from his confessor's approach?

## Role Play (in a group)

Role play a spiritual direction session in which one person is Ignatius and another is his spiritual director.

✞ What in Ignatius' experience would you focus on? What questions might you ask Ignatius?

After the role play, reflect on the experience, individually, and then discuss the following questions:

1. What touches you most about Ignatius' experience? Did any new insight come alive for you through role playing?

2. What strikes you most about the spiritual direction session and the spiritual director?

3. What did you learn? What was reinforced about spiritual direction?

4. Through role playing, what differences do you notice between spiritual direction and the sacrament of reconciliation?

## Significant Insights

✞ What three significant insights about the Rules for Discernment did you gain? What was reinforced through Ignatius' intense desolating experience?

---
3
---

# Ignatius' Discernment of Consolations

Although Ignatius suffered terribly throughout his scruples experience, he learned a great deal about consolation, desolation, and temptation. In particular, he learned several valuable lessons: consolation is a gift that God freely offers; desolation can be so severe that it can even cause total despair; attentiveness to the specific way temptation can occur enables him to take concrete steps to counteract the temptation; God uses interior movements and attentiveness to free him of disordered attachments. "God treated [me] just as a schoolmaster treats a little boy when he teaches him," Ignatius wrote. God always dealt with him like this.[1] Through the experience of interior movements Ignatius developed a deeper understanding of himself and of God's ways.

With God's help, Ignatius also learned about the nature of consolation itself—the sifting out of the different experiences of consolation. Ignatius experienced the various manifestations of true consolation that originated in God and the false consolation that grew from his own self or the "enemy." As Ignatius continued to experience God moving in his heart, he noticed differences in the manifestations of true consolation, differences in the immediate cause of true consolation, and differences between true and false consolation. In this chapter, I will examine several of Ignatius' experiences of true consolation in light of the Four Manifestations of Consolation (316) as well as the different causes of true consolation (330). I will also explore the differences Ignatius observed between true and false consolations in relation to the Second Week Rules (328–36).

## Experiences of True Consolation

When Ignatius began to experience God while recuperating from his leg injury, he felt consolation that lasted a very long time. But he also experienced a fleeting delight that left him dry and dissatisfied. God was moving in Ignatius in an implicit way; Ignatius did not yet have an explicit sense of God as person and personal. God was purifying Ignatius' inner being, which resulted in Ignatius experiencing consolation and desolation. This purification, which alternated between consolation and desolation, enabled Ignatius to experience and perceive God more clearly and more explicitly. The holy woman's prayer for Ignatius ("May our Lord Jesus Christ appear to you some day!")[2] began to come true. Ignatius shared several explicit experiences of God—experiences of true and deep consolation in which God was not only felt but seen. These experiences reveal the varied ways that consolation can be achieved. Their key aspects are summarized below (Again, the following paraphrases of Ignatius' words from a first-person perspective and, as in previous chapters, important Ignatian phrases appear in boldface):

### The Trinity

I have a great devotion to the Trinity and daily prayed to each person of the Trinity. When I was praying one day **my understanding began to be elevated** as though I saw the Holy Trinity under the figure of three keys. This was accompanied with so many tears and so much **sobbing** that I could not control myself. **I experienced great joy and consolation** as I talked about the Trinity to others. The result was that all through my life this **great impression** has remained with me to **feel great devotion** when I pray to the Most Holy Trinity.

### God Creating the World

Another time there was **represented to my understanding** with **great delight** the manner in which God had created the world. It had the appearance of something **white** out of which rays were coming, and it was out of this that God made light. But I did not know how to explain these things, nor did I remember well the **spiritual illumination** that God impressed upon my soul.

### Jesus in the Eucharist

At Manresa, where I remained almost a year, after I began to **feel God's consolations** and saw the **fruit produced** in the spiritual growth of the people with whom I dealt, I gave up those outward extremes I formerly adopted and trimmed my nails and hair. One day when I was hearing Mass during the elevation, **I saw with the inner eyes of the soul** something resembling **white rays** that came from above. Although I cannot explain this after so long a time, **I clearly saw with my understanding** how Jesus Christ our Lord is present in that most holy sacrament.

### The Humanity of Jesus and Mary

When I was at prayer, I often and for a long time **saw with the inner eyes** the humanity of Christ. The shape that appeared to me was like a **white body,** not very large or very small, but I saw no distinction of members. . . . I also **saw** our Lady in like form. . . . These things gave me, at the time, **great strength,** and were always a striking **confirmation of my faith,** so much so that I often thought to myself that if there were no Scriptures to teach us these matters of faith, **I was determined to die for them,** merely because of what I had **seen.**

## Great Illumination of Understanding

> I was on my way to a church in Manresa. The road ran along close to the river. Moving along in prayer, I sat down for a moment with my face toward the river. As I sat, **the eyes of my understanding began to open.** I beheld no vision, but **I saw and understood many things**, spiritual as well as those concerning faith and learning. This took place with **so great an illumination that these things appeared to be something altogether new.** I cannot point out the particulars of what I then understood, although they were many, except that **I received a great illumination in my understanding.** This was so great that in the whole course of my past life right up to my sixty-second year, if I were to gather all the helps I had received from God, and everything I knew, and add them together, I do not think that they would equal all that **I received** at this time.[3]

## A Deepening Understanding

Though painful, Ignatius' desolating experience enabled him to become enlightened. Through this experience, God freed Ignatius of the obsession—"disordered attachment"—to confess his sins over and over. By doing so, God created in Ignatius the interior space to experience a higher being in more explicit ways. Previously, his "understanding was still blind," and he was "without any knowledge of the inner things of the soul." Ignatius' desolating experience, in which it seemed God was asleep and perhaps even nonexistent, was really God's way of "awakening him as it were from sleep" and liberating him. God was very present and moving within Ignatius, but Ignatius' own blindness—caused by his disordered attachment, that is, his obsession to confess his sins—prevented him from seeing God. But now Ignatius had the interior freedom not only to allow God to work but also to recognize how God was working. His interior blindness was transformed into interior seeing.[4]

In each of these experiences, then, Ignatius mentions in various ways how he was able to see through his understanding. He referred again to *sentir,* a felt understanding in which, through grace, he could see and feel with his interior senses. Therefore, as his understanding was elevated he could see the Trinity. With his understanding he could also see white rays as God created the world. With the inner eyes of his soul he could see white rays coming from Jesus in the Eucharist and the humanity of Jesus and Mary personified as a white body. These experiences of understanding and seeing culminated and became integrated by the river at Manresa. It was there that his understanding was so illuminated that he could see clearly and, in an entirely new way, comprehend all spiritual and theological truths.

Thus, whereas before, Ignatius' understanding was blind, now it could see. Whereas his interior self was bound by the darkness of a disordered attachment, now it was freed to see God moving in explicit ways. Ignatius was so convinced these experiences emanated from God that he was determined to die for them. Thus, a remarkable transformation occurred since his experience with the Moor. He could not make a decision grounded in a discerning heart until the moment when his interior senses became so enlightened that he was willing to die for what he saw. Such transformed understanding could only occur through explicit experiences of consolation.

## Four Manifestations of Consolation

We experience consolation because of God's personal involvement with us. God, always present within implicitly, moves interiorly in a given moment, reveals something specific about Self, and communicates divine love. God's active presence results in a reaction, an awakening of understanding, an irruption of feeling within. God's transcendent and pervasive presence is immanently and specifically revealed, and we have an affective reaction.

Rule 316 describes four manifestations of consolation that vary in nature and intensity. All four manifestations are descriptions of affective reactions to God's self-communication in our interior selves. The first two expressions occur infrequently and are rather intense. The latter two are more common and pervasive experiences of consolation:

I call it consolation when an interior movement is aroused in the soul: by which it is inflamed with love of its Creator and Lord, and as a consequence, can love no creature on the face of the earth for its own sake, but only in the Creator of them all. . . . when one shed tears that move to the love of God, whether it be because of sorrow for sins, or because of the sufferings of Christ our Lord, or for any other reason that is immediately directed to the praise and service of God. . . . every increase of faith, hope, and love. . . . all interior joy that invites and attracts to what is heavenly and to the salvation of one's soul by filling it with peace and quiet in its Creator and Lord.

The First Manifestation of Consolation describes a lively and total affective union with God. God's love is experienced so completely that we are "inflamed with love" of God. As the Annotations said earlier: ". . . it is more suitable and much better that the Creator and Lord in person communicate Himself . . . , that He inflame us with His love . . . "(15). The word *inflame,* in both the Annotations and the Rules, indicates a vibrant, lively, burning, and intense love for God that only God can arouse within. The consequence of that burning love is enlightened understanding and complete interior freedom during the consolation—that is, no inordinate attachment to any reality, bad or good, occurs. We are so inflamed with God's love that all other loves are seen in their proper perspective and loved only in the context of our total love for God. We do not love others less; rather, we love more because all our love is contained in God's total love. God's love integrates all our loves. Therefore, in this moment of all-enveloping consolation our disordered attachments become ordered attachments because God's vibrant love eradicates any disorders.

Ignatius may have experienced this all-encompassing expression of consolation when seeing Jesus and Mary with his inner eyes. His willingness and determination to die for what he saw revealed the all-absorbing inflammation of God's love.

The Second Manifestation of Consolation indicates a strong affective reaction—shedding tears—that results from experiencing God's love and that leads to a deeper love of God. Ignatius mentions several specific types of love that can cause tears, such as sorrow for sin or being moved by the sufferings of Jesus. Thus, consolation can be painful. It hurts to know that we have offended a God who loves us so much, but that is exactly why we experience sorrow. It is painful to see clearly with the eyes of our heart how much Jesus has suffered for us and others. Tears of joy may be mixed with tears of pain. Pain may be a primary reason for tears or, on the contrary, tears may flow from joy and gratitude. For example, we can be moved to tears while experiencing God's overwhelming love in Creation or in the love of another human being. However, here Ignatius gives two reasons to be rooted in pain—sorrow for sin and the sufferings of Jesus. Thus, the intense consolation of tears can be ascribed to a variety of relational and affective reasons, including pain, joy, gratitude, and love.

During Ignatius' experience of the Trinity, he was moved to "so many tears and so much sobbing that he could not control himself." He experienced intense consolation as "his understanding began to be elevated." His implicit experience of God was becoming explicit: his soul, which was previously "blind" began to "see," and his "rough and uncultivated understanding" was beginning to be "elevated." As his understanding became more enlightened through God's explicit self-communication, Ignatius' reaction was so deep and intense that he was moved to uncontrollable tears.

Further, when seriously ill, he "melted into tears" as he thought about dying because it brought him so much joy and consolation. He could feel the complete contrast between suicidal thoughts during desolation and the joyful feelings of death during consolation.

The Third Manifestation of Consolation concerns an increase of faith, hope, and love. Because consolation is an interior movement, an affective reaction, Ignatius is referring here to a growing interior fullness of faith, an affective increase that is both spiritual and emotional and one that creates more space in our hearts to receive God's loving presence and that allows God to flow through us to others. Even though difficult at times, there is an ease about believing, hoping, and loving when we experience this increase. Such an increase is not dry knowledge or assent of the will about spiritual realities; rather, it is felt knowledge and assent of the heart that fills our entire being and moves us to greater love of God, of ourselves, and of others.

Ignatius experienced this affective increase in his desire to travel alone on a ship to Barcelona rather than with a companion. He said he desired the three virtues of faith, hope, and love. He wanted "to place all confidence and affection and hope in God alone. He spoke thus out of the fullness of his heart." Ignatius was feeling an affective increase of faith, hope, and love that moved him to want God as his sole companion. Further, he experienced an increase of faith through seeing Jesus and Mary with his inner eyes when he said that such an image gave him "great strength" and was a "striking confirmation of his faith." He is referring to a kind of faith that is more than an intellectual assent; it is an expansive and vibrant growth in faith.

The Fourth Manifestation of Consolation is also deeply interior and a feeling that draws us to the life of God. It is an interior joy—a joy of the heart, a joy experienced in the center of our being that spontaneously moves us toward God-centered realities. This interior joy results in our being filled with peace and quiet in God and is an experience of stillness, a quiet being with God. It becomes a more common and pervasive experience when we embrace God's loving presence.

Experiencing many tears during his interior understanding of the Trinity, Ignatius continued to feel a sense of joy and peace in God's presence: "The result was that all through his life this great impression has remained with him, to feel great devotion when he prays to the Most Holy Trinity" and filled him with a pervasive sense of consolation. Ignatius experiences this interior joy when, in his prayer, he feels "great delight" in the manner in which God created the world.

Thus, Ignatius experienced consolation in a variety of ways. Not only did he recognize the difference between consolation and desolation but also he felt the difference in the various manifestations of consolation itself. God was moving in Ignatius' interior, which resulted in a variety of interior reactions. Ignatius' experience of God was not dry or lacking in feeling; rather it was alive and full of emotion.

## Causes of True Consolation

The *Spiritual Exercises* are organized into four "weeks," which are based not on actual days but on specific graces sought. Thus, according to Harvey D. Egan, the First Week refers to the purgative way, the Second Week to the illuminative way, and the Third and Fourth Weeks to the unitive way.[5] In the First Week Rules, Ignatius describes four manifestations of true consolation. In the Second Week Rules, he distinguishes between Consolation without Previous Cause (in which God is the only cause) and Consolation with Previous Cause (in which, along with God, our exterior senses, such as thinking, imagining, and feeling are part of the cause). In Rule 316 Ignatius describes the different manifestations of consolation. In Rule 330 he describes the different immediate causes of true consolation:

> God alone can give consolation to the soul without any previous cause. It belongs *solely* to the Creator to come into a soul, to leave it, to act upon it, to draw it *wholly* to the love of His Divine Majesty. I said without previous cause, that is, *without any preceding perception or knowledge* of any subject by which a soul might be led to such a consolation through its own acts of intellect and will. (my emphasis)

Consolation without Previous Cause is a totally God-inspired experience; no other spiritual, psychological, or physical reality can precipitate it. God does four things during this consolation: (1) comes into us freely; (2) leaves us freely; (3) acts within us, that is, addresses specific realities that need attention, moves us to deeper understanding of God or our own self, and affects our interior senses so we see God, hear God, and touch God; and (4) draws us completely into divine love. Although we may have been praying or thinking of God, we did nothing to bring about this powerful experience—it is God's doing completely, and all we can do is receive this beautiful gift of God's total loving presence.

The four manifestations of consolation described in Rule 316 can be precipitated by using our own intellectual, affective, and imaginative powers along with God's action. Or they can result from nothing other than God's action. In Consolation with Previous Cause, the love of God, sorrow for sin, increase of faith, hope, and love, and attraction to heavenly things may be proportionate to the intensity of our desires and actions during prayer. By opening ourselves to God through our own natural powers during prayer or at other times, we give God the inner space to move. This, in turn, can result in one of the four consoling reactions described in Rule 316.

Although consolation may be experienced in any of these four ways, nothing is done to specifically cause consolation in Consolation without Previous Cause. We may have been praying or thinking of God when this consolation occurred, but nothing we did during our prayer resulted in this consolation; it was totally God's doing. We know this to be true because Consolation without Previous Cause differs from the usual experiences of consolation. It occurs unexpectedly; it is disproportionate to anything taking place in our prayer or our life; one does not cause consolation through personal effort nor does one hold onto it in any way; we are totally transparent in God's presence, wholly drawn into God in that there is no inner clutter between God and ourself. In this experience, we are so absorbed in God that we lose ourself, yet, in the process, we feel ourself more deeply. It is losing the false self that is really finding our true self in God.

Therefore, any of these consolations are Consolation without Previous Cause when they are a total, free, disproportionate experience of God, and we have done nothing to cause them. They are Consolation with Previous Cause when they are in proportion and result, in some way, from our own acts of intellect, imagination, and will. Rule 330, then, expands the description of consolation by focusing on the cause, that is, how an "interior movement is aroused in the soul." In contrast, Rule 316 focuses on the affective result of God's interior movement, that is, what happens when God moves interiorly whether with or without previous cause.

Ignatius' experience by the river on the way to Manresa is one of his most powerful experiences of Consolation without

Previous Cause. Through looking into the water of the river (exterior senses), he began to experience deep understanding (interior eyes). He understood more deeply matters of the spiritual life, faith, and learning: "This took place with so great an illumination that these things appeared to be something altogether new." He received "so great an illumination" that even up to his sixty-second year were he "to gather all the helps he received from God, and everything he knew, and add them together, he does not think that they would equal all that he received at that one time." The unexpectedness of this experience reveals the free movement of God within Ignatius. The sense of newness indicates this experience of understanding was disproportionate to his usually inspired understanding. The totality and depth of understanding show how God "wholly" drew Ignatius into the divine presence in a transparent way; that is, nothing within him was blocking his understanding. The profound and lasting impact, however, indicates how this experience transcended anything Ignatius could have conceived through his own intellect. Although Ignatius was contemplatively gazing into the river for a moment, it was not his contemplative stance that caused such an overwhelming and total experience of God; it was God's free and direct movement within him. All Ignatius could do was receive.

Although this was probably one of his most powerful experiences, Ignatius most likely had other experiences of Consolation without Previous Cause. For instance, his experience of the Holy Trinity was disproportionate to his prayer at the moment, as it overwhelmed him with love of God and drew him so completely and transparently into God that this "great impression remained with him" throughout his life. He may have also experienced another Consolation without Previous Cause during his recuperation period when he unexpectedly envisioned Mary and Jesus, a vision of such "abundant consolation" that resulted in so great a disgust for his sins of lust, that lustful thoughts and images lost their power over him. The unexpectedness of this vision, the total renunciation of his past life, and the lasting effect of it seem to indicate a consolation that was caused by God's power alone and nothing Ignatius had done to provoke it.

## Discerning between True and False Consolation

Ignatius' experience of interior movements was not only a way in which God purified him but also a way in which God taught him more specific realities about the spiritual life. Through desolation, Ignatius learned how the enemy can tempt him, and through various consolations, Ignatius realized the varied ways God moved within him. As the "inner eyes of his soul" were opened even more through true consolation, he learned the differences between true and false consolation. The following excerpts represent three experiences Ignatius underwent in which he became more acutely aware of how subtly he could be pulled away from God by spiritual realities and false consolations. The first experience occurred after his painful struggle with scruples, the second while he was studying in Barcelona, and the third while attending lectures in Paris:

### Great Illuminations and Spiritual Consolations

Besides my seven hours of prayer, I busied myself with certain people who came looking for me to discuss their spiritual interests. All the rest of the day I spent thinking of divine things, especially those that I had either read or meditated on that day. But when I went to bed I received great illuminations and spiritual consolations that made me lose much of the time I had set aside for sleep, and that was not much. I looked into this matter a number of times and gave it some thought. Having set aside so much time for dealing with God, and besides that even all the rest of the day, I began to doubt whether these illuminations came from God. I concluded that I had better not have anything to do with them and devoted the time that I had set aside to sleep. So this I did.[6]

### New Light on Spiritual Things and New Delights

Returning to Barcelona I began my studies with great diligence. But there was one thing that stood very much in my way, and that is when I began to learn by heart, as has to be done in the beginning of grammar, I received new light on spiritual things and new delights. So strong were these delights that I could memorize nothing, nor could I get rid of them however much I tried.

Thinking this over at various times, I said to myself: "Even when I go to prayer or attend Mass these lights do not come to me so vividly." Thus step by step I came to recognize that it was a temptation. After making my meditation, I went to Church and asked my teacher to listen to me for a moment. I gave my teacher a faithful account of what had taken place in my soul, and how little progress I had made until then for the reason above. And I made a promise to my master with the words: "I promise you never to fail to attend your class these two years, as long as I can find bread and water for my support here in Barcelona." I made this promise with such effect that I never again suffered from those temptations.[7]

## A Multitude of Spiritual Ideas

In Paris I took a course in philosophy. Just as I began the lectures, so also began once more the same temptations that beset me when I studied grammar in Barcelona. Whenever I attended lectures I could not fix my attention upon the lecture because of the multitude of spiritual ideas that came upon me. Seeing that I was thus making little headway in my studies, I went to my teacher and gave him my word that I would not fail to attend the whole course, if I could find enough bread and water to keep myself alive. After making this promise, all these devotions ceased, and I went on with my studies in peace.[8]

## The Second Week Rules for Discernment

The purpose of the Second Week Rules is to help us to understand the "different movements produced in the soul," to gain

a "more accurate discernment of spirits," and to help those
who are more in a Second Week experience of God (328).
The "more" mentioned three times in the first paragraph of
the Second Week Rules reiterates the "more" of the grace of
the Second Week Contemplations: ". . . to ask for an intimate
knowledge of our Lord, who has become man for me, that I
may love Him more and follow Him more closely" (104). The
Rules for the Second Week are intended for those who have
committed their hearts and lives to God—to developing a personal relationship with God and living out the consequences
of that relationship in their daily lives. They are for those who
are not seriously trapped in outright acts of sin but who have
allowed their hearts to be purified by God. Although areas of
their hearts continue to need purification, their deepest selves
are united with God in an intimate relationship. They are trying to know, love, and serve God with their whole hearts,
minds, souls, and beings.

Because these people are striving earnestly to be in total
union with God, they are more aware of obvious temptation.
Thus, their temptations occur in more subtle ways. Ignatius
refers to this in Rule 329, where he describes true and false
consolation:

> It is characteristic of God and His Angels, when they act
> upon the soul, to give *true happiness and spiritual joy,*
> and to banish all the sadness and disturbances which
> are caused by the enemy.
>
> It is characteristic of the evil one to fight against such
> happiness and consolation by *proposing fallacious
> reasonings, subtleties, and continual deceptions.* (my
> emphasis)

The Second Week Rules, then, focus on consolations and
discerning among consolations, whereas the First Week Rules
describe the interplay between consolation and desolation
and what to do while in desolation. Further, the Second Week
Rules emphasize the subtle and deceptive ways that we can
be drawn away from God over a period of time, whereas the
First Week Rules emphasize the more obvious and immediate
ways that we can be tempted.

In the three experiences already mentioned, Ignatius underwent subtle and deceptive temptations that took the form of consolations. Now, more deeply rooted in God and spiritual realities rather than worldly pursuits, his temptations were of a similar nature, that is, around spiritual things. In the first, Ignatius became preoccupied with the "great illuminations and spiritual consolations" that he experienced in bed at night. But the deceptive part of this was that these consolations caused him to lose sleep, which affected his daily service of God. In the second and third experiences, the deception was such that the "new light on spiritual things and new delights" and the "multitude of spiritual ideas" prevented him from studying rather than helping him to carry out his commitment to learn more in order to help others grow in their spiritual lives.

### Deception in Consolation with Previous Cause

Rule 331 more thoroughly explores the cause of consolation and explains why we undergo false consolation:

> If a *cause precedes,* both the good angel and the evil spirit can give consolation to a soul, but for a quite *different purpose.* The good angel consoles for the *progress* of the soul, that it may advance and rise to what is more perfect. The evil spirit consoles for purposes that are the *contrary,* and that afterwards he might draw the soul to his own perverse intentions and wickedness. (my emphasis)

In Consolation without Previous Cause, there can be no deception because God is the sole source of the consolation. However, in Consolation with Previous Cause ("If a cause precedes . . ."), there can be deception because this consolation can either be caused by God or by realities other than God. Thus, Ignatius' descriptions of consolation are becoming more precise.

What is the *purpose* of consolation and distinguishing between true and false consolation? True consolation from

God moves us closer to God and allows us to live for God. False consolation, which arises from our sinfulness or our own thoughts and fantasies, eventually moves us away from God and the service of others. The illuminations and consolations Ignatius experienced while trying to sleep left him weary and prevented him from giving himself as fully the next day; thus they were leading him away from advancing in a life of service. The spiritual insights that came while he was studying and listening to lectures were contrary to his deeper desire to be better educated in order to minister in a more effective way. Thus, due to the outcome of the consolation, he could distinguish its cause.

Rule 332 elaborates on the nature of the "fallacious reasonings, subtleties, and continual deceptions" of false consolation, that is, consolation not caused by God:

> It is the mark of the evil spirit to assume the *appearance of an angel of light.* He begins by suggesting thoughts that are suited to a devout soul, and ends by suggesting his own. For example, he will suggest *holy and pious thoughts* that are *wholly* in conformity with the sanctity of the soul. Afterwards, he will endeavor *little by little* to end by drawing the soul into his *hidden snares* and *evil designs.* (my emphasis)

This Rule gives the *picture,* the *process,* and the *progression* of false consolation. The picture is one of darkness, sinfulness, and evil that takes on the appearance of light. That is, the false consolation is attractive, uplifting, and enlightening and appears to be bringing us closer to God and our true self. When we are in intimate union with God, we are more likely to see crude temptations and less apt to notice temptation occurring in the guise of a spiritual reality that is attractive and life-giving. Therefore, darkness takes on the appearance of light and goodness.

How does the appearance of darkness as light occur? The process takes place in our thoughts. The affective state may be similar in true and false consolation, that is, I may be feeling delight, joy, and love for God. The thoughts flowing from this consoling affective state may be holy and pious and totally congruent with our intimate union with God. But little by little, the progression of holy thoughts leads toward "hidden snares"—the thoughts are drawing us away from God in almost unnoticed and secretive ways ("covert deceits"). Thus, darkness seems light and consonant with our relationship with God. The process is slow, it happens over time, and it is not immediately obvious. The progression is such that the original thoughts are in tune with God's ways, but they end up leading the person away from God.

Rule 333 elaborates on the process and progression and describes what we must do to increase our awareness:

> We must carefully observe the *whole course of our thoughts*. If the *beginning and middle and end* of the course of thoughts are *wholly good* and directed to what is entirely right, it is a sign that they are from the good angel. But the course of thoughts suggested to us may terminate in something *evil,* or *distracting,* or *less good* than the soul had formerly proposed to do. Again, it may end in what *weakens* the soul, or *disquiets* it; or by *destroying the peace, tranquillity, and quiet* which it had before, it may *cause disturbance* to the soul. These things are a clear sign that the thoughts are proceeding from the evil spirit, the enemy of our progress and eternal salvation. (my emphasis)

This rule complements Rules 319 and 326 of the First Week Rules. One way to counterattack desolation is through "examination" (319). Rule 333 suggests a more refined form of examination—recognizing the entire spectrum of thought from beginning to end—in order to counterattack false consolation. Both examinations have the same purpose—to help us see how we are being tempted to move away from God.

Rule 326 encourages bringing hidden realities out into the light of another spiritual person. Rule 333 complements 326 by encouraging us to bring our thought process into the light of our own awareness. Both suggest bringing the entire picture, process, and progression into conscious awareness in order to dissipate the power of darkness.

Having explained that moving away from God's light into darkness occurs gradually ("little by little"), Ignatius suggests a way of examination that incorporates the entire process.

He suggests that we carefully observe the "whole course" of our thoughts—the "beginning, middle, and end." If the entire movement is consonant with God's desires, our graced desires, and our growing intimate relationship, then these are truly from God. If the middle or end of our thoughts are dissonant with God's thoughts, even in the slightest way, then false consolation is present. A significant portion of the beginning of the consolation may be God-inspired, and a small dimension may be from our own darkness. However, darkness that resembles light could grow larger as the consolation reveals itself over time. For example, a consolation that is 75 percent God's action (true consolation) and 25 percent darkness (false consolation) in the middle and end portion could become just the reverse—that is, 75 percent from our own darkness. Or, even if the 25 percent false consolation remains the same throughout the entire process, that same percentage could be drawing us—little by little—further away from God. Therefore, we need to observe the full reality of the consolation in order to differentiate between what belongs to God and what belongs to our own darkness appearing as light. Sifting apart, differentiating, and discerning our consolations is essential for a more total union with God.

Rule 333 elaborates further. We can be sure that the consolation is false not only if it leads us to something evil or sinful but also if it leads us to something "distracting or less good" than our former attitude, behavior, or way of life. It is also false if it "weakens" our interior life and "disquiets" us, "destroys our peace, tranquility and quiet," or disturbs our single-hearted spiritual pursuits. Thus, any consolation (whether total or part) or "good and pious thought" that in the end results in disturbance of interior peace indicates that false consolation is operating and is, ultimately, attempting to draw us away from union with and service of God.

Ignatius experienced the dynamics of these two Rules in all three experiences. The great illuminations, new light on spiritual things, and multitude of spiritual ideas appeared to be from God's light and about holy realities. Possibly some of these illuminations were God-inspired. However, he observed the entire course of his thoughts. In the first experience, he "looked into this matter a number of times and gave it some thought." In the second, he thought over the beginning, middle, and end "at various times," and thus "step by step he came to recognize that it was a temptation." Through this careful and continuous reflection, Ignatius became aware of the end result: the great illuminations were preventing sleep, which he needed in order to serve God. The new lights were interfering with studying and listening to lectures that would help him serve God more effectively in the long run. Ignatius not only examined these experiences on his own, he also brought the latter two experiences to the attention of his teachers (326). This helped him to see the process of consolation more carefully and to counteract their progression by promising not to entertain the great illuminations and spiritual thoughts.

## Deception in the Afterglow of Consolation without Previous Cause

Most of the Second Week Rules elaborate on the deceptions that can be present in Consolation with Previous Cause. Realities other than God could be causing the consolation—that is, our own sinfulness and twisted thinking. Rule 330 focuses on a consolation in which there can be no deception within the consolation itself because God is its sole source. There is no need to look for deception because there is none. However, even though no deception exists within this consolation, there can be deception during the *Afterglow*. The deception is not innate in the consolation itself, as might happen in the case of Consolation with Previous Cause, but rather it could emerge from our interpretation *after* the consolation dissipates. In Rule 336, Ignatius states we must attentively and cautiously distinguish the actual time of the consolation from the period afterward. During the time after, due to the fervent feelings we have from being drawn into God's love, we might make a decision based on our own reasoning rather than from a God-inspired reason. Or the decision could arise from deception—darkness looking like light and grace. Thus, even with Consolation without Previous Cause, we need to examine the full spectrum of the experience—the source, the experience itself, and the time after. We need to discern, separate, and sift apart our most powerful consolations to assure there is no deception anywhere—beginning, middle, or end.

## Conclusion

As Ignatius grew in a more intimate relationship with God, he became more keenly discerning not only of contrary movements of consolation and desolation but also of similar movements of consolation. Whereas before his soul was blind, now the eyes of his understanding were open. He noticed differences in the experience of consolation itself—different manifestations of consolation, different causes of consolation, and various outcomes of consolation. He became aware which consolations brought him closer to God and which slowly and subtly drew him away from God. Ignatius was developing a keen discerning heart. God taught him through interior movements, and Ignatius, in turn, instructed us by writing down key aspects of his inner experience in his autobiography and in the Rules for Discernment.

## Experiencing God

### Reliving a Consolation without Previous Cause

In God's presence, remember a time that you experienced an unexpected, out of the ordinary, and very powerful experience of God's love that made a deep and lasting impression on you.

Savor the richness of the experience, and relive it in your memory, feeling, imagination, heart, and mind.

✝ What were the circumstances of the experience? What was God's presence like in the experience?

✝ What were some of your feelings, thoughts, and desires?

✝ What difference did you notice within yourself as a result of this experience?

As you relive the experience, be attentive to God's presence with you now. Share with God any feelings that arise, and listen to God's response.

## Noticing your Consolations in "Ordinary Time"

In God's presence, notice the ways you have been experiencing consolation in "ordinary time" (choose a time period—a week, a month, a few months).

✞ In your daily life, how do you usually experience God's presence?

✞ What are your usual affective reactions? joy? peace? love? hope? tears? a sense of well-being?

Savor the richness of your consolations. Express gratitude for God's presence with you. Ask God for the gifts of fidelity and strength in times of desolation.

## Getting Lost Along the Way

In God's presence, remember a time or a decision you made in which you thought you were going in the right direction, but later discovered that you got lost along the way. You learned that what seemed to be God's will and what seemed to be congruent with your deepest self was not right after all.

✞ What were the circumstances?

✞ What were your thoughts and feelings? What were the subtle deceptions that were going on?

✞ What was God's presence like at the beginning, middle, and end of the decision?

✞ How long were you lost? disoriented?

✞ What helped you to realize that you were moving in the wrong direction?

✞ What did you learn from this experience about yourself? about God? about false consolation?

As you ponder this experience, be attentive to God's presence with you now. Share with God any feelings that arise, and listen to God's response. Ask God what you need in order to avoid this type of false consolation again.

# Questions for Reflection and Discussion

1. Which of Ignatius' true consolations is most moving to you? Which one(s) can you relate to most in your own experience?

2. What similarities and differences do you notice in Ignatius' five experiences of true consolation?

3. What similarities and differences do you notice in Ignatius' three experiences of false consolation?

4. What are some of the values of true consolations that are necessary for the ongoing development of our relationship with God?

5. What are some of the benefits for the ongoing development of our relationship with God that can be derived from experiencing false consolation?

# For Spiritual Directors

## A Written Dialogue on True Consolations (individually)

Write out a spiritual direction conversation between Ignatius and yourself as his spiritual director on one or more of his five true consolations.

✟ What and how would you focus on in Ignatius' experience?

✟ What questions might you ask Ignatius?

## A Written Dialogue on False Consolations (individually)

Write out a spiritual direction conversation between Ignatius and yourself as his spiritual director on one or more of his three false consolations, keeping in mind the above questions.

## Role Play on True Consolations (in a group)

Role play a spiritual direction session on one of his true consolations in which one person is Ignatius and another is his spiritual director.

✝ What in Ignatius' experience would you focus on? What questions might you ask Ignatius?

After the role play, reflect on the experience individually, and then discuss the following questions:

1. What touches you most about Ignatius' experience? Did any new insight come alive for you through role playing?

2. What strikes you most about the spiritual direction session and the spiritual director?

3. What did you learn? What was reinforced about spiritual direction?

### Role Play on False Consolation (in a group)

Same procedure as above.

### Significant Insights

What three significant insights about the Rules for Discernment did you gain or were reinforced by Ignatius' experiences of true and false consolation?

# Part II

# Environment

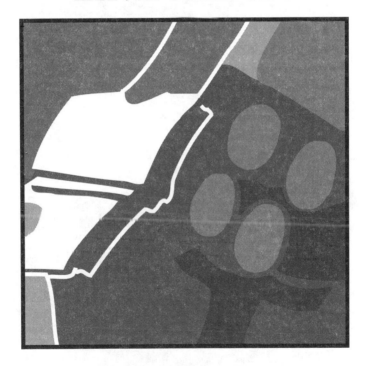

**Growth in Our
Personal Relationship with God**

**Spiritual Direction as Fostering
Our Relationship with God**

---
| 4 |
---

# Growth in Our Personal Relationship with God

As we relate to God in an affective way, the skeletal description of Ignatius' Rules for Discernment is enfleshed. As we grow in a conscious relationship with God, the lifeblood of the dynamics of the Rules is enlivened. As God's implicit presence within and around us becomes explicit in our experience, the rich meanings of the Rules become operative. Without the lively experiencing of God, the Rules remain an archaic description, a skeleton, of experience. Our personal relationship with God is what moves a *past description* into a *present experience*. Our vibrant experience of God is what brings the skeleton out of the closet, so to speak. Thus, when we relate with God in a personal way, Ignatius' Rules for Discernment become operative, meaningful, and understandable.

Our affective, conscious, and explicit experiencing of God is the foundation for our personal relationship. Our relationship with God is "personal" because it involves our entire being: our heart, mind, spirit, body, affectivity, desires, and actions. It is "real" because it moves through the various dynamics and dimensions of relational growth. In this chapter, I will discuss some of these dynamics and dimensions and reflect on these in relation to the *Spiritual Exercises*.

## Dynamics of Relational Growth

Growth in relationship with God occurs through mutual self-revelation: God reveals divine presence to us more fully, and we share ourselves more generously. God's objective self-communication through creation, Scripture, life circumstances, and relationships becomes subjective and alive in our experience. Further, God's felt involvement causes interior reactions in us. Spontaneous movements toward and away from God also take place. As in any important relationship, at times we feel joy and delight; other times, fear and struggle. Sometimes we surrender; at other times, we pull away from God's self-communication. Whatever the interior reactions, lively experience is happening within us, and a real relationship is growing. Although each of these elements—God's self-revelation and our interior reactions and response—usually occur simultaneously, I will explore each element separately in order to describe the dynamic of self-revelation in our relating with God.

As we grow in relationship, God reveals Self to us in concrete, fuller, richer, and deeper ways. The transcendent God becomes affectively immanent. Truths we have learned about God change to living realities.[1] Experiencing God involves being attentive to God's self-communication: "It is through the Holy Ghost, this 'finger of God,' that the hand of the All High touches us, and gives us His gifts, His gift, which is Himself."[2] Although God's touch is mediated through outer realties—such as creation—and inner realities—such as our imagination—it is immediate in that we feel God's closeness. Thus, Ignatius indicates God's immediate self-communication: ". . . it is more suitable and much better that the Creator and Lord in person should communicate Himself to the devout soul, that He inflame it with His love and praise, and dispose it for the way in which it could better serve Him in the future."[3] Experiencing God involves allowing God's self-communication to take place in our hearts and lives, as exemplified in the following contemporary examples. (The names have been changed to protect confidentiality.)

Joan affectively experienced God in creation as she prayed in a park one morning. She said: "God was just there in nature—being. Quiet. Present. I sensed God in various parts of creation—the trees as they blew in the wind, the rippling lake, the geese as they flew overhead. God was united to everything there. I felt a oneness with God and nature. There was no separation."

By reading a scriptural passage, Beth's experience of God became alive. As a leader in her parish, she struggled with a serious decision she had to make. The passage of Jesus healing the hemorrhaging woman appealed to her.[4] "I felt weighed down, burdened, bent over like the woman in the gospel," she said. "I felt Jesus say to me, 'You are free of your infirmity.' Although this burden continued to be there, I felt freer. I could stand up straighter, and deal with it."

God's presence becomes affectively alive in us through our awareness of God's self-revelation in a given moment. God becomes real for us as we affectively respond to God's self-communication. St. Bernard says, "He is life and power, and as soon as he enters in, he awakens my slumbering soul; he stirs and soothes and pierces my heart . . . Only by the movement of my heart . . . did I perceive his presence."[5] The more deeply we allow God to enter into our person, the more complete are our reactions: our mind, heart, spirit, feelings, and body become engaged. Ignatius refers to our total involvement: "We use acts of the intellect in reasoning, and acts of the will in movements of the feelings; greater reverence is required on our part than when we are using the intellect in understanding."[6] In his suggested mode of contemplation, Ignatius encourages us to "pass through the five senses of the imagination" in our interaction with God "to see the person with the sight of the imagination, . . . to hear with the hearing what they are or might be talking about, . . . and to smell and to taste the infinite fragrance and sweetness of the Divinity."[7]

Joe, in describing a deep experience of God, said: "It was like God picked me up and held me and has not let me down ever since. I could feel God's embrace—very warm, strong, gentle, and loving. I felt, and still feel, very secure yet free in that embrace." Similarly, by taking to heart the statement, "In Christ we live and move and have our being," Jim experienced a deep interior sense of God's presence: "I experienced a deep certitude that God is inside of me, a part of me. I feel God becoming more a part of me this week. I feel God deep inside me as I go about the activities of my day. God's presence

in me gives me great joy and comfort. One of the brothers I
live with even remarked that I seemed especially happy this
week. It's like a joy wells up within me. It's wonderful." Both
Joe and Jim affectively participated in God's self-revelation.

God's self-revelation causes a variety of interior reactions.
Some result from a movement toward God, such as joy,
peace, or a growing desire for closeness. Others occur because of a spontaneous movement away from God, such as
restlessness, fear, lack of spiritual desire, or resistance. At
times we feel God's presence: "When I contemplate all these
things I am filled with awe and wonder at his manifold
greatness,"[8] noted St. Bernard. At other times we feel God's
absence: "But when the Word has left me," he continued, "all
these spiritual powers become weak and faint and begin to
grow cold, as though you had removed the fire from under a
boiling pot."[9]

As discussed in chapter 1, Ignatius began to notice these
reactions within himself during his convalescence. When he
was thinking about worldly things, he felt much delight; but
afterwards he was "dry and discontented."[10] When pondering
the lives of the saints, not only was he "consoled" when he
had these "thoughts" but even after he remained "content and
happy."[11] Ignatius continued to notice differences in his reactions. At another time in his life, "various emotions came over
him and caused discontent in his soul . . . He struggled with
this conflict of desire for a long time."[12] He found "great plea-
sure and consolation" in seeing a beautiful creature in the air,
but "when it disappeared he was saddened."[13] He experienced "the same interior state of great and steady happiness"
and then a "harsh thought came to trouble him."[14] "He began
to experience great changes in his soul" sometimes feeling "so
disagreeable that he took no joy in prayer . . . and at other
times exactly the opposite came over him."[15] Ignatius was
experiencing the dynamics of a growing affective relationship
with God.

Julian of Norwich, the fifteenth-century English ascetic,
vividly describes this movement and countermovement:

> Our Lord revealed to me a supreme spiritual delight in
> my soul. In this delight I was filled full of everlasting
> surety, and I was powerfully secured without any fear. . . .

I was at peace, at ease and at rest, so that there was nothing upon earth which could have afflicted me.

This lasted only for a time, and then I was changed, and left to myself, oppressed and weary of myself, ruing my life . . . I felt that there was not ease or comfort in me except hope, faith, and love, and truly I felt very little of this. And then God gave me again comfort and rest for my soul, delight and security so blessed and so powerful that there was no fear, no sorrow, no pain, physical or spiritual, . . . which might have disturbed me. And then again I felt the pain, and then afterwards the joy and the delight, now the one and now the other, again and again . . . And in the time of joy I could have said with Paul: "Nothing shall separate me from the love of Christ"; and in the pain, I could have said with Peter: "Lord, save me, I am perishing."

This taught me that . . . God wishes us to know that he keeps us safe all the time, in joy and in sorrow, and that he loves us as much in sorrow as in joy. . . . In this time I committed no sin for which I ought to have been left to myself, nor did I deserve these sensations of joy; but God gives joy freely as it pleases him, and sometimes he allows us to be in sorrow, and both come from his love.[16]

Thus, as in any human relationship of deep love, at times we feel great joy and comfort because of another's presence in our lives. At other times we experience the burden of the relationship, we feel fearful to become more deeply involved, or we sense little of that person's support. Many times movement toward and away from God occurs simultaneously. The more real, deep, and mutual our relationship with God, the more subtle the "pulls."

## Dimensions of Relational Growth

Several key dimensions exist in God's self-revelation and our response to it. The primary dimension is desire: God's desire for us and our desire for God.[17] That is, God's desire for us awakens our desire for God. Our desire to love God is not merely a human exigency:

It was God himself who placed this desire in human
hearts, so that they yearn to see and love him face to
face. It was God himself who structured human beings
in such a way that they are permanently open to hearing the voice of God as it comes to them through
things, their own conscience, other human mediations,
and God himself . . . The natural desire to love God . . .
is the call which God places within human beings.
They hear that call and cry out for God. The cry of
human beings is merely an echo of God's voice calling
them.[18]

Frequently, desire begins with a vague attraction to God
and spiritual realities. For instance, often when people begin
spiritual direction, they express a desire for a personal relationship with God without a clear sense of who God is for
them. As they come to understand more about a personal
God, their attraction strengthens and their desire deepens.

Our desire for God is not a prelude to religious experience
but, in itself, is a rich experience of God. It is not only the
door opening toward a spiritual relationship but also a new
beginning, for in the strength of our longing our relationship
has already begun. As St. Gregory remarked: "He who with
his whole soul, desires God, certainly already possesses the
One he loves."[19] Union with God grows as desire deepens:
"The greater desire becomes, the more the soul rests in God.
Possession increases in the same proportion as desire."[20]
Ignatius expresses our desire for union with God as generosity and openness: "It is very helpful to him who is receiving
the Exercises to enter into them with great courage and generosity towards his Creator and Lord, offering Him all his will
and liberty . . . "[21] Further, he reveals the deepening of our
desires through the development of the "grace" ("what I want
and desire") in the Four Weeks of the *Spiritual Exercises.*[22]

Another essential element of relational growth is experiencing the various dimensions of God's love. As mutual desire
grows, so too does an openness to experience God's love.
God continuously reveals the "breadth and length and height
and depth of Christ's love."[23] God's love is revealed objec-
tively in specific ways.[24] Thus, this objective reality must be
subjectively experienced.

From the outset, God reveals the depth and uniqueness of divine love. "Mary," for example, prayed for a long period of time ("You are precious in my eyes.")[25] "I feel how uniquely precious I am to God," she said. "Each part of me is important to God—my thoughts, my feelings, and my body. It makes me want to value myself more." As God reveals the fullness of unconditional love, we realize that God's acceptance of us does not depend on our moral rightness or wrongness.

It is in this environment that the dynamics of the *Spiritual Exercises* take place. The *Spiritual Exercises* enable us to see God as Creator and ourselves as God's creatures. It helps us gain deep inner freedom ("indifference") in order to choose God and to find God in all things. It helps us to grow more aware of our sinfulness and our tendency toward darkness and to become freer of "disordered attachments" so that we can respond to God more completely. Interiorly, we notice and ask God to change self-centered and limiting attitudes —"disordered tendencies"—that prevent us from loving ourselves and others as well as God. Exteriorly, this transformation is expressed in our daily lives as we strive to respond to God's desires for us.[26]

The weeks of the *Spiritual Exercises* come alive through our affective knowledge of God's love. In the First Week this knowledge enables us to become aware of our sinfulness and uproot our disordered tendencies so that we can live a life more deeply committed to God. When "Maria" first began spiritual direction, she spoke of the specific way that God manifested Himself to her. She had decreased her commitment to God and the Church for several years. She sensed through liturgies and prayer that God was encouraging her to "Come to me. Return to me." As she lingered with God's invitation, Maria began to realize that God felt like a "fatherly friend" who loved her and desired to be part of her life. As she experienced God as "comforting and soothing," she began to feel sorrow. "I feel a lot of remorse for the years that I didn't bother with God or the Church. I feel sadness," she declared. God's desire for Maria to "return" deeply affected her:

> The "compunction of the heart," . . . always tends to become a "compunction of love" . . . Compunction is an act of God in us, an act by which God awakens us,

a shock, a blow, a "sting," a sort of burn. God goads us
as if with a spear; He "presses" us with insistence, as if
to pierce us. The love of the world lulls; but, as if by a
thunderstroke, the attention of the soul is recalled to God.[27]

As we experience the depths of God's love for us, we
grow more aware of our darkness and sinfulness. We realize
more keenly our unworthiness to receive that love. The light
of God's love illuminates dark areas. Its intensity frees us to
look deeper at our sinfulness:

It is to the love of God that we should cling. The soul
hardened by egoism becomes tender, the cold soul is
warmed and cleansed of its rust. Returned . . . to its
true center of gravity, . . . it is simplified, rectified,
freed. The soul cannot remain long (here). It is dazzled
by what it perceives of God; the light of God repels it
and it falls back upon itself, wearied and as if it
were struck by lightning . . . It takes up again its life of
desire in the midst of temptations, all the stronger and
more numerous for its having been admitted to a higher
plane. The soul, illuminated by God's light, the soul
which knows God, perceives in itself all that is impure
and contrary to God.[28]

So he has begun to pluck out and destroy, to build up
and to plant, to water dry places and illuminate dark
ones; to open what was closed and to warm what was
cold. . . . so that my soul may bless the Lord, and all
that is within me may praise his holy name.[29]

The "grace" of the First Week opens us to experience
God's merciful love. What we "ask for and desire" is intense
sorrow for our sins and the ability to understand the root of
our disordered tendencies.[30] Sorrow for sin and illumination
of our blind spots occur through experiencing God's unconditional love.

As we allow God's merciful love to purify us, we become
less self-centered and more aware of God and others. Our
growing freedom enables us to be more explicitly attentive to
God and to respond more completely. The "grace" of the
Second Week becomes operative: we grow in an "intimate

knowledge of our Lord," that we may "love him more and follow him more closely."[31] We are not satisfied with only being
saved by God; we desire more. We desire greater intimacy
with Jesus through knowing, loving, and working with him.
Thus, relating with God shifts from a doing-for to a doing-
and-being-with. That is, not only does God do for us and we
do for God, but now we work with God and God works with
us in bringing others closer to God. Mutuality grows. Our connection changes into a more vulnerable giving-and-receiving
relationship on both sides.

As we grow in mutual relationship with God, we want to
share with others our life-giving love. The love that God and
we experience mutually overflows into a desire to "labor
together" to help others experience God's saving love.[32] Our
desire to work with God has many faces. At times we do
works of mercy; other times we strive to change oppressive
social structures. We use our personal gifts and talents to help
concretize God's desire for justice: "Loving Him you will be
an imitator of His goodness and don't be surprised that a
human being can become an imitator of God."[33]

As our relationship unfolds, we encounter moments when
we are tested, either through interior struggles or exterior circumstances. We experientially realize the cost of discipleship
and the pain of commitment. We encounter darkness again,
but this darkness results from the struggle to remain faithful
when the cost of fidelity seems overwhelming. We experience
how deeply demanding is our relationship with God. We must
not only labor with but also suffer with God. The Third Week
of the *Spiritual Exercises* expresses this dimension: we experience "sorrow with Christ in sorrow, anguish with Christ in
anguish."[34] The "more" of the Second Week becomes a deeper
"more," as we suffer with God.

Our faithful commitment in hard times reaches completion
during the Fourth Week in the overwhelming joy we experience with God. In abandoning all, we receive all: not only
darkness but light; not only suffering but joy. God's joy
becomes our joy. We receive the "grace to be glad and rejoice
intensely because of the great joy and glory of Christ our
Lord."[35] Through suffering with God, we experience a deeper
and more pervasive joy.

As these dimensions of relational growth deepen, we realize more fully how God's presence permeates our personality, our life circumstances, and our culture. Our relationship with God does not unfold separately from but grows integrally in the atmosphere of our life experience: "God is present always, the relationship with him is constant, and growth is possible anytime," remarks Thomas N. Hart. "There is no area of human life in which God is uninterested . . . Our relationship with him, then, is not a special activity, but a constant reality."[36] We find God in all things as we realize that our relationship is not something added onto our life experience but something innate in it.[37]

The contemporary author and theologian Leonardo Boff describes it this way:

> Grace can be grace for us today only if it emerges from within the world in which we ourselves are immersed. Only then can it signify what it is meant to signify in Christian terms: the reality of God's free love and his liberating presence in the world. Grace appears within our concrete world, liberating us from a decadent human situation and for a fuller, divinized one . . . Only by immersing ourselves in the reality around us can we experience its aspects of gratuitousness and grace.[38]

## Conclusion

The more personally we relate to God in our life and world, the more concretely we find God in all things. The deeper we can respond to God's touch in our innermost being and life circumstances, the more integrated we grow and the more keenly we personify St. Irenaeus' expression: "The glory of God is a person fully alive, fully alive in Christ on the way to the Father."[39] Our aliveness happens in relationship with God, with ourselves, with others, with life circumstances, and with the world. But our relationship with God is the permeating reality of all other relationships. It is in this environment that we develop a discerning heart. It is here too that the Rules for Discernment come alive and are understandable.

# Experiencing God

## Getting in Touch with Your Desire for God

St. Gregory says: "He who with his whole soul, desires God, certainly already possesses the One he loves. . . . The greater desire becomes, the more the soul rests in God. Possession increases in the same proportion as desire."

In God's presence, let yourself be in touch with your desire for God.

✠ What is that desire like? How strong is your desire for God?

✠ "As the deer longs for the running waters, so my soul longs for you, O God!" (Ps. 42:2) How would you image your desire for God? How would you articulate it if someone asked you about it?

✠ Has your desire for God changed through the years? How has it changed?

Express to God your desire. Ask God to increase your desire if it needs to be strengthened.

## Becoming Aware of God's Desire for You

✠ Spend time looking at God. Who is God for you now? How is God present with you at this moment?

✠ What is God's desire for you like? Listen to God express this desire.

✠ Jesus said: "How often I have yearned to gather you, as a mother bird gathers her young under her wings . . . " (Mt. 23:37). How would you image or express God's desire for you as you are sensing it now?

✠ Let yourself feel God's desire for you. How do you feel as you get in touch with this desire? joyful? grateful? fearful?

Share this feeling with God. Ask for a greater awareness of and openness to God's desire for you.

### Remembering and Reliving an Experience of God

Remember a time when you felt touched by God, possibly similar to one of the people mentioned in this chapter—Joan, Mary, Beth, Joe, or Maria. Bring to mind the outer circumstances and the inner details of the experience. Linger with and relive the experience in your memory, feeling, imagination, heart, and mind.

☩ What were the circumstances of the experience, that is, were you by yourself, on the beach, on a retreat, at a liturgy, going through a hard time in your life?

☩ What was God's presence like in the experience?

☩ What were some of your feelings, thoughts, and desires? What difference did you notice within yourself as a result of this experience?

As you relive the experience, be attentive to God's presence with you now. Share with God any feelings that arise, and listen to God's response. Ask God for what you desire now in your personal relationship.

## Questions for Reflection and Discussion

1. Prayerfully reflect on your own growth in your relationship with God. Together with God, contemplate your relationship. What characterizes your relationship? Is it mutual, or is it one-sided? What are its joys, blessings, and strengths? In what specific ways do you need to grow in your relationship with God?

2. Do you experience a variety of reactions in your relationship with God, such as what Julian of Norwich describes or what Ignatius experienced? What are some of your usual affective reactions that move you toward God? What are some of your reactions that are a spontaneous (not necessarily intentional) movement away from God? Remember or share an instance of your varied reactions.

# For Spiritual Directors

Prayerfully reflect on each of your directees. Contemplate each of them in the presence of God.

✞ How would you describe their desire for God?

✞ What do you sense is God's desire for them?

✞ Where do you sense each of them is in their relationship with God? in relation to the Four Weeks of the *Spiritual Exercises?*

✞ What must individuals do to deepen their relationship with God?

1. Write out or role play with someone a spiritual direction session in which you are helping your directees articulate their desire for God and for a deeper prayer life. How might the session unfold? What are some key questions you might ask?

2. State three significant insights that you gained or that were reinforced about an individual's growth in a personal relationship with God.

---
| 5 |
---

# Spiritual Direction as Fostering Our Relationship with God

Spiritual direction helps to foster growth in our relationship with God. It helps us to respond to God's self-revelation as we experience it affectively in order to deepen our relationship with God and to live a more integrated life. Directors form a supportive relationship with directees and nourish a contemplative atmosphere that enables directees to express freely their vulnerability, their pain, their joys, and their gratitude and to share these with God; to contemplate God's felt presence in prayer and life; to savor, relive, and respond to their experience of God; and to notice interior changes and the effects of these changes in relationships and life circumstances.[1] In this chapter, I will briefly describe the qualities necessary to maintain a fulfilling spiritual direction relationship and the atmosphere that directors need to create in order to help people explore their experience of and relationship with God.[2] I will also make reference to Ignatius' view of the role of the spiritual director in the Annotations and in other parts of the *Spiritual Exercises*.

## The Relationship Between Director and Directee

For individuals to share openly they must establish a solid relationship with their director. Various qualities of person and presence can help solidify the relationship between directee and director.

Spiritual directors strive to become companions of their directees, not teachers, gurus, or problem solvers. Writes Alan Jones:

> With us who are consciously responding to a call to be a companion, the medium is the message. We cannot convincingly "talk" about companionship without "being" a companion. We are a word about the Word. We are not to offer dogma. We are to offer ourselves.[3]

Companionship is personified by the feminine image of the midwife. The literal meaning of midwife is "with woman." As a midwife facilitates the birth of a child, so too a director accompanies another individual in the growth of a lively relationship with God.[4]

As companions, spiritual directors journey along a path of deep empathy. They are engaged wholeheartedly in the other person's experience. They strive to enter into the other's world as if it were their own without losing the "as if" quality.[5] This empathetic presence means directors allow the struggles, joys, hopes, and spiritual experiences of their directees to touch them affectively. It involves creating the inner space to receive the unique stories of other people.

Spiritual directors must care deeply about their directees. Some directees are naturally more likable than others, but directors need to convey to all of them that they care. Such caring often frees people to share more openly. Their love, as God's love, can heal: "It is unlove that makes people unwell," notes Thomas N. Hart, "and it's love and love alone that can make people well again."[6] Listening is a particular expression of caring. Directors listen *actively* with interest, sensitivity, and compassion; not *passively* with detachment and guardedness. "To listen attentively to another and to go with another in companionship are expressions of love," Hart continues. "To do either without love is an empty gesture and bears no fruit. The helper loves the other."[7] Sincere care and reverence evokes trust and confidence from directees. They soon realize that directors consider what they share to be unique, precious, and sacred.

One of the most enabling qualities of presence is to be natural, to be oneself, to laugh, and to cry spontaneously when touched by another person's story and to express understanding and compassion. Directees can sense when directors are not being natural and relaxed, and this can block their free sharing. The more relaxed spiritual directors are, the more they enable directees to be themselves in their weakness and strength.

Commitment to the direction relationship and process is also essential. As in any caring relationship, psychological realities are going to take place, including transference and countertransference.[8] As people grow in their relationship with God, various expressions of resistance occur. Directees must feel confident that their directors will stand solidly with them in the ups and downs of their struggles. Spiritual directors need to know that their directees are deeply committed to their own growth so that when desolating experiences occur, directees are willing to work through them with God and in spiritual direction. A solid foundation of committed trust must develop over time.

The primary purpose of spiritual direction is to help people grow in an affective, conscious, and explicit relationship with God. The more deeply these five qualities of relationship—that is, companionship, empathy, care, naturalness, and commitment—exist in the director-directee relationship, the more freely can directees grow in a lively relationship with God through spiritual direction.

## The Atmosphere of Spiritual Direction

As a relationship of trust forms, directors strive to foster an atmosphere in direction sessions that frees people to share openly as they grow affectively with God. They attempt to create a conducive environment for people to notice more clearly God's self-communication and their reactions to God. Directors help individuals to share openly and pay attention to God's presence by fostering a contemplative atmosphere and by taking an evocative approach.

Spiritual directors create a contemplative atmosphere by helping people be more attentive to God's specific revelations in their life, in their prayer, and in their interior reactions. Directors help individuals to observe, ponder, relive, and respond to their experience of God. According to William A. Barry and William J. Connolly, "the spiritual director is most interested in what happens when a person consciously puts himself into the presence of God."[9]

Contemplation is attentiveness to and absorption in God in a given moment in life or prayer. Directors must not focus on realities that should be there or might be there or will be there in the future, but on what exists at the present moment. They help people to see what actually is happening between God and themselves, to linger with what they are observing, and to become more absorbed in God. By helping people to pay careful attention to their life and religious experience, directors assist them to become less self-absorbed and more other-absorbed. The result is deeper interior freedom. As people grow freer interiorly through becoming less self-absorbed, they are able to make choices from a less self-centered stance. Contemplation is a lingering process that enables absorption in God, growth in inner freedom, and the ability to make the right decisions.

Ignatius' spiritual life developed through this attentiveness to and lingering with his inner experience. His conversion experience occurred in the context of *staying with what is* for a long period of time. As he was recuperating from his leg injury, he read the lives of the saints and thought about them for hours: "This succession of such diverse thoughts, either of the worldly deeds he wished to achieve or of the deeds of God that came to his imagination, *lasted for a long time, and he always dwelt at length* on the thought before him." (my emphasis)[10] By dwelling on worldly deeds at certain times and the deeds of God at other times, his entire being—mind, heart, imagination, memory, desires—became absorbed.

Ignatius refers to lingering "with what is" in several places in the *Spiritual Exercises*. For instance, in the Annotations he suggests shortening or lengthening the Weeks because "some [people] are slower to find what they seek . . . and some are more diligent than others."[11] Today he might say something, such as: "Just stay where people are in their prayer; try not to hold them back nor move them beyond their felt experience of God." He exhorts directors not to move directees to the Second Week until they have experienced the fullness of the First Week.[12] He suggests explaining the Rules for Discernment only "as far as a person needs them."[13] Further, he recommends that directors not explain the Second Week Rules until the person has experienced interior movement, because "those of the Second will be harmful to him, as being a matter too subtle and too high for him to understand."[14] Thus, Ignatius firmly encourages spiritual directors to stay with the directees' present experience of God and to help them to become deeply absorbed in what is most alive so that their affective relationship with God will influence their inner capacity to respond to God's presence in a given moment.

Ignatius also underscores this "staying with" through the process of "repetition." He encourages directees to repeat prayer exercises: " . . . we should pay attention to and dwell upon those points in which we have experienced greater consolation or desolation or greater spiritual appreciation."[15] Earlier in the *Spiritual Exercises,* he refers to the reason for repetition: "It is not knowing much, but realising and relishing things interiorly that contents and satisfies the soul."[16] It is *depth* of experience that matters, not *quantity* of insights. Spiritual directors help people linger with their experience of God in the moment so that this relishing can take place.

The following verbatim conversation is an example of a spiritual director "dwelling upon" or staying with a directee's consolation (D = Director; J = Jill):

J1:   The struggle and darkness has been so great, as you know. But that night when I walked on the beach, something really special happened.

D1:   I'm really happy to hear that. Would you like to share with me what happened on the beach?

J2:   Well, I was talking to God again about all the mid-life stuff I've been going through, just sharing some of the recent pain I've been experiencing, which I've told you about. It was a full moon that night, which I always love. As I was talking to God, all of a sudden it was like the moon moved right down inside me. It was like the light and the brightness of the moon leapt down out of the sky and pierced my darkness.

D2:   The light and brightness of the moon pierced your darkness.

J3:   Yes, it's like the moon moved right through my insides and lightened up my darkness. It was so overwhelming and surprising.

D3:   You were so overwhelmed and surprised. Can you say more about that?

J4:   I know God has been with me, but I haven't felt God's presence in such a strong way in a long time. But that night I was overwhelmed with God's presence. It truly felt like God was in the brightness of the moon and moved strongly inside of me, like God's light pierced my darkness.

D4:   It was like God's light pierced your darkness.

J5:   Yes, it was such a strong and deep sense of God's presence. It was so piercing—God's light broke through all the heavy darkness I've been feeling. It was so wonderful.

D5:   It really sounds wonderful, Jill. God's presence was strong, deep, and piercing—breaking right through your darkness. How did you feel when that happened?

J6:   I felt so reassured by God—and hopeful. I felt for the first time in a long time that I'm going to get through this struggle. I felt so confident that God is not going to let my darkness win.

D6:   You felt reassured and hopeful.

J7:   Yes, and I felt so much lighter and freer. I even skipped along the beach for awhile. I haven't skipped since I was a kid!

Through the process of "staying with" this powerful consolation, Jill's director helps her "relish" the affective sense of God's presence and to become aware of her felt reactions. The experience is more meaningful and comes alive through sharing it with another.

It is also important for a spiritual director to help a directee "pay attention to and dwell upon" experiences of desolation or resistance, as expressed in the following conversation (D = Director; B = Brian):

B1:   I've really had a hard time praying the past few weeks. I can't sit still. When I go to pray, I start thinking of a million other things than God. I really want to pray, but I get so distracted.

D1:   Can you say something about your distractions; for instance, are there one or two things that keep coming to your mind?

B2:   Yes, now that you mention it. There is one thing that keeps plaguing me. It's my relationship with Joe, a co-worker. It's a real mess now. We keep having strong disagreements over . . . (the director listens to Brian's story and his feelings connected with it).

D2:   So you feel a lot of anger toward Joe, which you have told him about, and all that anger seems to surface when you go to pray. Have you shared your anger with God?

B3:   No, I haven't. I just seem to get caught up in my thoughts and feelings about this situation and forget God is there. I need to do that—go back to prayer and tell God how I'm feeling about all this.

D3:   Yes, I think you need to do that and especially tell God your anger. Also, Brian, when you feel you've said all you need to say to God for that moment, try to remember to be attentive to God, to listen to God, to see if God has anything to say to you.

B4:   Yeah, thanks for reminding me. I can forget to listen to God sometimes.

Brian's director helps him explore the desolation, which is in the form of restlessness and distractions. Through "paying attention to" the desolation in this exploratory way, Brian's director helps him to be freer and to create the inner space so that consolation can return.

Besides fostering a contemplative atmosphere, spiritual directors also take an evocative approach. They help directees to uncover and confront inner experiences, struggles, and joys

since there is greater power and richness when people discover an inner reality themselves. By being evocative rather
than didactic, directors allow God to stir the individual heart
and mind, rather than merely instruct people about God and
spiritual matters. They are like stagehands helping to set the
stage for God's action. By being evocative rather than direc-
tive, directors let people move at their own pace.

Ignatius emphasizes an evocative approach in his description of how spiritual directors give meditations and contemplations. He suggests that the director's explanation be brief in
order to allow a person's own "reasoning" to reach clarity and
understanding and to be "enlightened by Divine power." The
directee will gain "more spiritual relish and fruit" than if the
director had "much explained and amplified the meaning of
the events."[17] In this way, directors help persons become
open to God's self-communication. Thus, they allow God to
speak for God's own Self rather than speaking for God.
Afterward they help directees ponder what God said and did.

Ignatius uses a rich image to exemplify the spiritual director's evocative stance. Directors do not influence a person one
way or the other, "but standing in the center like a balance,
leave the Creator to act immediately with the creature, and the
creature with its Creator and Lord." They let God "communicate Himself to his devout soul, inflaming it with His love
and praise . . ."[18] Standing in the center like a balance, directors unobtrusively help God and individuals to become more
directly involved with one another.

How does this contemplative and evocative stance happen
concretely? Spiritual direction focuses upon the dynamics of a
personal relationship with God as it is experienced at a given
moment. Directors help persons be attentive to God's self-revelation. Initially, they may ask directees: "When you pray,
who are you conscious of—God as Father, Mother, Creator,
friend, Jesus, Holy Spirit?" or "Who is God for you now in
your life?" or "How does God seem to be present with you
when you pray?" These types of questions help people to
begin noticing God and God's self-revelation.

By helping individuals to carefully ponder God, they
notice concrete dimensions of God's self-revelation. For
instance, Mary noticed specific qualities of God's care (D =
Director; M = Mary):

D1:  God is like a Mother friend who listens to you. Can you say more about that?

M1:  God is really interested in what I'm saying.

D2:  Interested in what you're saying.

M2:  Yes. God really cares about what's going on in my life and is concerned about me.

D3:  God cares and is concerned about you.

M3:  Yes, as I'm talking about it I'm realizing God as Mother friend wants to be involved in things I'm doing and my worries.

Sometimes this evocative approach helps directees notice God in a "visual" and "auditory" way, as in Lyn's experience (D = Director; L = Lyn):

D1:  What is Jesus like as he and you hold your heart in your hands?

L1:  He's very gentle and understanding.

D2:  Gentle and understanding.

L2:  Yes, he knows how fragile my heart is right now. He holds it very gently, like it's a fragile piece of glassware that could shatter into a million pieces. He's so tender.

D3:  He's aware of how fragile your heart is now, so he holds it tenderly and gently.

L3:  Yes, it's like his hands are barely touching it because it's so delicate. It's like he's saying to me, "There's no hurry to let go of it." He really understands my hesitancy.

The spiritual director repeats key words and underscores  specific movements for several reasons. First, directees then know they have been heard and, therefore, feel affirmed. They feel the director is right with them in their experience.  Second, the underscoring prompts individuals to say more. They feel encouraged to describe their experience in more detail, and they want to continue to share. Third, it helps  them to savor and relive the richness of the experience and to feel God's presence as they are sharing. The experience comes alive again as directees describe it. Fourth, it assists directees to notice interior facts and gain insights that they were not aware of until they started sharing their experience.[19]

Spiritual directors help directees notice a pervasive movement. For example, God might reveal a particular dimension of divine love, such as unconditional acceptance, over a long period of time. An underlying motif may pervade the relationship; for instance, Jesus may invite a person to work with him to bring about peace and justice in the world. The director underscores the pervasive movement and encourages the person to elaborate:

> The past several months, Joan, you have been sensing God inviting you to work with the poor in Central America for a year or two. Would it be helpful to look at that invitation again today to see if the invitation is clearer and to see how you are feeling about it?

Spiritual directors also help persons notice and feel their interior reactions to God's self-communication and to share these with God. Any growing love relationship is reciprocal.[20] In order for their relationship with God to grow, directees must consciously let God know their specific reactions to God's self-expression. However, in order to reveal their reactions to God, individuals need to feel their feelings and be attentive to positive and negative reactions. Directors can help people get in touch with their reactions by asking questions, such as:

✝ How do you feel, Lyn, when God says, "There's no hurry to let go of your heart"?

✝ How do you feel, Mary, as you sense that God wants to be involved in things you're doing and worry about? When you sense God cares?

✝ How did that affect you, Dave, when Jesus said, "They didn't want me either"?

✝ How do you feel, Mary, when Jesus says, "Come to me"?

✝ What happens in you, Joan, when you see Jesus sweating and working so hard among the poor?

By focusing on feelings through questions like these, directors can help directees explore their interior reactions more carefully. The more clearly individuals feel and acknowledge their reactions, the more fully they can share these with God as well as gain a clearer sense of direction in their prayer, in their decisions, and in their life.

To encourage continued dialogue between God and directees, spiritual directors invite them to express their feelings to God through questions and underscoring, such as:

☦ You feel secure and grateful when God listens to you. Did you think of telling God that?

☦ Do you think you could tell God that you are afraid to let go of your heart?

☦ You feel comforted that Jesus experienced the same type of struggle as you. Did you let him know that?

☦ You felt remorse for staying away so long when Jesus said, "Come to me." Did you share your remorse with him?

☦ You feel a desire to help Jesus when you see him working so hard. Have you told him about your desire?

In this way, directors help directees to share *from* their feelings, not just *about* their feelings. That is, they encourage people to share their feelings with God as they are feeling them, not only after they feel them. Sharing reactions and feelings as they occur frees a person interiorly to be attentive to God's response. This sharing enables the affective relating between God and person to continue in an explicit way.

People grow in intimacy by continuing to be attentive to God's response to their response. For example, a director may ask: "How did God respond to you when you shared you were fearful?" A directee might answer: "God understood and is in no hurry."

A director may underscore the conversation by asking: "You told God how afraid you are to give your heart?" A directee might then reply: "Yes, and God just keeps accepting me with all my fears. God just wants me to feel love."

Through this continuous attentiveness-and-response pattern, the cycle of dialogical prayer and reciprocal relationship develops. One's relationship with God continues to grow more affective, personal, and alive.

Spiritual directors help directees to be aware of and explore their resistance. As in any meaningful relationship, at times resistance takes place in our relationship with God. For instance, people unconsciously will resist acknowledging their feelings, by rationalizing, intellectualizing, spiritualizing, or doubting an experience or by talking compulsively, forgetting, or denying negative feelings. Or they may delay praying, experience many distractions during prayer, fall asleep while praying, feel bored during prayer, or doubt a previous experience of God. Some examples of resistance might include:

✝ It's been a real effort to pray lately. I just feel kind of blah and bored most of the time.

✝ I started wondering if that powerful experience of God's love I had last week was real or was it in my imagination. I didn't feel God's presence much this week.

✝ Do you know when I went to share with God all that anger and hurt I got in touch with in direction two weeks ago, I couldn't remember what I said. Isn't that strange? I thought I'd never forget what I said!

✝ I realized I'm not as angry at God as I thought I was because it must have been God's will that this happened.

✝ I couldn't pray at all this week. Every time I went to pray, I was completely distracted.

Directors need to be patient and encouraging when directees resist. Ignatius reminds the director: "Let him not be hard and dissatisfied with him, but gentle and indulgent, giving him courage and strength for the future."[21] They must patiently continue to help directees acknowledge their feelings and address God. They need to help directees to contemplate their resistance as they would a lively experience of God in order to help them understand the reasons for their behavior. For instance, by helping a directee to calm down and notice what underlies compulsive talking, the person might observe: "I'm afraid if I slowly share this experience with you, I will be overwhelmed and lose control." Or, by helping a directee to look at distractions in prayer, the individual might admit: "I'm afraid if I really get into this, God might ask of me more than I can handle." Or, by helping a directee to explore an inability to sit still and pray, the person might confess: "I'm really angry at God for not healing my arthritis, and I'd rather not get into it during prayer. God always seems to win anyway, so why bother!"

By helping directees notice, explore, feel, and understand the reasons underneath their resistance, spiritual directors help them to be freed from the binding strength of resistance, to share the underlying feelings and reasons with God, and to become affectively aware of God again.

Spiritual directors assist people in gaining experiential insights about God and God's ways in the human heart. These insights evolve from experiences of God; that is, the experience itself reveals truths about God and about themselves. Insight is gained in a revelatory way, not through an analytical or figuring-out process. Therefore, the experience interprets itself.

An example of a directee's experiential insight about God might be:

> I realize from this experience that God is faithful to me no matter how much I run away. This experience enables me to understand God's unconditional love. God keeps loving me no matter how unworthy I feel and no matter how much darkness is in me. God's love for me does not depend on my feelings and actions.

Examples of growth in self-knowledge through experiences of God include:

> I realize through this desolating experience how powerless I am over my compulsive tendency to work so hard and my great need for God's strength in this area of weakness. God's constant love for me is enabling me to see in a deep way how lovable I am. It is helping me to appreciate my own giftedness in working with the homeless.

As people grow more absorbed in God and interiorly free, they begin to notice changes in themselves and in various aspects of their lives. Directors help people recognize inner and outer changes and to see how these changes are affecting their lives and their relationships with other people. They help them explore differences in themselves and examine the feelings and ramifications of these differences. For example, directors might help directees discover specific changes in their lives:

☩ I notice I'm changing. Because of my upbringing, I didn't share my feelings with anyone. Now I'm being more open with my feelings with some people.

☩ Something's different. I'm much more sensitive to my wife's needs and feelings rather than just being caught up in my own.

☩ Even the three Sisters I live with are noticing a change in me. They told me the other night that I'm much more open about what's going on in me and willing to express my anger rather than holding it in.

☩ My relationship with God is so different than it was a year ago. Before, God was kind of distant and uninvolved. Now I feel God close to me in so many events in my life.

☩ My prayer life is much more alive than it used to be. I think it's because I'm more honest with my feelings rather than hiding them, and God is more real to me. I am aware of more aspects of God's presence.

Discovering and rejoicing in these changes enables directees to realize experientially that their affective relating with God permeates every dimension of their lives. Their relationship with God is not only precious in itself but also it undergirds all their life experiences.

Lastly, spiritual directors help people to make prayerful decisions. They assist people to notice the inner dimensions of feeling, thought, and desire and the outer circumstances of a particular decision. They help them to explore the advantages and disadvantages of a decision in the context of their experience of God. They keep them in touch with God's desires as well as their own. So a director might ask:

☩ Can you share with me pros and cons discovered this week in your prayer as you prayed about your decision to work with AIDS victims?

✝ What is going on in God's heart concerning your desire to enter religious life? Do your desires and God's desires seem to be congruent with one another?

✝ What was God's presence like as you prayed about the possibility of becoming a spiritual director? What were your specific feelings as you prayed?

Spiritual directors in a contemplative and evocative way continuously strive to help directees be aware of God, be aware of themselves, and be aware of the concrete circumstances involved in any decision.

## Conclusion

Spiritual directors offer their directees a sacred gift by being a caring companion and a contemplative presence. Through spiritual direction individuals receive the support and space necessary in order to pay attention to and respond to God at their own pace and in their own time. A caring presence and contemplative atmosphere in spiritual direction enables directees to experience the fullness of life and the ramifications of intimate relating that occur through developing a personal relationship with God. It is only in this lively and intimate experience of feeling, movement, struggle, enjoyment, and resistance as one relates with God that Ignatius' Rules for Discernment are understandable and meaningful.

## Experiencing God

### "Staying With" an Experience of God

Ignatius encourages us, when we pray, to "pay attention to and dwell upon those points in which we have experienced greater consolation or desolation or greater spiritual appreciation" (*repetition*). Staying with an experience in this way helps to deepen a consolation and can bring clarity to a desolation. We grow more aware of God and our own reactions.

Call to mind a significant experience of prayer that you had recently, a time that you felt God's presence and felt a reaction within yourself. Remember the circumstances of the prayer time and the details of the prayer experience.

✞ How long did you spend in prayer? Did you go back to that significant experience and "dwell upon" it, or did you move onto something else during your subsequent prayer time?

✞ How did you feel "staying with" the prayer experience?

In God's presence, practice this important dynamic of repetition. Stay with the above prayer experience. Savor the experience. Linger with it. Let God come alive again for you in the experience.

As you stay with it, share with God any feelings that arise. Be attentive to God's response.

### Sharing an Experience

In God's presence, remember a moment you shared an experience of God with another person; for example, perhaps time spent with a friend, a spiritual companion in a faith sharing or prayer group, or a spiritual director.

✞ Did you talk about the experience or from the experience? Did you report it or relive it, that is, enter into it again as you shared?

✞ How did you feel as you shared the experience? Did it come alive again for you in your imagination and feeling? Did you notice anything new about it as you shared it?

✞ Did you feel God's presence as you shared?

✞ What was the person or group like as you shared? Were they listening empathetically? Or did they seem distant from you?

Share with God any thoughts or feelings that come to your mind. Be attentive to God's presence and response.

## Questions for Reflection and Discussion

1. What do you find helpful in the way someone listens to you? What is it about someone's presence or manner that invites you to say more, to continue sharing your story?

2. How well do you listen to others? In what ways could you grow in your ability to listen? Ask one or two close friends what they find helpful in the way you listen and how you might listen better.

3. If you have a spiritual director, what is it about this person's presence, manner, and approach that is helpful for you while sharing your experience of God?

## For Spiritual Directors

1. Of the several qualities mentioned in this chapter, which are needed for a solid spiritual direction relationship? Which do you feel you already have? Which qualities do you need to deepen? What other qualities do you have that are not mentioned in this chapter?

2. How would you describe your presence and approach in spiritual direction? In what ways are they similar to what is described in this chapter? In what ways are they different?

3. Write out or share an example of "staying with" an experience of one of your directees (repetition in the *Spiritual Exercises*).

   What benefits or "fruit" did your directee gain from your "staying with" the person; for example, a more vivid sense of God's presence in the experience, a deeper awareness of individual reactions? a new insight? How did you feel in this "staying with" process?

4. State three significant insights that you gained or that were reinforced about spiritual direction during the process.

# Part III

# Enfleshment

**Contemporary Experiences of
Individuals in Spiritual Direction**

---
6
---

# Exploring Five Contemporary Experiences of God

Ignatius developed the Rules for Discernment from his own experience and from listening to people as they developed a personal relationship with God. During the last four centuries spiritual directors have made use of the Rules in a variety of ways. Some directors may recommend them in order for directees to better understand their experience of God in prayer and life. Others may offer them to help directees to make important decisions or changes in life-style. Still others may use them to discern their own interior movements. A few might use them as ways to observe movement and counter-movement in their directees. Or they may do all of the above. Whatever method spiritual directors use, their intent is always to help their directees be attentive to God so that they can deepen their relationship with God and make choices based on a growing inner freedom.

In the experiences of the people that follow in the next five chapters, spiritual directors use the Rules mostly as a way to enable directees to recognize and understand interior movements toward and away from God so that they can respond more freely to God's self-revelation. I will reflect on each of the five experiences in light of the dynamics of the Rules and the Annotations.

## Experiential Process and Approach

The process I use in presenting each individual's experience is the same process I used in exploring Ignatius' experience and reflects the purpose of the Rules themselves: recognition, understanding, and admitting or rejecting (313). Recognition (noticing and awareness) is a *description* of each person's experience of God over a period of time. Understanding (savoring and exploring) indicates *relationships* to the Rules and the Annotations. Admitting or rejecting (responding) contains reflections on what the directee *did do* or what the directee *can do* with consolations or desolations as well as thoughts on the director's *approach* in facilitating growth in relationship with God.

The important dynamic of repetition in Ignatian prayer is operative in my approach. As stated previously, repetition for Ignatius means that "we should pay attention to and dwell upon those points in which we have experienced greater consolation or desolation or greater spiritual appreciation" (62; 118). It is a way to savor, relish, and deepen God's concrete action in our hearts and lives, as will be exemplified by the experience of these five people. In these experiences, I "pay attention to and dwell upon" certain key points about the Rules and about the approach of the director by repeatedly illustrating dynamics of the Rules and Annotations. My purpose for doing so is to enflesh their richness and to demonstrate how their universal dynamics operate uniquely in people's experiences. That way the Rules can be more practically applied in our own sifting out of interior movements and can assist spiritual directors as they help their directees to discern.

## Illustrations and Examples

These five experiences not only have similar features, they also clearly illustrate the various experiential aspects of the Rules and Annotations.

First, they all represent *kataphatic* rather than *apophatic* experiences of God.[1] The kataphatic way of prayer involves images, memory, interior and exterior senses, thoughts, and reason. However, the apophatic way strives to eliminate all references to images and thoughts and does not draw on these inner dimensions. It fosters a direct and simple presence with God.

Second, the five experiences focus on immanent rather than transcendent experiences in order to illustrate clearly the dynamics of closeness and distancing between God and the individual.

Third, each person's experience echoes some of the same dynamics of other people's experiences in order to demonstrate the uniqueness, yet universality, of a dynamic. For example, in several of the spiritual direction sessions I illustrate the dynamic of Rule 326, which describes bringing something hidden out into the light.

Fourth, each person's experience highlights two or three specific aspects of the Rules.

Fifth, each chapter demonstrates various aspects about the role of the director. Verbatim excerpts of conversations from genuine sessions are used that exemplify the evocative approach of the director in order to show interior movements in directees and illustrate specific aspects of the Rules.

Sixth, to assure confidentiality, facts about background and life experience of these five people have been changed. However, their experience of God remains intact. Similarly, spiritual directors have been chosen from a variety of areas.

## Overall Dynamics and Underlying Principles

In addition to exploring specific manifestations of the Rules and Annotations with each person's experience, I also "dwell upon" some key dynamics of movement and countermovement and the underlying principles contained in the approach of the spiritual director. The key dynamics and common principles stated below will be explained and illustrated throughout the remainder of the book.

### Key Dynamics of Movement and Countermovement

As people grow in a personal relationship with God, they experience interior reactions to God's self-communication. These reactions can move individuals toward God (315, 316) or they can draw them away from God (315, 317). In Rule 316, Ignatius says, "I call it consolation when an interior movement is aroused in the soul . . . ," but in Rule 317, he remarks, "I call desolation what is entirely the opposite. . . ." Therefore, I use interchangeably the terms *movement* and *consolation* (interior reactions toward God) and *desolation* and *countermovement* (interior reactions away from God).[2]

Experiencing God involves the alternation of movement and countermovement. Therefore, God is acting dynamically in countermovement to free a person from an area of darkness, sinfulness, and unfreedom. Often God's felt presence is hidden from an individual as he or she experiences countermovement (1, 6, 62, 118, 322).

Individuals usually experience an overall movement toward God for a specific period or during a directed retreat. This pervasive movement has many concrete manifestations of consolation (316). Likewise, they often experience a pervasive countermovement with concrete expressions of desolation (317).

Usually movement and countermovement are experienced around an "inordinate attachment" (1) or unfree area in a person's psyche or life experience. The unfreedom can be an *obvious* area of temptation, such as struggling to honor a marriage commitment when strong sexual feelings for someone else emerge. Or it can be a *subtle* area of darkness that has obvious effects on a directee's relationship with God and others, such as a desire for attention from those in authority. Movement and countermovement, operating as a means for God to free the person of a disorder, are valuable in our growth in relationship with God. Many different experiences of desolation and consolation can occur around this underlying unresolved issue or area of weakness over a period of time until the person is freed (327).

Bringing out into the light a hidden, dark, or shameful area or issue can free people signficantly from the power of that darkness and uncover their interior senses to accept God again (326).

A movement away from God is usually related to a movement toward God. The countermovement can be *obviously opposite* the movement (First Week Rules); for example, a person experiences deep peace and then moves into great restlessness. Or a countermovement can be *apparently similar* to a movement. That is, what seems like a movement can, ultimately, be a countermovement (Second Week Rules). For example, a desire to serve God as a missionary, which looks and feels like a movement toward God, could be an excuse to avoid important life issues and to run away from one's authentic self.

People who have a long-term personal relationship with God (Second Week) usually experience a subtle countermovement of "evil under the appearance of good" (332). Therefore, they need to examine carefully the "beginning, middle, and end" of their "thoughts" (333).

Individuals whose relationship with God and primary experience of discernment are Second Week can also experience the consolations and desolations characteristic of the First Week.

Although remarkable in itself, Consolation without Previous Cause (330) is a *normal* experience for those growing in relationship with God.

Healthy decisions, transformed attitudes, and changed behavior flow naturally from the freeing and clarifying experience of movement and countermovement.

## Underlying Principles in the Approach of the Spiritual Director

In direction sessions spiritual directors provide a contemplative and evocative atmosphere that facilitates the directees' exploration of concrete experiences of God (2).

Directors offer an encouraging presence that assists people to bring out into the light the desolating experiences that bind them (326). The director is a "balance at equilibrium" (15). Spiritual directors help directees to savor movements and explore countermovements (17).

As the session proceeds, spiritual directors discern when to focus on movement toward and when to explore movement away from God. Certain questions can assist directors in this on-the-spot decision, such as will the directee grow in freedom by savoring the consolation or exploring the desolation?

Directors can unobtrusively operate from various aspects of the Rules and Annotations so as not to interfere with directees' experiences in a given moment. In other words, directors do not have to mention a given Rule as such to directees but can simply use the dynamic of the Rule while directing the session.

Directors can help directees concretely deal with counter-movement (319, 325, 326, 333). Further, directors help directees develop a discerning heart, that is, help them to recognize differences in themselves and in interior reactions that occur as they grow in a personal relationship with God.

## Conclusion

The experiences of the five individuals we will soon meet—Fran, Laura, Bob, Bill, and Pam—constitute a colorful tapestry that reveals God's life-giving goodness and suggests how the Rules and Annotations can facilitate the growth of God's loving presence. Woven together, all five persons have common "threads" of experience but bring unique "colors" to this tapestry. For instance, all are consciously forming a personal relationship with God while experiencing different dimensions of relating. Four of the five people experience being drawn wholly into God's love, but in various ways. Each grows more conscious of movement and countermovement through spiritual direction, although their need to explore one or the other varies greatly. In direction sessions, all benefit from acknowledging hidden realities that shut them off from God's explicit presence, although a variety of obvious as well as subtle nuances affect the binding power of their "secret." Their experiences of God, unique and precious in themselves, together enflesh the rich dynamics of the Rules and the Annotations.

Since these individual experiences engage their whole person I encourage you to read these stories with your total self. Strive to let the experiences come alive in your mind, heart, and imagination, as if they were sharing them with you. This empathetic reading will result in learning felt insights, not only intellectual ideas. At the end of each chapter are suggestions for experiencing God, which will give your heart an opportunity to be stirred and will open you more deeply to God's self-revelation.

# 7

# Fran's Experience of God in Peace and Struggle

Fran is beginning a personal relationship with God. This is her first experience of spiritual direction, which she will receive during an eight-day directed retreat. Her retreat illustrates:

1. A person just beginning to articulate an affective experience of God to another person;

2. The clear alternation between consolation and desolation;

3. The director helping to savor the consolation;

4. The director assisting to explore the feelings and underlying reasons for the desolation.

## Background

Fran, married twenty-eight years and divorced one year, has four children, who are sixteen, eighteen, twenty-three, and twenty-eight years old. After five years of a very painful struggle, Fran has been feeling more at peace with herself. Although always a woman of deep faith, she has been consciously "working on" her relationship with God during the past year. She meditates for one hour each morning.

# Session 1

Fran shared with Doris, her director, information about her background, her present situation, and her prayer life. She is deeply concerned about her married daughter, who has a drinking problem but denies it. She is also worried about her unmarried son, who is also having some personal struggles.

Even though these concerns weigh heavy on Fran's heart, she feels at peace within herself. She shares the following:

> This year was probably the first year I have experienced such peace. I feel like this time of my life is for me. I immediately felt drawn to come on this retreat when I saw it in my parish bulletin. My drawing was confirmed when I received my money from my settlement and the confirmation notice from the retreat house. I feel so right about being here.
>
> I feel a deep peace within myself. There are these concerns about my children, but underneath that there's the deep peace. It's a kind of experience I've never had before in my whole life. I feel right about myself and right about how things are going.

When Doris asked her what she wanted to gain from the retreat, she replied, "I want to grow closer to God. I feel such peace when I'm involved in things about God, like prayer and talking to my close friend about God. Also, I have several meditation books that I use in the morning, but I feel like I'm jumping around a lot. I could use some help in how not to do that."

Doris then asked her who she is aware of when she prays. "I pray more to Jesus than to the Spirit," Fran answered. "The Father is still a little scary to me. When I pray to Jesus it seems we're always by the ocean. That's why I'm so happy to be here." She was not able to elaborate about her experience of Jesus.

## Movement, Countermovement, and the Rules

Fran's underlying orientation is movement toward God (315). She is striving to grow closer to God in concrete ways.

Although many concerns affect her, she experiences a deep peace: "This [peace giving] God does by making all easy, by removing all obstacles so that the soul goes forward in doing good" (315). She feels drawn to do something concretely "good" for her own spiritual growth after such a consistent struggle for so many years.

Her movement toward God "invites and attracts to what is heavenly" and "fills her with peace and quiet in her Creator and Lord" (316). Life struggles cannot dissipate her deep peace.

## Approach of Director

Doris gives her the opportunity to talk about her concerns and feelings about her children. Bringing these emotions into the open at the beginning of the retreat helps, temporarily, to free Fran of their burden so that she can concentrate on her interior space and be attentive to God's action within her (326).

Doris helps Fran to articulate her interior experience of deep peace so that she can feel more deeply its richness through sharing and can notice more clearly its pervasiveness in her life even amidst struggle. Doris also helps her to become aware of her desires for retreat, invites her to share these with God, and encourages her to be aware of God's desires for her on retreat.

Lastly, Doris begins to help Fran look at God by asking her who she is aware of when she prays. Through helping her to pay attention to God, she is encouraging her to be aware of the relational nature of prayer. This simple question can help Fran to become less self-absorbed and more God-absorbed.

# Session 2

Fran's first full day of the retreat was filled with consolation, peace, and joy. Doris invited her to talk about her experience of peace:

F1:  I feel such a deep peace. It's hard to put into words. It's hard to express.

D1:   Well, you used one word to describe the peace so far. It's very "deep." That's a good start! Are you able to say what that deep peace feels like in you?

F2:   (Pauses and reflects for a moment) It feels like it's inside my whole body, going through my whole body. It feels like a deep happiness—that's what it is. I feel very happy to be here with God, happier than I've ever been in my whole life.

D2:   It goes through your whole body—the feeling of deep happiness.

F3:   Yes, it's like a surge—a surge of happiness.

D3:   A surge of happiness.

F4:   Yes. I've felt this before at daily liturgy, but it only lasts for a moment. Usually after communion, I feel a surge of deep peace, a rightness about myself, my life. It's like a surge going all through me.

D4:   It's like a surge of deep peace and rightness going all through you.

F5:   Yes, it feels like it's coming out from deep within me. It's overflowing and overwhelming. It overwhelms me at times. It's so hard to express it. I'm not used to talking about things like this, so it's hard to put into language. It's so overwhelming.

D5:   Yes, I can understand how it's difficult to talk about. You'll notice as the retreat goes on, it will become a little easier. But even now you're doing really well expressing what's happening within you. (Fran smiles.) So it's like an overflowing surge coming from inside of you, and it's overwhelming.

F6:   Yes, it just overwhelms me. It's just too much to take at times. I feel so close to God then, a sense of his presence. And then I start feeling unworthy of God's love.

D6:   You start feeling unworthy of God's love.

F7:   Yes, I feel like I don't deserve this—don't deserve the peace he's giving me.

D7: You feel like you don't deserve the peace God's giving you.

F8: Yes, it's like I feel God so close, and then I feel unworthy. I say to myself: "Who do you think you are that you can grow close to God and feel such peace?" My life has been such a mess up to now, and two of my kids are still a mess, and I don't deserve such peace.

D8: (Doris explores Fran's feelings of unworthiness for a few moments.) Have you thought about sharing with God your feelings of unworthiness? We've all been taught that God knows everything, but in forming a relationship with God it can be helpful to share our feelings in a conscious way with God in order to help us be more aware of God's presence.

F9: No, I never thought of doing that, but I'll try that.

D9: You said before, Fran, that there's times you feel so close to God when you feel that peace that you feel a sense of God's presence. Are you able to say what that closeness, that sense is like?

F10: No, not really. It just feels like peace.

D10: (Realizing she is not able yet to discuss the sense of God in her experience of peace, Doris returns to the peace.) Is there anything more about the peace that you feel, Fran, as you're sensing God's presence with you? It's like a deep happiness within you, and it overflows from deep within you. It's a surge going all through your whole body. And it's overwhelming. Do you notice anything else? As I mentioned before, I'm helping you to notice more about your experience in order to enable you to feel the richness of God's gift of peace to you and to help you to continue to be open to God's touch. That's why we're taking our time here.

F11: Yes, it really helps to talk about it. I can feel the surge and happiness again as we're talking. (Pause) It's also a warmth. I feel warm inside when I'm feeling such deep peace. I can feel that warmth now. And a deep sense of rightness. I know it's right. I feel so right about God and where I am now in my life.

D11: (They linger with the warmth and rightness for a few moments.) How do you feel now, Fran, having talked about the deep peace you experienced yesterday in prayer?

F12: I just feel so grateful to God for letting me feel so much peace after so many years of struggle. It's such a gift and I feel so unworthy of it, but I'm grateful. And I feel grateful to you for taking the time to listen to me. That means a lot to me.

D12: Thank you, Fran. I'm glad you are finding this helpful. I'm really happy for you that you are experiencing such deep peace. Truly a gift! (Pause) I'd encourage you to share with God your gratitude as well as your feelings of unworthiness and any other feelings that arise in your prayer. And you may want to be aware of how God is present with you as you share your feelings.

## Movement, Countermovement, and the Rules

Fran experienced movement toward God in the form of a vibrant and life-giving peace: "I call consolation . . . all interior joy that invites and attracts to what is heavenly and to the salvation of one's soul by filling it with peace and quiet in its Creator and Lord" (316). The peace Fran felt in prayer was not masking deep feelings but rather revealed an interior motion that is dynamic. She used many rich words to describe her experience of peace—"deep," "like a surge of happiness going all through her," "a warmth." It was an intense experience of peace, that is, overwhelming and, at times, too much to take. It resulted in feeling right about herself and her life. She felt close to God.

Fran began to experience countermovement. Her overwhelming experience of peace also resulted in feelings of unworthiness. She felt she did not deserve such peace because her life had been such a mess; she felt so ordinary. Feeling close to God caused interior realities to emerge that have not been consciously touched by God. Fran's feelings of unworthiness—and her acknowledgment of those feelings—allowed her to let God be involved in these dark areas.

Thus, Fran's movement precipitated countermovement. The countermovement involved an area not yet freed and affectively linked with God. It pointed toward a dark and vulnerable place that needed to surface in order to be touched by God's love. The countermovement, then, is a momentary affective reaction drawing a person away from God's felt presence, a felt presence that occurs because the individual allows God to touch inner areas. It occurs *because* of God's felt presence. Therefore, although one pulls away from God, the countermovement does not indicate a lack of spiritual presence but rather reveals God's personal involvement.

## Approach of Director

Doris helped Fran to describe her deep experience of peace for several reasons:

1. To savor the richness of the peace and to enjoy the experience once again. Just as rich and intimate experiences in human relationships are meant to be enjoyed, so too are our experiences of God; they should be enjoyed and savored for their own sake.

2. To enable the experience to take deeper hold within her. Through sharing her experience with Doris, Fran felt the peace again; this, in turn, deepened the reality of her experience of God.

3. To affirm the realness of her experience. Doris' careful listening and deliberate lingering enabled Fran to gain confidence and to discover that the experience was real and alive. Doris did not have to say in words that Fran's experience was real. Her acceptance of the experience helped Fran to feel its reality.

4. To notice specific aspects of the experience in order to develop Fran's capacity to recognize dimensions of her interior life in an ongoing way. The more specifically Fran accepts God's felt presence and the more she pays attention to her reactions in direction sessions, the more she

will be able to be aware of them on her own. Doris encouraged Fran to look specifically at God's presence. She
invited Fran but did not pressure her. She realized Fran
was able to notice a great deal about the peace but was
not yet aware of God's concrete presence. Doris is confident that, in time, Fran will be able to contemplate God's
presence more vividly. Thus, Doris invited Fran to look at
God for several additional reasons:

a. To become more aware of God in her experience in
order to feel the relational dimension of prayer;

b. To gain a "feel for" God's specific self-communication.
God does not just communicate divine presence to people
in general but also reveals divine love in a personal and
heartfelt way; and

c. To grow less self-absorbed and more absorbed in God.

Doris also helped her to explore her feelings of unworthiness (see lines D6–D8):

1. To help Fran accept her feelings and acknowledge the
   underlying reasons for this countermovement, which is as
   much a part of her as the experience of peace;

2. To encourage Fran to share these negative reactions with
   God in a conscious way in order to open herself to "God's
   dealing directly" (15) with this interior reality. Ignatius says
   that the director should be "kept faithfully informed about
   the various disturbances and thoughts" in order "to propose some spiritual exercises in accordance with the
   degree of progress made and suited and adapted to the
   needs of a soul disturbed in this way" (17). By exploring
   the countermovement, Doris suggests a concrete "spiritual
   exercise," that is, she encourages Fran to bring these disturbances into conscious dialogue with God.

Further, Doris invited Fran to share both her negative and
positive reactions with God for two reasons:

1. To involve God in an affective way in all dimensions of
   her interior life. By encouraging Fran to let God know specific reactions to God's felt presence, Doris helped her to
   form the habit of keeping all her interior reactions, positive
   and negative, in conscious dialogue with God;

2. To become more attentive to God's felt presence and specific response as she shares her reactions. This attentiveness enabled Fran to realize experientially that prayer is not just thinking, or having strong feelings, or noticing one's own reactions. It is a relationship, which means that a person must bring one's thoughts and feelings into heartfelt dialogue with God, must allow God to respond to one's sharing, and must be attentive to God's response. Prayer requires both awareness of self and God as well as sharing of self with God.

## Session 3

Fran's second day of her retreat differed from her first full day. The following is a summary of her experience as she shared it with Doris:

> Yesterday was very different from the day before. I felt very unsettled, restless. A lot of memories kept coming to me from way back in my childhood and all the way to the present. Different memories of injuries I caused people; for example, a hurt I caused someone when I was a little girl (she shares the hurt). I hadn't thought about that for years.
>
> Different hurts came to me that I caused during my teenage years, my marriage, and with my children (she describes further). I was feeling many regrets, particularly about my marriage and the pain that I caused my husband. I was feeling the part that I did wrong in the marriage (she mentions several examples). For so long I've been aware of what he did wrong.
>
> Also, regrets about my sister came back. My sister was very sick for several years when I was going through my crisis in my marriage. I had the sole responsibility of taking care of her, and it was such a burden at times. There were times I would be patient with her but also times I'd be very impatient with her. There were times I'd feel strong anger and resentment toward her. I never said that to anyone before. Yesterday, I felt really sorry for having those feelings toward her. She couldn't help that she was dying of cancer.

It's very strange that all these memories kept coming up. I didn't know what to do about it, so I just let them come up. Was that all right?

It started as soon as I left you yesterday, when I started telling God that I felt unworthy of his love. I asked him what makes me feel unworthy, and then all of these memories started popping up.

It was happening during my prayer times, which was very interesting. It was when I took those prayer times which you suggested that all the restlessness and turmoil, and all these memories surfaced.

But last night it was all different. I went into the chapel and all those memories, the regrets, and sorrow were gone. I felt a deep peace and calmness within me. I felt God filling me with a quiet calmness and joy, and I felt him listening to me. It was amazing how quickly I changed.

And today I feel like I'm waiting, just waiting for the Lord to direct me, to reveal himself to me.

In addition to helping Fran explore her experience, Doris offered the following:

It's not unusual that this type of experience happened, Fran. It's not unusual that one day of the retreat is very different from the other. Notice that it was when you were sharing with God your feelings of unworthiness that these memories and feelings arose. It seems the Lord was showing you the reasons for your unworthy feelings—the regrets and sorrow you have. Possibly you needed to feel sorrow and regret for specific injuries and feelings so that you could be freed of their binding power. Often a deep experience of peace and God's presence, as you had the day before, can unleash dark areas that need to be brought out into the light of your consciousness, God's presence, and in the presence of another. This unleashing and awareness can open you even more deeply to God's felt presence.

Just know that God was working as much yesterday in the turmoil, restlessness, and struggle as He was the day before when you felt such deep peace and joy.

And notice how the peace and joy returned last night after letting all those memories and feelings surface in your prayer times.

## First Week of the *Spiritual Exercises*

Without Fran being aware of the dynamics of the First Week and without her director giving her the First Week Exercises, Fran was able to experience the grace and dynamics of the week. She experienced "regret" and "sorrow" related to specific injuries she caused during her life. She became acutely aware of her wrongdoings in her marriage and felt "regret." She experienced great "sorrow" over her resentful feelings toward her dying sister. Many specific memories arose and deep sorrow grew when she asked God what made her feel unworthy. God seemed to respond by allowing her to feel pain and sorrow over particular wrongdoings and resentful feelings. God brought into her conscious awareness specific areas of darkness and sinfulness that needed to be soaked in merciful love.

Some dynamics of the Second Exercise (55–61) occur, again without Fran's knowledge of the exercise. Fran experiences the grace of ". . . a growing and intense sorrow and tears for my sins" (55). The First and Second Points then occur: "First Point. This is the record of my sins. I will call to mind all the sins of my life, reviewing year by year, and period by period . . . Second Point. I will weigh the gravity of my sins, and see (their) loathesomeness and malice . . . " (56, 57). In asking what makes her feel unworthy of God's love, Fran spontaneously remembered particular wrongdoings and sinful attitudes in her life, beginning with her childhood. These memories were very specific. She felt not only sorrow for her wrongdoings but also the weight of their gravity and malice. For instance, in relation to her dying sister, she felt the burden of her deep resentment and impatience.

God's active involvement led Fran to become aware of painful memories of hurting others. She became affectively and vividly aware. Such keen affective awareness and deep sorrow resulted in her being freed from the binding power of her sinfulness and gave her the inner space to experience God's peace and calmness again in the evening.

## Movement, Countermovement, and the Rules

On Fran's second day of her retreat, she immediately began to feel "unsettled," a vast difference from the peaceful feeling of the previous day. Her prayer times were permeated with "restlessness and turmoil" as sinful memories emerged, which contrasted greatly with the "peace and surge of happiness" of the day before. She experienced "darkness of soul, turmoil of spirit, . . . restlessness rising from many disturbances" and felt "separated" from God (317); that is, although God's activity precipitated those memories—resulting in turmoil—she did not feel God's closeness. However, God was just as present and active, but in a different way. God's presence brought to light sinful areas, which resulted in emotional chaos rather than a sense of peace. The deep experience initiated the painful memory of injuries. Only through facing her darkness and feeling sorrow for her wrongdoings did peace return.

Not only is Fran's desolation the opposite of consolation but also her desolation is precipitated by her consoling experience of peace. The desolation did not happen in isolation, but in relation to the consolation. God's activity resulted in her experiencing deep peace all through her being, a sense of congruence. From this congruent experience, incongruent areas emerged. The experience of peace brought to her consciousness unpeaceful inner areas that caused turmoil.

## Approach of Director

Doris helped Fran in two ways. First, she helped her to talk about each of the painful memories and her sorrowful feelings surrounding them. She helped her to verbalize those specific details and feelings around a particular memory. For instance, Doris helped Fran articulate specific attitudes she held toward her sister and her sorrow for harboring these feelings rather than merely expressing general opinions about her sister's illness. God's action precipitated some inner realities but not others. Doris helped Fran explore what was alive in her prayer, in her thoughts, and in her memory (17).

Second, Doris explained to Fran the dynamics of consolation and desolation and some possible reasons for these dynamics. "If the one who is giving the Exercises should perceive from desolations, . . . and from consolations that the exercitant has need of them, he should explain to him the rules . . . for the understanding of different spirits" (8). In understandable and nonthreatening language, Doris explained the Rules for several reasons: to help Fran to be free to let God work, whether that be peace or turmoil; to alleviate her concerns about whether it was "right" to allow her memories to arise; and to underscore something Fran already hinted at, that is, that God was showing her "reasons" for her unworthy feelings. Doris explained in a tentative and open-ended way, using words such as "seems" and "possibly," which left Fran free to have the final say and allowed her the freedom to deeply savor and integrate the experience.

## Session 4

F1:  It was a very peaceful day for me again yesterday. That peace returned. It felt like a leap within me at times. A leap starting here (points) in my heart.

D1:  You felt a leap within you at times coming from here (points) in your heart.

F2:  Yes, it's like it comes from deep within me and then goes out.

D2:  It comes from deep within you and moves out.

F3:  Yes. It's like a joy that comes out of me. It's so overwhelming at times.

D3:  It's a joyful leap that comes out of you, and it overwhelms you at times.

F4:  Yes, I feel so filled with peace when it happens. And I know God is with me.

D4:  You know God is with you. Can you say anything more about your knowing?

F5:  Not really. It's hard to put into words. I know God's there because I know it's not me. I know this leap is not coming from me. That's how I know it's God. It's different from anything else I've ever felt in my life. The peace and joy that I'm feeling during these days, and since I've started following the Lord, is so different from anything else I've ever experienced. I just know it's coming from God, and it's not me.

D5:    So the leap, the joy, the peace are different from anything you've ever experienced in your whole life.

F6:    Yes. I've had so many problems in my life with my husband and children, and I've been so bound down and burdened by them. But it's different lately. There are still a lot of problems, but I feel different. I don't feel weighed down like before. I feel a deep peace. The problems are there, but a deeper peace is within me. The problems can't penetrate that peace. I think I'm just realizing this as I'm sharing now with you. During this year, and now on retreat, the many problems in my life do not penetrate that deep peace. This is so new and different for me.

D6:    How does that feel, Fran, noticing that now—that your problems do not penetrate your deep peace?

F7:    Gosh! I'm thrilled! This is all so new to me. It's great! And it's so helpful to talk about it with you. (They linger with her feelings.)

D7:    Fran, you mentioned a few times that the word "come" keeps coming to you. Can you say anything more about that?

F8:    The last few days the word "come" keeps coming up in me. I asked the Lord what do you mean by that, like "Come where or what do you want me to do?" But I don't receive any answer from God.

D8:    How does that feel—not receiving an answer?

F9:    All right. I feel like I'm just waiting—but maybe a little curious.

D9:    Do you sense anything about God when God invites you to come, like do you notice any quality about who it is who invites you to come?

F10: No, not really. I know it's God, but I don't notice any-thing about him. I just sense him saying, "Come."

D10: Isaiah 55 is an invitation from God to "Come." The Lord says, "Come to the water, you who are thirsty"; "Come, receive grain and eat"; "Come heedfully, listen, that you may have life." (Doris suggests ways to pray with this passage.)

F11: As you read those verses, I can feel that leap again. (Fran's eyes fill up.) I'm feeling so filled up right now. My heart is leaping again. Gosh! That's just where I'm supposed to be.

D11: Gee, that's wonderful that you're feeling that leap again as you listen to these words! Keep letting that happen. And as you're listening to these words, see if you sense God saying these words to you, and see if you notice anything about God as God invites you to "Come."

F12: Yes, I will. I feel so excited. I feel that leap of joy again. I know this is from God.

## Movement, Countermovement, and the Rules

Again, Fran experienced strong movement: "all interior joy . . . filling her with peace . . . " (316). The peace and joy are like a "leap," a "surge," and they are overwhelming. It is different from the peace that she experienced in the past in that life struggles, though painful, cannot penetrate it.

She also felt a quiet movement in sensing that God invited her to "Come." Her experience of God is beginning to change from a pervasive sense of peace and joy to a specific invita-tion. This quiet movement grew stronger as Doris suggested Isaiah 55 and mentioned several verses that contain the word "come." Movement toward God occurs not only in Fran's prayer but also during her direction session. God's presence can be affectively experienced in a spiritual direction session as well as in one's prayer times.

Fran knows and feels that the peace and joy she experi-ences is from God. She knows that it is God who is inviting her to come. However, she is not yet able to notice God's

presence in a specific way. Through spiritual direction, as
Fran notices more about her experience of peace and the
invitation to come, she will probably grow more aware of
who is giving her the peace and offering the invitation. Her
prayer, then, will grow even more relational.

The peace that a directee feels can also be a form of resistance. That is, someone may describe a peaceful feeling that
is really a cover-up of intense feelings, such as anger, fear, or
guilt, that the person cannot acknowledge at the moment.
This type of peace is duller and flatter than Fran's rich and
alive experience. God's presence is not sensed. Although Fran
cannot yet articulate God's presence, she feels very close to
God and experiences the peace even in the midst of struggle.
Fran's overwhelming experience of God's peace frees her
interiorly to face turmoil. Resistant peace prevents struggle,
pain, and turmoil from emerging.

## Approach of Director

Doris again evocatively underscored key words and phrases
in Fran's experience in order to help Fran become more familiar with it, own it more personally, feel it more deeply, and
relive its richness. Fran's savoring is like a rose blooming
forth, and each aspect of her experience like a petal. As each
petal opens up, the rose becomes more beautiful and full. So,
too, as each aspect of an experience of God reveals itself, it
grows fuller, richer, and deeper. Doris suggested a scriptural
passage that is congruent with God's invitation to "come." The
passage helped Fran to linger longer over this invitation. She
mentioned only one passage to Fran rather than several
because "it is not much knowledge that fills and satisfies the
soul, but the intimate understanding and relish of the truth"
(2). An abundance of scripture passages could distract Fran
from the quality and depth of God's action within her.

## Session 5

During the fourth day of her retreat, Fran experienced the
alternation of consolation and desolation. Throughout the
morning, Fran felt deep peace and joy. She continued to read

Isaiah 55, and the words kept filling her. During the after-noon, however, she experienced a great deal of restlessness and many "worldly temptations." She tried to recreate the feel-ings of peace, but it was very difficult. In the evening, those feelings returned as she sat in the chapel.

During her direction session, Fran mentioned that she desired to experience God's love more deeply, to know and feel God's love for her. Doris suggested that she pray with Isaiah 43:1–7. A few verses—"I have called you by name; you are mine and I love you"—moved Fran to tears. She felt that God was saying those words to her at that moment and felt overwhelmed by God's love for her.

## Session 6

F1:  My whole day was filled with peace and joy. I didn't experience any of that restlessness I did the previous day. I went to chapel after our session and just kept reading that passage. I kept feeling filled with God and with peace and joy. I felt God saying to me, "You are mine"; even that he loves me with my guilt. God's love felt so complete. It was hard to believe that God could love me with my guilt. I felt so overwhelmed with God's love for me.

D1:  (After helping Fran savor this experience for awhile, Doris asked) Did you have any sense of how God was when God said to you, "You are mine" and when you experienced such complete love?

F2:  No, I just kept feeling overwhelmed with love, and my heart was leaping for joy again. That happened at com-munion in particular. Right before communion, as the host was coming around, I felt that leap. I felt like I was going to burst. It takes my breath away. (They stayed here. Later in the session, Fran continued to share her experiences.) I sensed Jesus sitting with me on the beach today. He walks over to me and sits down next to me. We talk. I do most of the talking, and he listens. I tell him I'm sorry for talking so much, and he gently touches my shoulder with his hand. His touch is very gentle and reassuring. Eventually he gets up and leaves. It feels peaceful, soothing to be there with him. (They stayed here.)

D2:  (At the end of the session) I encourage you to keep letting the Lord love you as he tells you "You are mine" and let him know how his total love for you feels. Also, you may want to spend some time with Psalm 139:1–18. Notice it says "God rests his hand upon me." In using this psalm, you may want to tell Jesus how you feel as he rests his hand upon your shoulder.

## Two Expressions of Movement

The movement of peace is precipitated by two experiences of God. First, Fran feels intense peace through experiencing God's total love: God loves all of her, her darkness and her light, which causes her to want to burst with joy. Second, Fran feels peaceful as she sits with Jesus and talks about her concerns. His gentle hand on her shoulder makes her feel soothed.

Also, Fran notices more specific dimensions of God as God reveals Self. In the first experience, she notices that God says, "You are mine" and that God's love is total, embracing all of her. In the second, she notices that Jesus listens; his touch is gentle and reassuring. Fran recognizes more clearly not only her own interior reactions but also the One who causes these reactions. Fran is growing less self-absorbed and more aware of God.

# Session 7

Fran felt a deep peace, joy, and sense of calmness. She remarked, "It's like a calm peace that fills me." A line from Psalm 139 stayed with her: "You know my soul full well." She had a deep sense of God knowing everything about her. She could not hide anything from God: "Before me and behind me you hem me in." She felt very strongly that "God knows me inside and out." She felt very peaceful and deeply experienced God's love for her.

The sense of God inviting her to "Come" was still with Fran. She was on the beach with Jesus again. He rested his hand on her shoulder and said "Come." He rose and left, but she did not go with him. She did not know why she did not follow him but as Doris helped her to explore her response, Fran felt a sense of fear. She was afraid of the unknown, afraid of what Jesus might ask of her. Doris encouraged Fran to share that fear with Jesus as they sat on the beach.

## Movement, Countermovement, and the Rules

Again, the movement precipitated the countermovement; they are completely opposite experiences (317). In the context of feeling peace and calm, Fran experienced fear. Her peaceful experience of God knowing everything about her and "hemming her in" changed to a contrary emotion: she felt afraid of God's invitation to the unknown.

## Approach of Director

Doris fulfilled two important dynamics of spiritual direction. First, she helped Fran get in touch with her fear. She helped Fran to recognize specifically the two related dimensions of her fear—fear of the unknown and fear of Jesus' expectations. What is hidden comes to light in the presence of another (326).

Second, Doris moved Fran one step further by encouraging her to share this fear with God and to be attentive to God's response. In this way, Fran fights the countermovement through prayer (319). By expressing her fear to God, her interior self becomes freer to accept God. Thus, by following these two principles, Doris helps Fran's movement away from God change to movement toward God.

## Session 8

The following is a summary of Fran's experience:

> I had a very calm and peaceful day again, but last night I had a disturbing dream. I dreamt I was in my house in Maryland, and my husband and I went back together. We were sitting in the kitchen. The woman that he's living with now called up. She was screaming and yelling on the phone because he left her. She was throwing his

things out of the house—his tools and his clothes. I said to her that she could have him back. I was feeling very calm in the dream.

When I woke up, I felt very upset and I couldn't get rid of the feeling. I went into chapel and asked God to take the feeling away. The main feeling I felt was hurt: I felt that deep pain and hurt that I felt when my husband first left me four years ago. I thought I had put all of that aside, but I guess there's still some things there. I really loved my husband. I still do, and I wish these human feelings would go away. I felt that same hurt as before, because I love him.

Now I feel more of a numbness but also a churning deep inside of me. When I was in chapel, Jesus and I were in the Garden of Gethsemane. We're still there. I sense his pain, his fear. The main thing I sense from him is his fear: the fear of being alone and the fear of what he had to go through. I keep asking God to take away this pain, as he did with Jesus. Jesus sweats and trembles and is in a lot of pain because of what he has to go through.

Doris helped Fran to explore the above experience as she talked about it. She also shared a few thoughts of her own at the end of the session:

I encourage you to stay with Jesus in his feelings of pain and struggle, Fran. And as you're with him, share with him your hurt and fears. I encourage you to let yourself feel your pain and hurt as fully as you can as you're asking Jesus to take these away. See how Jesus wants to be with you in your pain.

Feeling such great peace on the retreat and God's love for you may be helping these unresolved inner struggles to surface. Experiencing God's peace may be bringing to light areas that are still not at peace within you. Although you have worked through a great deal concerning your husband, there must be some more unresolved feelings that God's presence is bringing to light. I encourage you to continue to share these struggles with Jesus as you are both in the Garden.

## Ignatian Contemplation

God drew Fran into a contemplative stance *with* Jesus. At first, she spent several days with Jesus on the beach. She "sees," "touches," and "listens" to him. She "sees" him sitting next to her, "feels" his hand on her shoulder, and "listens" to his invitation to "come" as he walks away (101–109).

Fran was drawn even more deeply to be *with* Jesus. Jesus revealed deeper realities about himself—his fear, suffering, and struggle in the Garden—encouraging her to share her anguish with him. Thus, Fran responded by sharing vulnerable areas of hurt and pain with Jesus.

## Session 9

Fran spent the day with Jesus in the Garden talking out her fears and her struggles and being with him in his turmoil. Jesus assured her: "Do not be afraid. I am with you. I will not leave you alone." She felt peace again and confidence that Jesus would not leave her alone, that his presence would "hem her in," that his hand would be upon her as she struggled. She felt surprised that the painful feelings about her husband surfaced again near the end of the retreat. She was grateful that Doris was able to meet with her on a regular basis afterward in order to help her sort out her feelings. This human support, along with Jesus' assurance, helped her not to feel alone.

## Conclusion

Fran's retreat experience was a significant element of growing into a personal relationship with God. She learned that when God touches her heart and spirit, she has a variety of reactions, ranging from deep peace to great restlessness. As in any relationship, she learns that there are ups and downs. The alternation of consolation and desolation point to a real and deep relating with God. Because she is involved with God, her inner being is open to God's self-communication. This sometimes results in great joy and other times causes inner turmoil because of an area of darkness that needs to be redeemed. Fran's own tapestry of religious experience becomes more colorful and bright through this alternation of consolation and desolation.

# Experiencing God

### Reliving a Movement

Remember a time when you experienced a lively peace and a deep joy. Savor the richness of the moment, and relive it in your memory, in your feeling, in your imagination, in your heart, and in your mind.

✟ What were the circumstances of the experience, that is, were you by yourself, on the beach, on a retreat, or at a liturgy?

✟ What was God's presence like in the experience?

✟ What were some of your feelings, thoughts, and desires?

✟ What difference did you notice within yourself as a result of this experience?

As you relive the experience, be attentive to God's presence with you now. Share with God any feelings that arise, and listen to God's response.

### Exploring a Countermovement

Remember a time when you experienced a great deal of inner turmoil and disturbance (such as Fran's experience in session 3).

✟ What were the circumstances?

✟ What was God's felt absence like? Was there any sense of God's presence?

✟ What were some of your thoughts and feelings? Do you recognize the experiential reason—the area of unfreedom—underneath the turmoil?

✟ How was the desolation resolved?

✟ What did you learn about yourself and about God as a result of this experience?

As you pray about the experience, be attentive to God's presence with you now. Share with God your feelings, and listen to God's response.

## Questions for Reflection and Discussion

1. In what specific ways did Fran grow from the alternation of consolation and desolation? What did she learn about herself? What did she learn about God?

2. What other aspects or dynamics of the Rules for Discernment relate to Fran's experience? Describe the relationships.

3. Does Fran's experience remind you of any aspect of Ignatius' experience?

## For Spiritual Directors

1. What is most striking to you about Doris' approach in session 2? in session 4?

2. Write out or role play how the spiritual direction session might unfold in session 3, session 8. What might be some key questions to ask Fran?

3. Recall a directee that had a similar experience of God in peace and struggle. How did you help your directee savor the peace and explore the struggle?

4. State three significant insights about spiritual direction that you gained or that were reinforced by Fran's retreat experience. What were some key insights that you learned about the Rules for Discernment?

---

# 8

# Laura's Experience of God's Total Acceptance

---

Laura is beginning a personal relationship with God. Her experience demonstrates several things:

1. A First Week struggle around an obvious area of sinfulness (314) and an underlying area of unfreedom (315–17);

2. Various expressions of consolation and desolation, and the relationship between the value of consolation and desolation (316–17);

3. The role of the director in staying with movement and countermovement (17, 62) and the dynamics of the "secret" being revealed in spiritual direction (326);

4. How clarity arising from the experience of consolation and desolation naturally results in positive actions (318).

## Background

Laura, a graduate student in theology, is twenty-five years old. The following is an overview of ten direction sessions, on a weekly basis, with my reflections interspersed.

## Session 1

Laura expressed two desires for direction: (1) "I want to bring together my head and heart. In studying theology there's too much head stuff. I want to be more consciously aware of God in my life"; and (2) "I want more discipline in my prayer. I've been trying for years to pray for a half hour in the morning; I can never do it, and I'd like to try again." She thought of God as "female, as a big womb" but had no sense of God as a person.

### Movement, Countermovement, and the Rules

Laura's movement toward God is found in her desire for a felt and conscious relationship with God. She is striving to "rise in the service of God" (315). She experiences countermovement in her struggle to be disciplined in prayer: "inclination to what is low and earthly; restlessness; slothfulness" (317).

Laura has a predominately heady approach to God: God as a big womb. It is not coming from her *experience* of God, but is more an *idea* of God. This idea can move her toward God if it becomes a part of her felt experience. It can move her away from God, however, if it remains only an idea because she could become stuck in a certain notion or image of God and not allow room to let God reveal Self.

## Session 2

Initially, Laura was quite hyper, very talkative, and restless. After she spoke rapidly for the first ten minutes, she shared with Dave, her spiritual director, information about her struggle during the week to sit and pray. Finally she was able to relax and slowly read a book by Thomas Merton in God's presence. (Movement [M] and countermovement [CM] appear in boldface):

D1: Was there a particular time that was significant to you when you sat with this book in God's presence? Maybe a time when you **sensed God's presence?** (Focusing on M).

L1: (Smiles) Yes. One time I was sitting in my rocking chair in my room facing the window. I read a little bit and then just closed my eyes and sat still. I'm usually rushing; even when I read I'm rushing ahead.

D2: And did anything happen as you sat there, still, and with your eyes closed? (Exploring concrete moment.)

L2: I got more **relaxed**. I was anxious about so many things. I just relaxed. And **I asked God to be with me** (M).

D3: And did you sense God with you? (Concretely focusing on M.)

L3: Yes, I did (pauses). It was **like God was sitting there with me, relaxing** (M). That **sounds strange**, doesn't it? (CM).

D4: God was sitting there with you and relaxing. Can you tell me more about God there? What God was like? (Focusing on M).

L4: I hope I'm not **projecting my need to relax onto God**, (CM) but I **sensed that God needed to stop and relax** (M). **Is this something just in my imagination?** (CM).

D5: Well, let's just take our time and keep looking at God there, and stay with the experience before drawing any conclusions about it. Is that all right with you? (Invites her to linger with M rather than with CM.)

L5: Yes, that's fine.

D6: God sat there with you, and you sensed He needed to relax. Can you tell me any more about God's need to relax? (They focused on M for awhile.)

L6: I never thought about God needing to relax before. And, now that I think of it, God was showing me how to relax. **I became more relaxed as we were together there** (M).

D7: God demonstrated how to relax, which helped you to relax (evoking more feelings about M).

L7: Yes, it was like God wanted me to see that he needs to relax, too. And with all the work God has to do, seeing God's need to relax helped me to relax. **We just rested together** (M).

## Movement, Countermovement, and the Rules

Initially, Laura experienced countermovement in the form of anxiety and "restlessness" (317) as she attempted to pray. When God showed her how to relax, she experienced "peace and quiet in her Creator and Lord" (316). The "restlessness" is opposite the "peace" ("I call desolation what is entirely the opposite of consolation") [317].

Also, as she sensed God's need to relax (M), she questioned: "Is this in my imagination?" (CM). God's presence was mediated through her interior sense of sight. Laura observed God's action and slowed down as she contemplated the experience. Several times she moved toward reflecting on the experience and tried to determine whether or not it was real. Thus, Laura concretely experienced vacillation between movement and countermovement.

## Approach of Director

Laura's spiritual director, Dave, gently tried to help her to relive the richness of the experience before reflecting on it. There is a place for reflection: noticing movements, countermovements, and the connections between the two. However, to move too quickly toward reflection in one's prayer or in a direction session can lessen the fullness of God's self-revelation and diminish a person's response.

Spiritual directors, in the moment, spontaneously discern whether to stay with movement or countermovement in a session. Much of this discernment depends on the depth of the individual's conscious relationship with God. Usually people who are beginning an explicit relationship with God need to contemplate God's felt presence primarily in order to facilitate awareness of the Other and to move away from self-absorption. On the contrary, people in a long-term relationship with God, who habitually recognize God's specific presence may not need to focus as long in a direction session because their absorption in God is more constant in their lives and in their prayer. However, the director's decision is primarily based on the individual's particular needs at a particular moment.

As directors become more experienced, the choice between movement or countermovement becomes instantaneous according to the "felt need" of the directee and the "felt sense" of their own mind, heart, and spirit. The ultimate goal is an ongoing growth in relationship with God. Specifically, directors' intentions are: to help people grow more interiorly free in order to love God, to love others, and to love themselves more deeply ("to rid the soul of all inordinate attachments") [1] and to help individuals grow more consciously aware of God's presence in their prayer and life ("seeking and finding the will of God in the disposition of our life for the salvation of our soul") [1].

## Some Questions to Consider

1. Is lingering with the felt experience of God or addressing the disturbance at a particular moment going to, ultimately, move this person toward a closer relationship with God?

2. Is the person stuck in the desolation and therefore needs to talk about it before the individual can be open to God's self-communication?

3. Will exploring the countermovement distract from or will it help movement toward God?

4. In this moment, where does the stronger feeling exist— with consolation or with desolation?

5. In this moment, is exploring the movement or the countermovement going to help free the person in an area in which they are bound?

6. How developed is this person's relationship with God?

In this session, Dave chose to linger with the movement rather than discuss Laura's question about whether the experience was in her imagination (see D5) for several reasons: (1) to discuss this question at that moment would have distracted her from noticing God's need to relax; (2) for Dave to acknowledge Laura's anxiety could have prevented her from experiencing the fullness of the movement of God and of herself as they rested together; (3) Dave's felt sense indicated the need for her to concentrate on God rather than herself, which would have led her back into self-absorption; (4) she would be freed of her anxiety through recognizing God; and (5) she is just beginning an explicit relationship with God.

## Session 3

At the beginning of the third session, Laura was anxious and apprehensive. She told Dave: "I have to tell you something, and I've been a wreck all week about telling you." Finally, she blurted out: "I've been involved with Don for over a year. This is my first sexual relationship. Don does not understand my religious commitment. None of my ideals for myself are being lived up to." They had not been sexually active for several months (at the time of the session, Don was away at school). She does not see herself resuming the physical aspect of their relationship again. However, Laura never came to terms with her guilt regarding the period of time they were together. She talked about her relationship with Don at length: her feelings about him, about the relationship, about her role in the relationship, and about her sense of alienation from God because of this unresolved "sinful" period in her life. She mentioned that God was a light at the end of the tunnel, an image that she explored further with Dave.

D1: When you sense God at the end of the tunnel, what is God like there?

L1: (Slowly) Encouraging, confident in me, disappointed— God does not focus on my sexual involvement. He's disappointed, like a loving parent, because I'm not doing the best for me. (They focused here for awhile; she mentioned that God looked at her.)

D2: What does God see while looking at you?

L2: I have this big heavy lead coat around me weighing me down—all the things I've been telling you. God looks at me like a parent, inviting me to trust. (Pause) I'm afraid God will take off the coat, and I will be standing naked. I don't think I can do that. (They explore her fear.)

D3: Do you think you would like to take a little time now to tell God that fear? You could tell God in the quiet of your own heart. (They paused for about five minutes.)

L3:  After I expressed my fear, God embraced me with the coat on, with my fears and everything else. I don't have to have it all figured out before I come to God. I'm so surprised and relieved, and I'm so grateful for sharing all this with you.

## Movement, Countermovement, and the Rules

Relaxing with God caused Laura's anxiety about her relationship with Don to surface. Because of her attentiveness, God was able to touch deeper parts of her. The darkness of her sinfulness came into light as she experienced God.

Laura experiences a "sting of conscience" in one area of her life (314). She strives to grow in relationship with God (315), but the ramifications of the sexual dimension of her relationship with Don had been hidden from God and from herself (CM). She now feels guilty because "none of my ideals for myself are being lived up to" (M). This experience is painful, but necessary. A conscious relating with God, rather than superego reactions, evokes Laura's guilt. She is concerned with the effects this sexual involvement is having on her relationship with God, with Don, and with herself. The strong affectivity that surrounds her guilt and is rooted in relational growth with God indicates the need to explore her sexual involvement with Don from a spiritual perspective rather than from a moral one. Eventually, Laura shared her sexual involvement in the sacrament of reconciliation with her confessor—a concrete action that flowed from her interior reactions in relationship with God.

Laura's struggle to share this with Dave exemplifies Ignatius' description in Rule 326 of movement and countermovement operating together:

> When the enemy of our human nature tempts a just soul with his wiles and seductions, he earnestly desires that they be received *secretly and kept secret*. But if one *manifests them* to a confessor, or to *some other spiritual person* . . . , the evil one is very much vexed. (my emphasis)

The dark area wants to remain hidden because then it has power over people's inner selves and keeps them from God. But Laura's relating with God causes this dark area to emerge into the light of another person. Grace attained its fullness by turning weakness into strength through revelation to another person. By completing the revelation of her "secret" in a sacramental way, Laura grew in the kind of relationship with God described in Rule 315.

By Laura sharing with Dave this hidden area and expressing her concerns about the darkness, she was able to notice God more fully at the end of the tunnel. Previously she only had glimpsed God, but was so preoccupied with her "secret" that she could not stay with the image. Sharing her anxieties in depth with Dave created the inner space she needed to linger with God in this experience.

Laura experienced countermovement in the form of "darkness of soul, turmoil of spirit, restlessness, . . . separated, as it were, from God" (317). The movement and countermovement are related in a contrasting way: the darkness of alienation from God contrasts sharply with the image of God as light at the end of the tunnel while the fear of trusting God because God may take off the lead coat and leave her naked contradicts the relief she feels as God embraces all of her.

### Approach of Director

First, Dave helped her to discuss in depth the concrete facts and feelings about the "secret." Exploring the countermovement with her is itself a movement toward God and enables consolation to return.

Second, after the "secret" was revealed and her desolating feelings were released, Dave helped her to focus on what God is like at the end of the tunnel, how God sees her, and her reaction to God.

Third, after exploring fear ("dwelling upon desolation"), Dave invited Laura to share it with God during the session in order to allow the fullness of this concrete experience to evolve.

Fourth, Dave acted as a "balance at equilibrium" by facilitating "the Lord in person to communicate Himself to the devout soul" (15). Enabling openness to God's "communication in person" during a direction session can happen in several ways:

1. The director can take an unobtrusive, noninterfering stance and assist individuals to look at God, their interior reactions to God's presence, and God's response;

2. The director can encourage people to share with God their own feelings and thoughts that emerge during the session;

3. The director can invite people to look at God or share something with God during the session.

# Session 4

Again Laura was anxious at the beginning, indicating that countermovement was still prevalent. During the initial days after her last direction session, Laura felt God's embrace surrounding her as if she was encased in God's womb. She felt that God was very close; she experienced peace and calmness in her relationships and in her work and noticed she was no longer rude toward other people. She then felt a great deal of restlessness; she felt hypocritical and self-critical, and again she wanted to keep God out of some aspects of her life because she felt God could not accept all of her. She vacillated in and out of God's acceptance.

### Movement, Countermovement, and the Rules

The strong movement Laura experienced during the third direction session continued during the following three days, not only in her prayer but also in her life and relationships. The movement resulted in an attitudinal and behavioral change:

> It is characteristic of the good spirit to give courage and strength, consolations, tears, inspirations, and peace . . . by making all easy, by removing all obstacles so *that one goes forward in doing good* (315). (my emphasis)

However, since her deeper "disordered attachment"—her lack of self-acceptance—still needed time to be freed, desolation returned. "It is characteristic of the evil spirit to harass with anxiety [her restlessness], . . . to raise obstacles backed by fallacious reasonings" [her self-criticism leads to the thought that God cannot accept all of her] (315).

Again, countermovement is the direct opposite of movement: restlessness v. peace; keeping God removed from aspects of life v. feeling totally surrounded by God as if encased in a womb.

## Sessions 5 through 7

God's surrounding embrace continued to be a pervasive movement for Laura. It had concrete manifestations. For example, when she felt restless and anxious, "God's embrace became a restraining one; it's like the emotionally disturbed kids I used to teach. When they had a temper tantrum, I had to hold them tightly but with love until they settled down so they wouldn't hurt themselves or others. God does the same thing with me until I calm down and listen" (fifth session).

God consistently invited Laura to surrender in trust. She was unable to do so because her trust is not strong enough yet. She told God this in the sixth and seventh sessions.

During the sixth session, Laura mentioned several significant areas of growth:

> I'm beginning to realize that my relationship with God can be a part of my life. . . . I don't have to go off and do things on my own; God and I can be a team. I'm really feeling the difference within me—when I try to work things out on my own and just run ahead, I get confused, restless, and pushy. When I work things out with God, I feel peaceful, more integrated and whole. Things get clearer. I need to continue to slow down, relax, and look at things with God.
>
> God is so deeply committed to me. I feel sorrow when I leave God out of things.

In time, Laura shared with God more of her concern about her relationship with Don, rather than simply trying to work it out on her own. Her usual pattern is to end a close relationship when there are struggles, which she realizes is an easy way out. The unfolding dialogue with God moved her to express her feelings openly with Don, to work on their relationship rather than end it.

## Sessions 8 through 10

God embraced Laura's darkness as well. God's presence was like a "muted light." She said: "I can see my darkness, but it's like God is not letting the light shine too brightly so that I'm not overwhelmed with my darkness" (eighth session). Laura continued to deal with the negative aspects of her relationship with Don and more subtle sinful areas too, such as how giving herself to others often comes from a deep need to be accepted and how her lack of self-acceptance prompts her compulsively to seek acceptance from others. Through all this, God consistently and completely accepted her, much to Laura's amazement (ninth session). And when she was in God's embrace, Laura pervasively experienced God saying to her: "You're enough."

L1: God accepts the humanness in the liturgy. He accepts my humanness, my hostility and anger. God is saying to me, "You're enough."

D1: "You're enough."

L2: Yes. I don't have to be pure and perfect to come to God. God accepts me there.

D2: God accepts you with your hostility and anger.

L3: Yes, that's my humanness. God accepts mine and that of those at the liturgy. I didn't have to stay away from communion on Sunday, even though I had those hostile feelings. I'm seeing God wants an encounter with me; He's not looking at my sins. It's that embrace again; God accepts all of me, even the lead coat.

D3: How does that feel—that God accepts all of you?

L4: I still want to be perfect when I come to God. I'm resisting it. But I also appreciate it.

It was difficult for Laura to receive unconditional acceptance (tenth session). Laura continued to experience God's total acceptance and desire to be part of all aspects of her life. She was constantly amazed when she experienced God's all-embracing love. She struggled to accept it: at times she can embrace God's love, at other times she grew fearful of such a complete love and pulled away from it.

## Relationship between Movement and Countermovement

Several dynamics permeate the relationship between movement and countermovement. One is rhythm: whenever movement occurs, countermovement usually follows. This alternation of movement and countermovement takes place in varying intensities, that is, strong consolation and intense desolation or strong movement and subtle countermovement, which appears to be movement toward God (332). It occurs in various time frames, such as from morning to afternoon, day by day, week by week, month by month. In Laura's experience, strong countermovement usually followed movement.

Various reasons exist for this alternation. From God's perspective, one reason is that consolation is pure gift. We can open ourselves to that gift, but we cannot control when and how God gives it to us: ". . . it is not within our power to acquire and attain great devotion, intense love, tears . . . all this is the gift and grace of God" (322). In the fourth session, Laura shared her feeling that her entire life was in God's embrace for three days, but then this feeling suddenly changed. Even so, God's embrace was pure gift. From our perspective, experiencing God can shed light on the darkness within us. Love can loosen up an area of unfreedom and result in desolation.

A second dynamic is that the movement away from God relates to the movement toward God. It can be a contrasting, contrary, and opposite type of relationship (First Week Rules): "I call desolation what is entirely the opposite" of consolation (317). This dynamic is exemplified in Laura's experience.

A similar type of relationship may exist when the movement toward and away from God looks and, at times, feels the same, but its direction is different (Second Week Rules). "If a cause precedes, both the good angel and evil spirit can give consolation, but for a quite different purpose" (331).

# The Value of Consolation and Desolation

Consolation and desolation are valuable in uprooting disorders. The *pervasive movement* Laura experiences is God's total acceptance of her, concretely manifested in God's embrace and her positive response to this, such as accepting God's love, feeling peace within herself and in her relationships with others, desiring to share with God various aspects of her life, and feeling sorrow when she prevents God from becoming involved. The *pervasive countermovement* Laura experiences is not trusting and accepting God's total acceptance of her and leaving areas of her life removed from God's embrace. The *underlying disorder* or unfreedom is her own lack of self-acceptance, which is rooted in perfectionism and its effects. Laura experiences the grace of the First Week of the *Spiritual Exercises* during these movements and countermovements; that is, the grace of sorrow and forgiveness.

Disorders, areas of unfreedom, and "inordinate attachments" take various forms in our experience. For example, an individual may struggle in different ways with competitive tendencies. Or someone may continuously repress anger and act in passive-aggressive ways or perhaps even struggle with a compulsive need to achieve because of deeper feelings of inadequacy. Laura initially experiences pain over the sexual dimension of her relationship with Don. As she deals with it, she notices this is related to a deeper disorder: a lack of self-acceptance, which causes her to bend to others in order to be accepted (part of what was occurring between Don and herself), to be self-critical and a perfectionist, and to be hostile toward others.

God uses the interrelationship of consolations and desolations to bring to consciousness the various manifestations of a deep-rooted disorder. Ignatius says that the director should anticipate and expect movement and countermovement (17). If these do not occur, the director must explore the person's experience (6). He encourages us to linger in prayer in places where we experience "greater consolation, desolation, or spiritual appreciation" (62, 118). In her prayer during the ten-week period, Laura returned to the particular way she experienced God's embrace and to the concrete ways she avoided this embrace.

"Dwelling upon" these movements and countermovements evokes greater clarity concerning an area of unfreedom, notes Harvey D. Egan:

> The return to previous areas of special consolation and desolation helps the exercitant pinpoint areas of harmony and disharmony within himself in the light of God's saving word. These consolations and desolations accentuate the exercitant's spontaneous, yet often hidden, likes and dislikes which may or may not be in accord with the demands of his true self.[1]

Through consolations Laura experienced her authentic self; she accepted herself in darkness and in light. Because her self-acceptance is not complete, however, desolation continues to take place. For example, she loses sight of God and focuses on her imperfections. Through desolation, then, Laura experienced her refusal to be her true self and gained clarity about hidden areas where this refusal occurred. Writes Egan:

> . . . desolation can be understood as the repugnance which flows from the exercitant's deordination and resistance to the deepest demands of his own human nature. Desolation highlights the exercitant's often hidden resistance to full self-identity as well as those areas in the exercitant's being which prevent his authentic, human growth. . . . desolation indicates hidden areas of resistance to God's healing grace. Desolation exposes his disorder and truncation, and allows him, through frequent repetition of the points in which he received these desolations, to work out and heal the inordinate attachments in much the same way that a person works out a cramp from a muscle.[2]

Both consolation and desolation, then, are God-centered experiences. Consolation occurs, according to Jules J. Toner, when "the person feels God's loving presence, feels himself lovingly present to the lovingly present God. It is a conscious, affective, experience of loving communion with God."[3] Laura, for example, feels encased in the womb of God, feels God's embrace with her heavy lead coat.

Desolation is a God-centered experience of a contrary type: "It is as much a God-centered experience as consolation;

only it is God-who-seems-absent at the center of it, God apparently not loving me, God the beloved from whom I feel separated," writes Toner.[4] It is precisely because we have experienced God's felt presence in movement, he suggests, that we feel separated from God in countermovement: "Only insofar as a person's conscious life is God-centered or God-ward will a sense of separation from God generate spiritual desolation."[5] Because Laura has felt acceptance through God's embrace, she has grown to feel more acutely when she separates herself from that embrace and notices more experientially when she lacks trust in God.

The more pervasively we experience consolation, the more intensely we feel desolation and, concludes Toner, "the greater the extent to which his conscious life is such [God-centered] and the more intensely it is such, the more completely and more acutely will the sense of separation from God flood his consciousness with desolation."[6] The more vividly Laura experienced the various manifestations of God's embrace in her life, the more keenly she felt the difference when aspects of her life were not in God's embrace.

## Conclusion

Through movements and countermovements Laura grew in her knowledge of herself and of God. She learned that she wants to be perfect before approaching God. But God accepts her completely with her strengths and her imperfections. Nothing in her can keep God from embracing and loving her. She also learned that experiencing God's love results in hidden areas of sinfulness and darkness being brought out into the light—the light of God's presence, the light of her own awareness, and the light of another person's awareness.

## Experiencing God

### Reliving a Movement

Remember a time that you experienced God's embrace or God's total acceptance. Savor the richness of the experience. Relive it in your memory, feeling, imagination, heart, and mind.

✝ What were the circumstances of the experience? What was God's presence like?

✝ What were some of your feelings, thoughts, and desires?

✝ What difference did you notice within yourself as a result of this experience?

As you relive the experience, be attentive to God's presence with you now. Share with God any feelings that arise, and listen to God's response.

## Exploring a Countermovement

Remember a time when you experienced fear of letting God love you or that you had to have it "all together" before you could let God be close to you.

✝ What were the circumstances?

✝ What was God's felt absence like? Was there any sense of God's presence?

✝ What were some of your thoughts and feelings? Do you know the experiential reason—the area of unfreedom—underneath your fear?

✝ How did the desolation get resolved?

✝ What did you learn about yourself and God as a result of this desolating experience?

As you pray about the experience, be attentive to God's presence with you now. Share with God your feelings, and listen to God's response.

## Questions for Reflection and Discussion

1. In what specific ways did Laura change by revealing to Dave an area of sinfulness in session 3? Can you remember a time when you struggled to share something shameful with another person? What was that struggle like for you? How did you feel after you shared it?

2. What are some values in bringing dark, hidden areas out into the light of another human being? out into the light of God?

3. In what specific ways did Laura grow from the alternation of consolation and desolation? What did she learn about herself? What did she learn about God?

4. Besides those mentioned, what other aspects or dynamics of the Rules for Discernment relate to Laura's experience? Describe the relationships.

## For Spiritual Directors

1. At the end of session 2, what other questions might you ask yourself in discerning whether to stay with a directee's movement or countermovement in a given moment? What do you think of Dave's decision to stay with movement at that particular time?

2. In session 3, write out or role play Laura's struggle to share with Dave her sexual relationship with Don. What did you learn about the director's approach from this journaling or role playing?

3. Recall a moment when a directee had a hard time sharing something difficult or shameful with you. How did you feel as he or she struggled? How did you handle the session? Were you pleased or disappointed in how it went? Was your directee any different as a result of sharing this with you?

4. State three significant insights about spiritual direction that you gained or that were reinforced by Laura's experience. State some key insights that you learned regarding the Rules for Discernment.

# 9

# Bob's Experience of God's Extravagant Love

Bob has been in a close relationship with God for a long time. His experience illustrates:

1. Concrete expressions of movement and countermovement (316, 317);

2. Consolation without Previous Cause (330) and the After-glow (336);

3. The spiritual director savoring movement (15) and exploring countermovement (17);

4. Hidden fears being brought into the light (326).

## Background

Bob, a Christian brother, is forty-two years old. He has a deep personal relationship with God and has experienced God's love affectively. In spiritual direction sessions he is able to pay close attention both to God and to his interior reactions with ease. He has been in spiritual direction for many years.

# Session 1

Bob came into spiritual direction with a lightheartedness and exuberance. Mary, his spiritual director, knew by looking at him that something significant had happened to him.

B1: The other morning I was praying over the story of the woman who washed the feet of Jesus with expensive perfume. I was struck by the extravagance of her love.

M1: The extravagance of her love.

B2: Yes, nothing was too much for her to do for him. She took the most expensive thing she had and extravagantly poured it out on Jesus' feet (focused here for several moments). And then the most unexpected thing happened. I was all of a sudden overwhelmed with God's love. It was incredible.

M2: Gosh! Tell me about it.

B3: It was so unexpected and overwhelming and extravagant. God just extravagantly poured out His love on me. It was outrageous. I have felt for a long time God's love for me, but this was so extravagant.

M3: Wow! God extravagantly poured out His love on you.

B4: Yeah. It was totally accepting love; the kind of love that you don't have to do anything to earn. It was more than anything I could ever imagine. (They stayed here.)

M4: How did you feel, Bob, being so extravagantly loved by God?

B5: I felt so deeply consoled and strengthened.

M5: Deeply consoled and strengthened.

B6: Yes. I felt a deep inner strength, totally accepted by God, confirmed by God in who I am and what I'm about as a Christian brother. I even cried, which I have not done in a long time. I was so moved. God and I were totally one. There was no gap between us. (They lingered for awhile on Bob's reactions and on the total union and then focused directly on God.)

M6:  Are you able to say anything more about God's extrava-
     gant love for you? What was that like? Or what God was
     like as he loved you?

B7:  (Smiles) I was sitting on a comfortable chair in my room.
     It was like the arms of the chair became God's arms and
     wrapped around me—like a big hug!

M7:  Like a big hug.

B8:  Yes, it was like God wrapped His arms around me real
     tight, and I sunk down in His lap.

M8:  You sunk down in God's lap. How did that feel?

B9:  It was like we were totally enmeshed. There was no sep-
     aration between us. We were totally one. The very core
     of my being was one with God. I felt totally accepted by
     God. God is so pleased with who I am and how I am
     serving others as a religious. (Mary helped Bob savor this
     experience most of the session.)

## Movement and the Rules

The movement began with *attraction* to the woman's extravagant love for Jesus, which prepared Bob's heart for the experience of God's extravagant love. "I call consolation all interior
joy that invites and attracts to what is heavenly" (316).

A quiet attraction resulted in an intense experience of
God's overwhelming love: "I call it consolation when an interior movement is aroused in the soul, by which it is inflamed
with the love of its Creator and Lord" (316). Bob described
God's love as extravagant, totally accepting, and outrageous.
Bob's reactions were intense: he felt completely loved and
accepted, strengthened, totally one with God, and confirmed
in his vocation. He was not required to do anything in return.
Bob cried. "It is likewise consolation when one sheds tears
that move to the love of God, whether it be because of sorrow for sins, or . . . the sufferings of Christ, or for any other
reason . . . " (316). Bob was moved to tears by the feeling of
being so extravagantly loved by God and by feeling so totally
one with God. "It belongs solely to the Creator . . . to draw a
person wholly to the love of His Divine Majesty" (330).

## Approach of Director

Through an evocative and contemplative approach, Mary strived to help Bob stay with this powerful movement of extravagant love. By underscoring and asking appropriate questions, she helped him to be more aware of God and his interior reactions, to savor the richness of the experience, and to relive its fullness. She took an unobtrusive stance because "this produces greater spiritual relish and fruit . . . " (2).

Besides the sheer joy of feeling such deep love from God, there are several other reasons to notice, savor, and relive the experience. First, staying with a movement at length facilitates continuing movement toward God and ongoing growth in relationship with God. Second, it results in deeper understanding of the "truth" of God's self-communication in a given moment; for example, Bob experienced the "truth" of God's unconditional love. Third, it results in a depth of understanding, not merely a quantity of insight: "For it is not much knowledge that fills and satisfies . . . , but the intimate understanding and relish of the truth" (2).

Mary acted as a "balance at equilibrium" by not interfering with "the Creator and Lord in person communicating Himself to the devout soul . . . " (15). She maintained balance by helping Bob to focus on God and by helping him to recognize his interior reactions to God. This balancing approach is twofold: sometimes the focus is on God (see M3, M6, M8); other times the focus is on Bob's reactions (see M4, M9). Both sides of the scale are equally important because the experience happens in the context of two persons relating—God and Bob: "The director, . . . without leaning to one side or the other, should permit the Creator to deal directly with the creature, and the creature directly with his Creator and Lord" (15). Interiorly, Mary discerned when and how long to linger depending on the thoroughness with which Bob recognized God's self-revelation. Mary's discernment occurred in the context of her "felt sense" of Bob's "felt need" at a given moment.

Thus, spiritual directors need to be sensitively discerning as they facilitate directees' contemplation of a life-giving experience. On the one hand, directors can lead individuals to concentrate on God too quickly and not allow them sufficient time to notice fully their reactions. On the other hand, directors can stay too long with directees' interior reactions and lose sight of God in the experience.

## Session 2

B1:  I was praying with that powerful experience I told you about last week. I haven't had one of those in a long time. I wasn't feeling the intensity of the feelings I felt when it happened; at first I felt a sense of loss. But as I stayed with it, I could sense again the depth of God's love. I felt hollowed out, different, affirmed in my vocation, more open to God. I felt a strong desire to do something for God to express my love for him. And then I got distracted and could feel myself move from depth in my prayer to shallow thoughts.

M1:  Do you have any sense, Bob, of what was happening in you that moved you from deep prayer to shallowness?

B2:  (Pause) Well, actually I became afraid to pray deeply.

M2:  You became afraid to pray deeply.

B3:  Yes, I started thinking: "Does this powerful experience mean God is going to ask something of me?" I'm just getting settled, as I've mentioned to you, and I don't want to get unsettled. Then I got fearful that if I stay with the deep prayer I experienced, God might demand something of me. I know in my head and from experiencing God's love before that God's love is unconditional, but in some unfree place within me I became fearful.

M3:  You became afraid of what God might demand of you, that you might have to get unsettled.

B4:  Yes. I know, of course, from past experience that God's love is a free gift. But that experience of God's extravagant love was so powerful, like one of those experiences that initiate a conversion. I've had enough change in my life the past several years, I don't need another conversion right now (laughs).

M4:  Is there anything specific you are fearful that it might demand of you? any specific conversion or change? (Looking for a possible stimulus for this CM.)

B5:  Yes, it's related to that letter I got from my provincial several weeks ago. I just got settled into one area of education, and I don't want to have to change it because I might be stuck in school administration the rest of my life. (They explore this concern for awhile.)

M5:  Have you shared your fear with God that this experience might demand something of you? Have you shared this specific fear?

B6:  No, not really. I guess I got caught in my fear and forgot to share it with God.

M6:  Do you feel you could share your fear with God now that we have talked it out? Share your fears in prayer as specifically as you've shared them with me?

B7:  Yes, now that I've talked this out with you, I feel freer to share my fears with God and to listen.

### The Afterglow, Countermovement, and the Rules

Rule 336 describes what can happen in the period after a Consolation without Previous Cause:

> When consolation is without previous cause, there can be no deception in it, since it can proceed from God our Lord only. But a spiritual person who has received such a consolation must consider it very attentively, and must cautiously distinguish the actual time of the consolation from the period which follows it.

Bob experienced two types of reactions in the afterglow: a deep knowledge of God's love and a strong sense of affirmation and fearful thoughts and feelings. First, although the intensity of feeling was not present, a deep recognition of God's unconditional love continued within Bob. Also, he felt a profound affirmation of his vocation to religious life. God confirmed his primary commitment to serve as a Christian brother.

Second, Bob moved toward fearful thoughts in the afterglow: "It is characteristic of the evil one to fight against such happiness and consolation by proposing fallacious reasonings, subtleties, and continual deceptions" (329). It is not unusual that when people experience a powerful or intimate encounter with God, they move away from it due to an area of unfreedom. This countermovement can take the form of various "fallacious reasonings," such as "Am I worthy of such great love?" or "What will this consoling experience demand of me?" Individuals may *know* and have previously experienced God's unconditional love. However, their felt reaction and thoughts move away spontaneously and indicate a deeper area that needs to be freed through God's action. On one level of his being, Bob *knows* that God's love demands nothing of him. But in an unfree area, he *feels* fearful and wonders what this profound experience might require of him.

## Approach of Director

Ignatius encouraged individuals to "pay attention to and dwell upon those points in which we have experienced greater consolation or desolation or greater spiritual appreciation" (62, 118). This dynamic also takes place in spiritual direction. In the first session, Mary helped Bob to "dwell upon" points of greater consolation. In this session, she encouraged him to "pay attention to" the countermovement for several reasons: (1) to gain greater clarity of his underlying feelings and reasons for it; (2) to be freed of its power; and (3) to share the desolating feelings and "fallacious reasonings" with God in prayer in order to create inner space for movement back toward God.

Being attentive to the countermovement in the direction session also exemplifies the dynamic of bringing into conscious awareness that which is hidden (326). The "secret" can be something obvious, as in Laura revealing the sexual dimension of her relationship with Don. But it can also be a more subtle "secret." It can be a life circumstance, an interior reality, or a vague feeling that a directee is consciously or unconsciously holding back from self and the director. It diminishes a fuller awareness of one's interior reactions, and it keeps God hidden from one's affectivity and awareness. Bob was only vaguely aware of his fear of what God's extravagant love might demand of him. Through specifically exploring this fear with Mary's assistance, Bob was freed of its power and was able to bring it into conscious dialogue with God.

"It will be very helpful if the director is kept faithfully informed about the various disturbances and thoughts caused by the action of different spirits" (17). Specific responses in the session have this as their goal. In M1, for example, Mary attempts to get to the inner source of the difficulty by praying deeply; in M2 and M3, she underscores to evoke more feelings and content around the fear; and in M4, she specifically searches for a concrete reason for Bob's fear.

Further, a director explores the various motions in order to "propose some spiritual exercises in accordance with the degree of progress made . . . and suited to the needs" of the person (17). In M5 and M6, Mary helps Bob bring his specific fears into conscious dialogue with God. This explicit sharing is needed in order for movement to return.

## Consolation without Previous Cause

Bob's experience of God's extravagant love is a vivid example of Consolation without Previous Cause (CWPC). CWPC is an experience of consolation that goes to the core of one's being and unites one totally to God in that moment. Although "remarkable," it is also an experience, according to Harvey D. Egan, that belongs to the normal perspective of the spiritual life.[1] It is a profound experience but, it is not a rare occurrence.[2]

Through the centuries there has been great difficulty deciphering the meaning of Consolation without Previous Cause since Ignatius describes it in only two places in the *Spiritual Exercises* (330 and 336) and cites only a few examples of it in his *Autobiography* and *Letters*. The two descriptions in the *Spiritual Exercises* are extremely brief: "Ignatius has here accomplished a masterpiece of brevity but not of clarity," says Egan.[3] One of the reasons for Ignatius' brevity is because CWPC is so basic to the entire experience of the *Spiritual Exercises*. Rule 330 says:

> God alone can give consolation to the soul without any previous cause. It belongs solely to the Creator to come into a soul, to leave it, to act upon it, to draw it wholly to the love of His Divine Majesty. I said without previ-

ous cause, that is without any preceding perception or knowledge of any subject by which a soul might be led to such a consolation through its own acts of intellect and will.

A letter from Ignatius to a friend, Sister Teresa Rejadell, also discloses elements of CWPC:

> For a clearer understanding of this fear and its origins I will call your attention to two lessons which our Lord usually gives or permits. The one of them He gives, the other He permits. The first is an interior consolation which casts out all uneasiness and draws one to a complete love of our Lord. In this consolation He enlightens some, and to others He reveals many secrets as a preparation for later visits. In a word, when this divine consolation is present all trials are pleasant and all weariness rest . . . This consolation points out and opens up the way we are to follow and points out the way we are to avoid. It does not remain with us always, but it will always accompany us on the way at the times that God designates. All this is for our progress . . .
>
> For it frequently happens that our Lord moves and urges the soul to this or that activity. He begins by enlightening the soul; that is to say, by speaking interiorly to it without the din of words, lifting it up wholly to His divine love and ourselves to His meaning without any possibility of resistance on our part, even should we wish to resist.[4]

Consolation without Previous Cause is the "basis of Ignatian discernment," says Egan, a "key Ignatian experience," which "dominates his entire perspective."[5] Essentially, it is the becoming explicit of what is already implicit in our experience: "The Ignatian method," continues Egan, "evokes, intensifies and strengthens what is actually everyone's fundamental, yet most often anonymous, stance in the grace of Christ."[6] It is the "apex," the epitome of Ignatius' expectation that God "in person should communicate Himself to the devout soul, inflaming it with His love and praise" (15).

What characterizes this experience? Several things. It was not previously asked for, and it is disproportionate to what the individual desires from God at the moment of receiving it. It transcends the grace expected from the prayer or activity at hand, and it draws us wholly into God's love.[7] God alone enters, renders the specific meditation at hand transparent, and draws the person beyond what he or she wants and desires entirely into love.[8]

Although disproportionate to "what I ask for and desire," the experience is somehow proportionate and fitting because it is congruent with our deepest desires. "The actual fulfillment, however, is disproportionately proportionate to the actual expectation," writes Egan.[9] The disproportion signals us to observe this experience carefully. However, the quality of the religious experience—its intrinsic value and its ability to draw us entirely into God's love—is the criterion of CWPC.[10] God enters, envelops us in divine love, and empties us of everything, except God's presence. A sense of loss is usually associated with CWPC.  It is initiated from within the very core of our being, involving our deepest freedom and inmost center. This movement excludes all inordinate affections that hinder wholeness and unifies the entire person. According to Egan, it is a " . . . radically integral, fully human experience, unifying and summing up the one person in all of his depth and dimensions."[11]

The same letter from Ignatius to Teresa Rejadell indicates that there can be various kinds of CWPC: (1) a pure, transcendental experience of God in utter receptivity; (2) a pure openness to God that contains specific, nonconceptual felt knowledge guaranteed by God; or (3) an experience that supports within its pure openness to God a specific, conceptual, and verbal knowledge guaranteed by God. As CWPC approaches the "time that follows," it loses its God-guaranteed specification and explicitness.[12] At such times, CWPC is barely distinguishable from Consolation with Previous Cause.

While contemplating the great love of the woman washing the feet of Jesus, Bob was wholly and unexpectedly drawn into the "extravagant" love of God. The experience was disproportionate to his usual experience of Consolation with Previous Cause. He felt "totally accepted by and enmeshed" with God. The deepest core of his being was touched as he is overwhelmed by this transparent experience of God's love. As Egan says:

. . . gradually the mystery before him becomes more and more transparent, although this does not necessarily mean that all conceptual awareness must vanish. The (person) in his inmost center feels himself totally drawn beyond anything conceptual or individual into God's love. He becomes, as it were, Pure Openness and Receptivity. He experiences everything he is drawn to and united with God's love.[13]

Bob felt a sense of loss afterwards because the intensity of the union with God dissipated, although he continued to feel the depth of God's love. "During it, the person experiences a greatly heightened interior unity, simplicity, and presence," Egan points out. "A return to his normal state is experienced as a loss."[14]

Bob, like Ignatius, experienced a deep felt knowledge regarding the nature of God's personal love:

For Ignatius, "sentido" almost always means felt knowledge, personal knowledge, connatural knowledge, a knowledge flowing from love and the heart, a non-conceptual, non-verbal, mystical knowledge, often described as a "tasting" or a "savoring." Ignatius himself admits in a letter that there could be matters that could be better felt than put into words.[15]

The felt knowledge that Bob experienced was God's extravagant and unconditional love. His "interior sense of touch" became involved when he experienced the arms of the chair as God's arms wrapping around him, like "a big hug." He "savors" this embrace by sinking down into God's lap.

CWPC must be considered not in isolation, but in the context of the *Spiritual Exercises*. Harvey Egan says CWPC is for someone who is "elite," a person "from whom great things in God's service can be expected," someone "who has shown fervor and generosity during the First Week," and a person who can "cope with the 'subtle' and 'advanced' knowledge required for discernment" during the Second Week.[16]

From my practical experience as a spiritual director, I have a somewhat different perspective. First, by making the kind of person who receives CWPC "special"—that is, someone who is primarily in a Second Week stance—Egan seems to contradict the thesis of his book, which claims that CWPC is the foundation of Ignatius' mystical horizon:

> The CWPC presents itself as a key Ignatian experience which manifests in a highly concentrated way all the facets of Ignatius' mystical horizon. . . . Furthermore, the CWPC presents in a concentrated way not only Ignatius' mystical horizon, but also what is *most characteristic of everyone's* life in the grace of Christ (my emphasis).[17]

He neglects the experience of a significant group of people, that is, those primarily in a First Week stance.

Second, although CWPC is not discussed as such until the Second Week Rules, I view it as a powerful manifestation of the first kind of consolation mentioned in the First Week Rules:

> I call it consolation when an interior movement is aroused in the soul, by which it is *inflamed with love of its Creator and Lord,* and as a consequence, *can love no creature* on the face of the earth *for its own sake,* but only in the Creator of them all (my emphasis) (316).

People drawn wholly into the love of God are inflamed with God's love to the extent that God experientially becomes the root and foundation of their life in that moment.

Third, some commentators consider the first election, that is, one way of making a God-centered decision, as CWPC. In that description Ignatius says:

> When God our Lord so moves and attracts the will that a devout soul without hesitation, or the possibility of hesitation, follows what has been manifested to it. St. Paul and St. Matthew acted thus in following Christ our Lord. (175)

Although their experience of CWPC moved them ultimately to a total commitment to God, both Matthew and Paul would be considered in a First Week stance at the time they received this consolation since their lives and actions were not quite yet rooted in Christ.

Fourth, in my experience as a spiritual director for many different people, I have seen individuals at various junctures of their relationship with God experience CWPC, such as those just beginning a conscious relationship with God, those in a First Week stance, and those who strongly resist God's love. CWPC can break through strong resistance.

Possibly, CWPC is a more frequent occurrence among those in a more "advanced" relationship with God. However, people of various capacities of openness to God can also receive this pure gift. For example, Laura, who is primarily in a First Week stance, experienced CWPC when she felt God "embrace her with her heavy lead coat." She felt wholly drawn into God's love as she struggled with an area of sinfulness. God's total acceptance was unexpected and disproportionate to her usual spiritual experiences. It went to the core of her being. This CWPC continued to reveal itself through other experiences of God's embrace, which were mainly Consolation "with" Previous Cause. God frequently drew her to her deepest self and to the initial experience in order to reveal an all-accepting love, to transform her inner darkness, and to open her to an even fuller and deeper spiritual experience.

## Conclusion

Both Bob's and Laura's experience of God illustrate two unique aspects of Consolation without Previous Cause. Their experiences also demonstrate how CWPC is a normal, though remarkable, experience; show how people at different stages of growth in relationship with God can undergo this all-encompassing consolation; and reveal how CWPC goes to the core of one's being and unites one totally to God in that particular moment. Although this consolation affectively dissipates—and fears may arise in the period after the consolation, as in Bob's case—its impact and certainty endures throughout one's life. Indeed, Consolation without Previous Cause is a powerful experience of deepening the relationship between God and individuals. Its clarity, depth, strength, and effect on people cannot be denied or forgotten. A powerful touch of God, though taking place in a moment of time, lives on in individuals forever and becomes the foundation for developing a discerning heart.

# Experiencing God

## Reliving a Powerful Movement

In God's presence, remember a time that you experienced an unexpected, out of the ordinary, very powerful experience of God's love that made a deep and lasting impression on you.

Savor the richness of the experience and relive it in your memory, in your imagination, in your heart, and in your mind.

✝ What were the circumstances of the experience? What was God's presence like in the experience?

✝ What were some of your feelings, thoughts, and desires?

✝ What difference did you notice within yourself as a result of this experience?

As you relive the experience, be attentive to God's presence with you now. Share with God any feelings that arise and listen to God's response.

## Afterglow

✝ Remember how you felt after that consoling movement. Did you feel moved to serve God in any particular way? Did you become frightened by what it might mean?

✝ What was God's presence like in the Afterglow of this consolation? How was God's presence different from the actual consolation?

✝ What were some of your thoughts and feelings?

✝ What did you learn about yourself and about God as a result of this consoling experience?

✝ What makes this experience different from other consoling experiences?

As you pray about the experience, be attentive to God's presence with you now. Share with God your feelings, and listen to God's response.

## Questions for Reflection and Discussion

1. What did Bob learn about himself through this experience? after the experience? What did he learn about God?

2. Does Bob's Consolation without Previous Cause remind you of any of Ignatius' consoling experiences in chapter 3?

3. Do you think most people of faith experience CWPC during their lifetime? Do you think they usually remain aware of the experience or do they forget about it as time goes on?

## For Spiritual Directors

1. What is most striking to you about Mary's approach in each of the two sessions?

2. Has any of your directees shared with you a CWPC? What was that session like? What was your approach? What was God's presence like in the session? How was this experience different from other consoling experiences which that directee shared?

    If part of a group, role play your directee's CWPC so that you can feel the depth and richness within yourself once again.

3. State three significant insights about spiritual direction that you gained or that were reinforced by Bob's experience. State three key insights that you learned about the Rules for Discernment.

---

# 10

# Bill's Experience of
# Deeper Awareness

---

Bill has been relating to God in an affective way for several years. His eight-day directed retreat exemplifies:

1. Intense alternation between movement and countermovement, which gradually reveals a pervasive area of unfreedom (327);

2. Concrete ways of dealing with desolation (319, 325, 326);

3. Subtle countermovement of "evil under the appearance of good" (332–333);

4. A changed outlook and concrete actions resulting from the experience of consolations and desolations;

5. An example of Consolation without Previous Cause (330).

## Background

Bill is a single man in his early thirties who has been active in campus ministry and who, in recent years, has been experiencing deep loneliness. Several years ago he went through a discernment process over his vocational choice (priesthood v. marriage). At the end of this process, he came away with the realization that he wanted to be married, which gave him much joy and peace. Not long after, Bill began to feel depressed because he had not formed a lasting relationship.

## Session 1

Attracted to cornfields, Bill reflected on God's desire to feed the world with corn and bread and his own desire to feed others. Eventually, Bill's attention changed to Jesus' desire to feed him. He felt Jesus' personal care for him. For awhile, Bill started to feel filled up, like he was being fed (M). This changed suddenly: "I felt that tension again, confused and depressed, like screaming, frustration. . . . I feel like there's this big hole in me that needs to be filled. I feel so empty and needy and lonely." He began to think: "Is my desire for someone just to fill my own needs? Am I being selfish to want to have my needs filled?" (CM). Donna, his retreat director, encouraged him to share these feelings and thoughts with the caring Jesus.

### Connection between Movement and Countermovement

Bill experienced intense alternation of movement and countermovement. The feelings are contrary: Jesus desires to feed him, and he begins to feel filled. Then he feels a big hole inside himself; he feels empty and lonely. Bill's desolating feelings provoked desolating thoughts ("Is my desire for someone just to fill my own needs?"). Ignatius points to this dynamic: "For just as consolation is the opposite of desolation, so the thoughts that spring from consolation are the opposite of those that spring from desolation" (317).

## Session 2

B1:   The image of corn and bread changed to water last night. I was aware of the importance of water for sustaining life, like when I took a drink of water and listened to the rain today. I sensed that God was saying to me, showing me, that He is going to fill me and sustain me. (They stayed with this.)

Later, I went into the chapel and put my hand in the holy water font. It was empty. That was such a concrete expression of the tension I talked about yesterday. And so different from what God said about filling me.

D1: It was empty, different from God's desire to fill you.

B2: Yes, it felt barren, empty, and void, like I feel when I'm feeling that loneliness. (They stayed with God's desire to fill his emptiness.) Then I started remembering times in my life that God did sustain me—different images from childhood. (They stayed here.)

D2: What was that like for you to remember those times and images?

B3: I started to feel some hope. When I get into that lonely place I feel so hopeless. And then I sensed Jesus telling me again that he is going to sustain me and that he is filling me, as with water.

D3: What was Jesus like there as he kept telling you that?

B4: He was very reassuring, encouraging, satisfied with me, and hopeful. The hope I see in him helps me to be more hopeful. I especially felt his presence during liturgy. The hope, peace, and joy grew stronger and kept growing during most of the afternoon.

D4: The hope, peace, and joy kept growing as you felt his presence grow.

B5: Yes, when I heard the first reading about God forming a covenant with His people, I felt like I was being filled, and the hopeful feeling strengthened in me. I felt warm inside and filled with hope. Then that tension started to come back again, a lot of anger, that feeling of wanting to scream.

D5: You felt a lot of anger and felt like screaming.

B6: Yes, the anger is that I really don't want to be a priest. Why does that idea keep coming back to me? As the tension and anger came back I felt like a weight was on me. A real heaviness.

D6: A heaviness.

B7:  Yes, it feels like this big thing is weighing down on me. And I feel stretched inside, torn again between marriage and priesthood. (They spent time talking about how and when his original desire to become a priest began to grow.)

D7:  Do you have any sense of what brought on the tension and heaviness this afternoon? When and how it originated today?

B8:  I started thinking about creating space in me for others. Then the thought came to me: "I could probably create the biggest space in me for others by becoming a priest." Then the tension started to come back, the heaviness, feeling torn.

D8:  Are you still feeling that tension and heaviness now?

B9:  No, not really. In preparation for coming here, I read over my notes of the day. I noticed that most of the day was focused on covenant love, being filled, and hope. There's only this one small part of the day when the tension begins to grow—that seems to have been my pattern so far. (Bill described at length his discernment process of two years ago. The greatest movement occurred at the end of the process when he said aloud to his director: "I want to get married and be involved in full-time ministry." He felt like a big weight was lifted; he was exhilarated with joy and peace, a feeling that lasted for months.) I'm tired of dealing with this priesthood question.

     (Near the end of the session, as Donna encouraged him to share with God his strong feeling of not wanting to deal with this anymore, he said:)

B10: That tension and heaviness is coming back, and it's really strong in me right now.

D9:  The heaviness is strong in you now?

B11: Yes, I'm feeling stretched again; feeling like I want to scream. The heaviness. Feeling torn. (They explored these feelings.)

D10: Do you have any sense of God being there at all?

B12: Whenever these feelings come over me I lose sight of Jesus and sense an old-man God with white hair. A god who's angry and disappointed with me. He reminds me of my father. They have the same face. I sense my father is disappointed in me, too, because I didn't become a lawyer. He doesn't say that, but I know he is. (They stayed here.)

D11: This god is angry and disappointed with you, like your father. Do you notice anything else about him?

B13: He's cold, very cold. It's this angry, cold god who I sense will be angry with me if I don't become a priest. (They explored this a bit more.) It's really helping me to talk about it, because I'm realizing this cold angry god is not God. I know that's not God, but yet that god is often there when I feel this heaviness and loneliness. All of this must come from somewhere in my past and my unconscious because it comes up enough. But helping me to bring this out into the open brings clarity to me.

D12: (End of session) Bill, could you talk to Jesus—warm, caring, and satisfied with you—about this cold and disappointed god? Tell Jesus how you feel about this cold god, and listen some more to him.


## Movement, Countermovement, and the Rules

Bill's immediate concern is choosing between marriage or priesthood. A deeper issue is the importance of his own needs. The vacillation between movement and countermovement occur around the priesthood-marriage matter, lending greater clarity about the underlying reasons for his struggle.

The main movement consists of hope, peace, and joy when he senses Jesus as a caring, warm, encouraging, and satisfied figure, desiring to fill him. This relates to consolation:

> I call consolation every increase of faith, hope, and love, and all interior joy that invites and attracts to what is heavenly and to the salvation of one's soul by filling it with peace and quiet in its Creator and Lord (316).

What does "increase" mean here? Jules J. Toner discusses several possible meanings: (1) greater depth of hope in that it becomes "more interiorized, reaches more profoundly into one's personality, and involves a fuller commitment to Christ"; (2) firmer—that is, unshakable under trial; (3) greater purity—more from God and less from "good humanistic motivation"; (4) greater diffusion through our personality, coloring our ways of perceiving, reasoning, judging, imagining, and feeling reality; (5) greater effectiveness—increased influence on ways of choice and action; and (6) greater intensity of "affective feelings" and ease in that "all intellectual difficulties and all conflicting affections are put to rest." All these possibilities move toward increased integration. Although these interpretations could be included in consolation, Toner points out that Ignatius stressed increased intensity, especially affective sensibility. For example, Ignatius says: "For though God has taken from him the abundance of fervor and overflowing love and the intensity of his favors, nevertheless, he has sufficient grace for eternal salvation" (320). We, in ourselves, cannot "attain great devotion, intense love, tears, or any other spiritual consolation" (322).[1]

As a First Week phenomenon that occurs in some experiences, Toner stresses "greater intensity" because of the emphasis that Ignatius places on affectivity in consolation and desolation. However, the other dimensions of "increase" can also relate to a person's experience of God, although more observable, perhaps, over a period of time. What is most noticeable in Bill's experience is his intensity of feeling, that is, the affective sensibility. At the same time, hope deepens and becomes more firmly rooted in him. Growing hope affects the way he perceives reality and the way he reasons, feels, imagines, and makes choices. Consequently, growth in depth and integration occurs over a period of time because of the affective moments of hope.

Bill's countermovement has elements of both the First and Second Week Rules. A First Week dynamic is operative in that Bill experienced the opposite of the movement: hopelessness, tension, heaviness, feeling torn when starting to think about creating a bigger space for others through the priesthood, and encountering an angry, cold, disappointed god. Bill experiences:

darkness of soul [heaviness], turmoil of spirit [tension], inclination to what is low and earthly [cold, disappointed god], restlessness rising from many disturbances and temptations [feeling torn between priesthood and marriage], which lead to want of faith [losing the feel for a caring Jesus and seeing a cold god], want of hope [feelings of hopelessness], and want of love.

The soul is . . . sad [depressed feelings] and separated, as it were, from its Creator and Lord [losing the caring Jesus in his experience and focusing on a cold god] (317).

Both Bill's thinking and his feelings are affected: For "those who seek to rise in the service of God, it is characteristic of the evil spirit to harass with anxiety, to afflict with sadness, to raise obstacles backed by fallacious reasoning that disturb the soul" (315). Bill experiences fallacious reasoning when he thinks about creating "the biggest space" possible by becoming a priest and when he perceives God as being disappointed in him if he does not become one.

Ignatius develops more subtle aspects of fallacious reasoning in the Second Week Rules by describing "evil under the appearance of good" (332). In this dynamic the countermovement can be seemingly similar to movement. It is more difficult to distinguish good from evil because frequently what moves someone away from God appears to be good and, in fact, may be good. However, it may not be the "best" for this person, nor may it be the direction that God wants.

The "evil spirit," notes Ignatius, begins to draw us away from God by suggesting thoughts that are congruent with our underlying movement toward God, but ends by suggesting thoughts that lead away from God. These thoughts can be "holy and pious thoughts that are wholly in conformity" with our overall relationship with God. However, they can also "little by little" draw us away from God if we linger with them too long (332).

To gain clarity about how this dynamic operates, Ignatius suggests that we "observe the whole course of our thoughts." If the "beginning and middle and end" of our intellectual and affective components are leading to what is "wholly good . . . and entirely right," then we can be assured that this experience is congruent with our ongoing movement toward God. However, if the course of our thoughts might end in "something evil or distracting or less good," or if these thoughts may "weaken or disquiet" us or "destroy the peace, tranquility, and quiet" previously present, we can be certain that they are not from God (333).

In thinking about creating the "biggest space for others" through the priesthood (B8), Bill began to encounter "evil under the appearance of good." He had been experiencing consolation, but when he started thinking the "holy and pious thought" of entering the priesthood, he "ended" by feeling torn, heavy, and empty. His "peace and tranquility were destroyed." His experience of the warm and satisfied Jesus changed to that of a cold and disappointed god. In that moment, his relationship with God was "weakened."

Through talking about this cold and angry god (B13), Bill gained a clearer sense that this was not the true God. He observed the "beginning, middle, and end" and noticed more clearly that this image of god rose to his consciousness when feeling lonely and down over the priesthood question. He realized that this image destroyed his peace and moved him away from Jesus. Simultaneously taking place here was a more subtle expression of bringing a hidden reality out into the light in order to gain greater clarity (326). To repeat, through specifically describing this god and his feelings regarding it, Bill realized clearly that this was not God. Therefore, the image that emerged from his unconscious began to lose power over him.

## Approach of Director

Bill's director, Donna, encouraged him to linger over consolation and desolation. By helping Bill contemplate various qualities of Jesus and assisting him to talk about his reactions to Jesus—especially his "heavy" feelings and his attitude toward the "cold" god—she helped him to "pay attention to and dwell upon consolation" in order that consolation may return (62). This "dwelling upon" strengthened his felt sense of Jesus.

In such a way, Donna was "kept faithfully informed about the various disturbances and thoughts caused by the action of different spirits" in order to "propose some spiritual exercises in accordance with the degree of progress made . . . " (17). She suggested a concrete way of praying (D12) to help Bill "go against" the desolation (319).

A director "should encourage and strengthen him for the future by exposing to him the wiles of the enemy of our human nature" (7). A director does not necessarily have to point out these "wiles," although this is important to do at times. Through an evocative stance, a director can assist people to better identify their vulnerable areas. By helping Bill talk about his concerns, Donna is "exposing to him the wiles of the enemy."

"For it is not much knowledge that fills and satisfies the soul, but the intimate understanding and relish of the truth" (2). Donna facilitated Bill's observation and recognition of the real Jesus. She helped him verbalize what Jesus said to him; that is, the "truth." She did not suggest he read a passage from Scripture, which could have distracted him from the movements. Instead she encouraged him to share his feelings and perceptions with God and to be attentive to God's response.

"Remain firm and constant in the decision to which we adhered in the preceding consolation" (318). By exploring with Bill and helping him remember concrete evidence of his previous discernment, Donna assisted him to grow more firmly convinced of its authenticity and of the rightness of his desire to get married.

## Sessions 3 and 4

Bill came in feeling very down. The loneliness was so overwhelming at times that he wanted to cry but had a hard time doing so. He felt like packing up and going home.

B1:  I feel so deeply the need for someone. It feels like there's this big hole in me, a real big void.

D1:  Can you say more, Bill, about your need for someone? Is there any particular person that's been coming to mind?

B2:  Yes, as I'm feeling like this I'm feeling a deep desire to be close to Joan. I've been thinking of her a lot today.

D2: Tell me about her—who she is and what you've been
   feeling toward her and thinking about concerning her.

Joan is a college student who works closely with Bill on
campus ministry activities. They have a close friendship. As he
shared in direction, Bill began to realize that he is in love with
Joan. Although not terribly concerned over their age difference (twelve years), he felt some anxiety about what others
might think. He was eager to go home to discover how Joan
feels toward him.

Jesus continued to say that he will sustain him and fill his
needs. Bill compared the cold, demanding, unsatisfied god
with the caring and warm Jesus. He sensed from the former a
great deal of dissatisfaction with him; he sensed from Jesus a
healthy satisfaction. As the difference between these two
experiences grew, Bill realized experientially that the cold god
was not God. The difference moved him to talk more to
Jesus. It was this Jesus—the true Jesus—who eventually freed
him of the fear and burden caused by the dissatisfied god.

## Movement, Countermovement, and the Rules

Frequently, what is deeply hidden within us needs to be
revealed gradually to another person. We may share a certain
degree of the "secret" (326). That sharing frees us to experience consolation again and prepares our inner selves for
deeper unfolding. Self-revelation to another person provokes
more revelation. The "secret" can have both positive and negative aspects. Bill's realization of his true feelings for Joan was
a very positive experience for him but later, at the retreat, it
released a painful and more basic part of the "secret."

Bill's loneliness continued because more of what was hidden needed to be revealed. In talking about Joan, he realized
deep feelings of being in love with her. This acknowledgment
relieved his loneliness momentarily and moved him to want
to talk to both God and Joan about his true feelings.

## Session 5

Although the "black god" left him, darkness remained. Bill
talked about this with Jesus. In their conversation, Bill noticed

two "black cubes." One cube involved the question of priest-hood— he feared dealing with it. But eventually he said to Jesus: "I'm really afraid to deal with this, but I'm laying my life on the line for you." By addressing the issue, Jesus trans-formed the "black cubes" into "gray coals," that is, Jesus assured him of his love—being satisfied with him—no matter what Bill chose. Bill felt "exhilarated" because his trust in Jesus was growing.

The second "black cube" was even bigger and more com-plicated: his fear of dealing with his relationship with Joan in prayer because he might lose her.

B1: I kept telling Jesus how afraid I was to deal with it, and I kept sensing from him, "Trust me." So I finally did trust him and began to look at that black cube with him. And I was overwhelmed with God's love.

D1: You were overwhelmed with God's love?

B2: Yes, it was so powerful. It was like waves and waves were coming over me and filling me.

D2: Waves and waves were coming over you and filling you.

B3: Yes, and these waves were Jesus—him deep within me.

D3: Those waves were Jesus deep within you.

B4: Yes, I trusted to Jesus the thing I was most fearful of los-ing, so he kept filling me with himself. (They stayed here.)

D4: How did you feel, Bill, as Jesus kept filling you with himself?

B5: I felt exhilarated. I felt overwhelming joy. As Jesus kept filling me with himself, I was being filled with joy . . . and this freed me to keep dealing with my fear. In the blackness the word "unwanted" stood out as big as life. It all came together for me. My fear of bringing Joan up to Jesus had to do with my fear that she may not want me. The bottom line of my loneliness is feeling unwanted. (They explored his feeling of being unwanted by his parents and significant women along the way.)

The Lord kept inviting me to trust him with my fear of being unwanted. As I did, that covenant love kept filling me, and I had a deep sense that Joan and I were going to form a bond of covenant love. I don't mean necessarily marriage but that we would continue to be connected. Even if it didn't lead to marriage, I'm not going to be left with that feeling of being unwanted.

The main thing with all this is not so much the sense of Joan and me being bonded, although that is very important. The main thing is that I trusted the most fearful parts of me to Jesus and that he and I are bonded. I feel so deeply wanted by the Lord. That unwanted feeling is being healed. The Lord's love is deeper than my feeling of being unwanted.

### Movement, Countermovement, and the Rules

Bill's decision to share his fear of confronting the two black cubes exemplifies several dynamics of "going against" the desolation. A powerful fear urged him to keep his feelings hidden from a conscious dialogue with God. However, in sharing his fears with Jesus, Bill "faced his temptation boldly and did exactly the opposite" (325). In this way, his fears lost their power ("blackness" changed to "grayness"), and consolation returned ("joy and exhilaration").

Bill's sharing with Jesus exemplifies how prayer intensifies our activity against the desolation. Ignatius suggests fighting the desolation in several ways: by prayer, meditation, examination of ourselves, and penance (319). Since desolation encompasses all of us, these actions involve various parts of our being: prayer engages our affectivity; meditation and examining ourselves involve our thinking; and penance engages our behavior. Bill had done all of these. At times he needed to examine his feelings and thoughts on his own and with his director. This day he needed to share his feelings with Jesus in depth.

Bill's experience also exemplifies how God uses consolations and desolations to reveal and free a "disordered area" (1). In dealing straightforwardly with his fears of joining the priesthood and losing Joan, Bill facilitated the unpacking of his deeply rooted vulnerable area of feeling unwanted. His twin fears are symptoms of a deeper area of unfreedom. His fear of being unwanted is the "weak point that is continually being attacked" (327). In uncovering this area, he was able to be open to and feel the Lord wanting him.

Bill experienced Consolation without Previous Cause on the fifth day of his retreat. The feeling of being "overwhelmed with God's love, like waves and waves were coming over me and filling me" was disproportionate to his experience of Jesus filling him the previous four days. He felt "wholly drawn into God's love" (330). Bill's underlying "disorder" of feeling unwanted was freed for that moment as he felt totally accepted by Jesus. Nothing else mattered. He felt whole. Although he continued to experience Jesus during the remainder of the retreat, he felt a sense of loss and a longing to experience with similar intensity the feeling of Jesus filling him.

At that moment, Bill had a deep sense that he would form a covenant bond of love. During the following few days of the afterglow, his "own reasoning" operated strongly as he wondered if the deep experience meant that he and Joan were going to be married (336).

## Session 6

B1: Jesus and I were close together today. I sensed him on the cross saying to me: "See, I was unwanted too. I know how much it hurts to feel unwanted. I'm glad that you're sharing your unwantedness with me and that we can share it together. Your unwantedness is your cross, too."

D1: How did you feel as Jesus was saying that to you?

B2: I didn't have any strong feelings, like the joy I felt yesterday. But it was a sense of being really close. We spent all afternoon walking around together. We were joking as we walked along, and we were having a lot of fun. Jesus had his arm around my shoulder as we walked. He kept saying to me: "To know me is to be wanted. The more you know me, the more you will feel wanted." I kept sensing that his care and love were all that mattered.

D2: How did that feel to you?

B3:    It felt right, and I had such a deep desire to get to know him totally. Then the priesthood question started coming up again. The question was: "If I really get to know him that means I'm going to know more deeply how much he wants me; is that going to mean that I have to become a priest?" That really scared me. I really started to get confused. Then it seemed that Joan left the picture totally.

D3:    And how does that feel in you?

B4:    I don't like it at all. I don't want her to be out of the picture. But this fear comes up in me that the more that I sense that Jesus wants me, the more Joan will go out of the picture. He keeps inviting me to trust him, but I'm having a hard time letting go. (They stayed here. Donna encouraged Bill to share that fear with Jesus.)

## Movement, Countermovement, and the Rules

Again, in the midst of movement, a desolating question returned: does growing to know Jesus more deeply mean that Jesus will want him to be a priest? "Evil under the appearance of good" is operative here (332). Bill experienced true consolation and closeness to God. But the "beginning thought" arising from that movement "ends" in fear and confusion, "destroying his peace, tranquility, and quiet" (333). The connection between movement and countermovement is of a similar rather than opposite nature: Jesus loves and wants him (M); is this going to result in Jesus hoping he becomes a priest? (CM)

## Approach of Director

Donna explored the "various disturbances and thoughts" by eliciting more reactions to the movement and countermovement (17). She "proposes a spiritual exercise" (17) by encouraging Bill to share his thoughts and feelings with Jesus and to be attentive to his response.

## Session 7

Bill experienced a great deal of desolation during this session. "I feel horrible inside," he said. "It feels like nobody wants me, that Joan is not going to want me, that I'm never going to be wanted by anyone. I feel like I'm never going to have Joan." He tentatively shared these feelings and fears with Jesus but was not really attentive to Jesus' response. Bill explored with Donna his confusion and desolating feelings in order to attain greater clarity, to be freed of these burdensome feelings, and to share them with Jesus.

## Session 8

Bill felt that the retreat was unfinished, that there was more to come. Several deeply felt insights lingered with him:

1. He needed to begin to share his feelings with others—with Joan, his mother, and a few other people: "I feel like there's a bottle in me that has just begun to leak; I need to let out my feelings more."

2. His deepest desire was affirmed again: to get married and have a family.

3. The tremendous experience of joy and being filled by Jesus related to his willingness to trust Jesus with his two deepest fears.

4. Even if others do not want him, he has a deeply felt sense that Jesus wants him.

5. He recognized a felt difference between Jesus and the black, cold god. He experienced Jesus as the real God.

### Final Reflection

The first two insights exemplify how staying with interior movements result in decisions, changes, and confirmations that affect our outer life. Bill decided to share his deeper feelings with significant others. He chose again to orient his life circumstances toward meeting women with the hopes of eventually getting married. The last three insights exemplify concrete growth in relationship with God that is affected by movements and countermovements: deeper trust of vulnerability, greater security in God's personal love, and a clearer experiential sense of a living God. Though unfinished, Bill's retreat had a powerful effect on his life circumstances and his relationship with God.

## Conclusion

Bill experienced intense alternation of consolation and desolation around a deep area of unfreedom—a strong loneliness from feeling unwanted. By letting this unfreedom come out into the light in his prayer and in his spiritual direction, he more readily allowed Jesus to fill his emptiness; moreover, he realized his need to become freer from this heaviness. Bill also experienced a more subtle kind of countermovement— false consolation in the form of fallacious reasoning. With the help of his director, he looked carefully at the subtle way his attitude toward the priesthood can lead him away from God's desires for him. His growing awareness enabled him to grow freer and more able to acknowledge God's wishes. These painful struggles helped him to grow closer to a warm and loving God in Jesus rather than a cold, distant god. God gave Bill the gift of true knowledge, both of God and of himself through the various expressions of movement and countermovement.

## Experiencing God

### Reliving a Movement

Remember a time that you experienced a lively sense of Jesus—warm, loving, deeply caring, and concerned. Savor the richness of the experience, and relive it in your memory, in your imagination, in your heart, and in your mind.

✞ What were the circumstances of the experience? What was Jesus' presence like in the experience?

✞ What were some of your feelings, thoughts, and desires?

✝ What difference did you notice within yourself as a result of this experience?

As you relive the experience, be attentive to God's presence with you now. Share with God any feelings that arise, and listen to God's response.

### Exploring a Countermovement

Remember a time when you experienced movement away from God in the form of false consolation, such as perceiving a particular good as the best choice for you when it was ultimately leading you away from God and your authentic self; or fallacious reasoning where you thought that a certain sense of direction was the right one for you when it turned out not to be.

✝ What were the circumstances?

✝ What was God's felt absence like? Was there any sense of God's presence?

✝ What were some of your thoughts and feelings? How were these leading you away from God or from a right decision when they could appear to be leading you closer to God and a right decision?

✝ How was this false consolation resolved?

✝ What did you learn about yourself and about God as a result of this subtle countermovement?

As you pray about the experience, be attentive to God's presence with you now. Share with God your feelings, and listen to God's response.

## Questions for Reflection and Discussion

1. In what specific ways did Bill grow from his intense experience of the alternation of consolation and desolation? What did he learn about himself? What did he learn about God?

2. Through his experience of fallacious reasoning in session 2, what did Bill learn about God? about himself?

3. What specifically helps the gray, cold god to become weaker and the warm, loving Jesus to grow stronger in Bill's experience?

4. What specific things take place that help Bill become clearer about not being called to the priesthood?

5. Does Bill's experience of false consolation remind you of any dimension of Ignatius' experience? (See chapter 3.)

## For Spiritual Directors

1. What is most striking to you about Donna's approach in session 2? in session 6?

2. Write out or role play how you would handle Bill's idea of creating the biggest space for God through the priesthood in session 2.

3. Can you remember when one of your directees struggled with false consolation? How did you help that person? What approach did you use? What was the outcome? Did you use the Second Week Rules for Discernment? Role play the situation.

4. State three significant insights about spiritual direction that you gained or that were reinforced by Bill's retreat experience. State three key insights about the Rules for Discernment.

---

| | 11 | |
|---|:---:|---|

# Pam's Struggle to Achieve Intimacy with Jesus

---

Pam has a long-term relationship with God. Her experience indicates several things:

1. Movement and countermovement revealing more about an unfree area, as Jesus invites her into greater intimacy (the "more" of the Second Week);

2. The fullness of the "secret"—in this case, her self-hatred—gradually being revealed (326, 327);

3. Subtle countermovement in the form of "holy and pious thoughts" (332–33);

4. The evocative and contemplative approach of the director (15, 17);

5. An example of Consolation without Previous Cause (330);

6. Concrete manifestations of growth in freedom and in relationship with God through movement prevailing over countermovement.

## Background

Pam, a religious woman, is forty-eight years old. Pam's prayer has grown more contemplative during her initial four direction sessions. She notices additional aspects about God and her interior reactions to God. Although somewhat of a rigid person, she attempts to "go with the flow" in her life and during prayer. Her tendency is to "program times and ways of praying" inflexibly. After several sessions, Pam moved beyond merely experiencing the methods of prayer she uses to actually sharing the content of her prayer; that is, what happens between herself and Jesus. The pervasive movement in Pam's relationship with God has been one of intimacy and mutuality.

# Session 5

Pam shared with Jesus some situations about her life. When she listened, she sensed him saying: "I want to know about you." As she contemplated this, she began to become more aware. Jesus wanted to know who she is inside—that is, what was important to her and her attitude toward life—not just facts about situations. He also desired that she reveal to him the light side of herself—her gifts and talents—as well as her dark side—her struggles with certain situations (M). She felt hesitant to do so: it was easier to let him see negative rather than positive aspects of herself (CM). Her director, Dan, encouraged her to share her hesitancy with Jesus. She felt, during this session, a longing to be with Jesus (M), which Dan also suggested that she share in prayer.

## Movement, Countermovement, and the Rules

Pam experienced subtle countermovement between two goods manifested in two ways: sharing herself v. sharing about herself (choice one) or sharing negative v. positive aspects of herself (choice two). Both aspects are good. However, the Lord invited her to share "herself" and her "positive" qualities. But for Pam to move in this direction would "terminate in something distracting or less good and would weaken" her relationship with God (333). It is a subtle distancing from God at a time when Jesus is inviting her toward a greater intimacy.

# Session 6

P1:   Jesus is holding my hand and looking at me.

D1:   How do you feel as he holds your hand and looks at you?

P2:   I feel afraid. I ask him, "Why am I afraid?"

D2:   Does he answer you?

P3:   No, he just keeps holding my hand and looking at me.

D3:   What's he like as he holds your hand and looks at you?

P4:   He's very loving and caring.

D4:   Do you notice anything about his hand as it holds yours?

P5:   It's very gentle. It's holding mine like this. (Shows Dan.) He's not pulling me closer; he's just gently holding my hand.

D5:   How do you feel there as he gently holds your hand, without pulling you closer?

P6:   I feel very secure, comfortable. But I'm still more on the knowing rather than feeling level.

D6:   You feel very secure and comfortable there even though you're not feeling it real deeply yet.

P7:   Yes, I start thinking about different things and that I should be doing more with my time this year rather than just staying focused on Jesus (she's on a sabbatical year).

D7:   Can you tell me about Jesus' eyes, or his look, when he holds your hand and looks at you?

P8:   (Pause) His eyes are very piercing.

D8:   Piercing.

P9:   Yes. They look through me, like he really knows me deep down.

D9:   They look right through you.

P10:  Yes, but they're very loving, sensitive, and gentle.

D10:  What happens in you when he looks at you in this way?

P11: Well, it's funny. I keep looking and then quickly look away. You know how when you really like someone, and your eyes meet and you quickly look away? Maybe feeling embarrassed? It's that kind of thing.

D11: Do you feel embarrassed when Jesus looks at you?

P12: Yeah, I guess I do.

D12: Can you say anything more about your embarrassed feeling?

P13: Well, I think I'm really afraid.

D13: Afraid?

P14: I'm afraid I may not be good enough for him.

D14: You may not be good enough for him.

P15: Yes, I feel like he's not going to like what he sees, that I'm not good enough for him.

D15: Do you have any sense of what he might see if you really look at him and let him look at you?

P16: (Pause). I'm afraid there might not be anything there.

D16: You're afraid there might not be anything there.

P17: Yeah, I feel so small inside, and I'm afraid that if he really looks at me that he won't find anything there.

D17: Are you able to say anything more about that, Pam?

P18: No, it's just very scary. (They stayed here.)

D18: (Later) As Jesus gently holds your hand and looks at you, Pam, do you think you could share with him your fear— that you're afraid there won't be anything there if you really look at him? (Encouraging movement.)

### Relationship to the *Spiritual Exercises*

The grace of the Second Week applies here: "Ask for interior knowledge of the Lord, Who for me has become man, that I may more love and follow him" (104). Pam vividly experienced Jesus drawing her to a more intimate sharing of herself.

She concretely felt Jesus' desire to know her deeper feelings and inner life.

That Pam notices more details and savors this experience illustrates the deepening of prayer that occurs in the Second Week of the Exercises. First, Contemplation (for example, 110–17) occurs when Pam uses her imagination and senses— sight and touch—and notices specific details about Jesus' presence. Her feelings and inner life are also involved. Second, Repetition (118–20) occurs when she lingers with the experience on her own and when she savors and relives it with Dan. Third, the Application of the Senses (121–36) occurs when she continues to visualize and touch Jesus with the interior senses of her soul. Hugo Rahner notes:

> This means, then, that the senses are no longer being simply applied to the object of contemplation; what happens is that the soul moves outward and upwards until it finally comes to visualize and touch divine things directly—a state in which it fixes upon and embraces divine things without, as it were, any inter-vening agency.[1]

The more specifically Pam contemplates Jesus' concrete pres-ence, the more alive and life-giving her experience of Jesus becomes. Their mutual involvement touches deeper levels of her affectivity.

Ignatius experienced this too. After he tells about the Lord "awakening him as if from a dream," Ignatius reflected on five ways he experienced the Lord. On the fourth experience, he declared, "He saw with interior eyes the humanity of Jesus."[2] Later, he speaks of this type of experience again: "While he was there Christ appeared to him in the manner in which He usually appeared to him, as we mentioned above, and this comforted him very much."[3]

## Movement, Countermovement, and the Rules

Pam's reaction to Jesus' gentle invitation is very real: she feels attracted yet fearful of such closeness. Her fear that Jesus will not like what he sees could remain countermovement if she pulls away from him and does not express her fear to him.

However, she can continue to experience movement if she expresses her embarrassment and fear.

By exploring the countermovement with Dan, the "fallacious reasonings, subtleties, and continual deceptions" (329) are brought out into the light (326). The fact that these are being revealed is movement, but the content (see P14, P15, P16, and P17) of the revelation is countermovement. The power of the content is dissipated through the revelation to another person.

"In souls that are progressing to greater perfection, the action of the good angel is delicate, gentle, delightful. It may be compared to a drop of water penetrating a sponge" (335). Pam has been growing in relationship with God for many years. Her experience of Jesus here is not an "intense" consolation, as in the First Week Rules, but rather a very gentle, integrating, simple, and soft one.

### Approach of Director

In addition to helping Pam explore concretely Jesus' felt presence and the content of her reaction, Dan also encouraged her to share her fear with Jesus (D18). Keeping the countermovement in conscious dialogue with God facilitated movement to return.

## Session 7

P1:  I had a hard time settling down to pray this week. I started to get into my thing of having to make time to pray rather than just letting it happen. I tried going back to Jesus looking at me but I couldn't stay with it. I kept getting distracted. I couldn't get comfortable, and I just didn't want to be bothered.

D1:  You were distracted and didn't want to be bothered.

P2:  Yes, I just didn't feel like praying, which is unusual for me. (Later) I had a vivid dream the other night. I was in a restaurant, and there were people all around. I had to go to the bathroom real bad. I kept trying to get through the crowd to get there. I finally worked my way through to go. Everyone was listening to a man sing. He was singing Spanish music. But when I woke up the man was singing "My Cheri," which is French for "my dear." And there was a big pyx right in the middle of the room.

D2:   What stands out to you in the dream?

P3:   It was strange that the man was singing "My Cheri," a French song, when he had been singing in Spanish. And that I had to work so hard to get to the bathroom. And that the pyx was right in the middle. I've prayed about it a little since then. I sense that the song and the pyx are God saying "I'm here." He's very quiet, still, and relaxed. (They stayed here.) And having to find a bathroom before I went on the floor—I realized that I'm the one trying to control things, not God.

D3:   How does that make you feel?

P4:   I feel bad that I'm trying to control things again, that I want things to go a certain way. And I told God that.

D4:   Did you sense any response?

P5:   God just continues to be relaxed and still, saying "I'm here." This helps me to relax a little. (During the week Pam decides she wants to go back to Jesus, as he holds her hand and looks at her.)

### Movement, Countermovement, and the Rules

Pam experienced the "unquiet of different agitations" in her restlessness and inability to pray. She felt "tepid and separated, as it were" from God (317). The Lord was getting a little too close. Her distractions in prayer indicated she was retreating from the intimacy that Jesus invited her to enjoy the previous week. Unconsciously, she was trying to avoid staying with that experience. The dream was her unconscious telling her she was fearful of losing control. Sensing God's reassurance shifted countermovement slightly toward movement.

## Session 8

Pam shared her disappointment about not being accepted into a renewal program for next year. She had difficulty praying this week. However, she did not stay very long with her disappointment but moved rather quickly to a positive stance: "Maybe God has something else in mind for me" and "I should trust more." Pam and Dan focused on these thoughts, and, in various ways, she reiterated that she "should" trust Jesus more.

D1:   Pam, I'm wondering if you let yourself deeply feel your disappointment. I'm sensing as we talk that you are having a hard time staying with it and that in your prayer you moved rather quickly to the fact that you should be trusting God. What do you think? What's your reaction to what I'm saying?

P1:   Yes, you're right. I'm moving rather quickly to what I should be feeling. It's probably because it will hurt too much to stay with it.

D2:   Yes, I know what you mean. I do that many times myself. I move away for awhile when something hurts a lot. (Pause) Do you want to talk about your hurt and disappointment? Or would you rather not right now?

P2:   Yes, I think it would be good for me to talk about it. (Pause) When I did stay with it this week, I felt a lot of self-pity.

D3:   Self-pity.

P3:   Yes, I really felt sorry for myself. I don't want to wallow in self-pity, so I move away from it. But underneath that is a lot of hurt. I feel hurt by God.

D4:   You feel hurt by God.

P4:   Yes. I shared that in prayer a few times. God understood my feelings.

D5:   God understood your feelings?

P5:   Yes, God understands my disappointment and hurt (long pause). As I'm talking now, I'm realizing how I have a hard time letting God know all this because of my self-hatred. Underneath my disappointment and self-pity is self-hatred. I'm afraid if I stay with this with God, I'll find out I don't deserve to go to this program.

D6: You're afraid you'll find out you don't deserve to go to this program.

P6: Right. There's an underlying sense of unworthiness in me, self-hatred. I'm not aware of it all the time, but I'm just realizing again self-hatred is underneath all this. That's why, too, I have a hard time looking Jesus in the eye and letting him look at me. I'm afraid he won't like what he sees.

D7: You're afraid he won't like what he sees when he looks at you.

P7: Yes, I know that's not true. I've always suffered from low self-esteem. I'm just realizing again the self-hatred is still there. I thought I worked through that long ago.

D8: How do you feel realizing this, Pam?

P8: I'm surprised it's still there (pause). And I think that's the reason I have a hard time looking Jesus in the eye and why I struggle with sharing who I really am rather than things about me. I'm afraid he won't like what he sees. (They explore this fear for several moments.)

D9: (Near the end of the session) Do you think, Pam, you could tell Jesus you're surprised that the self-hatred is still there? And tell him you're afraid he won't like what he sees, and let him tell you how he feels about you there?

P9: Yes, I would like to. I'll be on retreat next week so I'll have plenty of time to talk to him.

## Movement, Countermovement, the Rules, and the Approach of the Director

The simple word *should,* as it operated in Pam's life, was a sign of a subtle but real movement away from God. Pam's assertion, "I should trust the Lord more," was another experience of "fallacious reasonings, subtleties, and continual deceptions" (329). This "false" kind of thinking prevented her from deeply feeling her disappointment and expressing it to God. Each time she said "should trust," Dan felt it was like "water falling on a stone" because of her sharpness and defensiveness, rather than "water falling on a sponge" (336).

Although Pam was thinking a "holy thought"—trusting God—it did not originate from God's invitation but more from her own rigidity and avoidance of hurt and disappointment. When Dan articulated the "beginning, middle, and end" of her thoughts, Pam realized that such attitudes were "terminating in something distracting or less good" (332). Avoiding her hurt and disappointment through *shoulds* was distancing her from God rather than bringing her closer. Sharing her disappointment, hurt, and self-pity with Dan was the beginning of movement back to God (326).

Also, the fact that Pam began to express these feelings to Dan facilitated the revelation of the fullness of her "secret." Pam noticed her self-hatred—something she was unconsciously hiding from herself and God. She had previous glimpses of this secret (for example, "He won't like what he sees if I really look at him"). However, the complete unfolding of the dark area occurred during this particular session. Then she desired to share with God her feelings and explore the residues of self-hatred that were still present within her.

## Session 9

P1:  As usual, I went with my agenda on the retreat. As I prayed I kept sensing that Jesus wanted me to be with him in his sufferings, which I wanted to also, but I wanted to talk over my shortcomings with him first. I didn't realize this until about the third day of retreat.

D1:  What happened that made you realize this?

P2:  My director must have noticed I was stuck. She suggested that I write out all my desires, thoughts, and feelings, then listen to God and write down what I sense are God's desires. I did a lot of writing that day and things got clearer. I realized how fixed I was in my agenda and became aware of Jesus' desire: "I want you to be with me in my sufferings."

D2:  He said, "I want you to be with me in my sufferings."

P3:  Yes. I told him that it's hard for me to believe that he wants me to be with him; that I felt unworthy and that shouldn't we take some time first to look at my sinfulness and get that out of the way so that I could be with him more completely.

D3:  How did Jesus respond to you there?

P4:  He said that right now he needs me to be with him.

D4:  He needs you to be with him.

P5:  Yes. He is going to go through a lot this week, and he needs me to be with him in his sufferings.

D5:  How did you feel when he said that?

P6:  I wanted to be with him. But I was afraid I'd fall short of what he needed. But I just kept sensing from him that he needed and wanted me to be with him. So I finally gave up my agenda and went with the flow.

D6:  What was that like for you when you went with the flow?

P7:  It was so beautiful and moving for me to be so close to him in his sufferings. Although we went through each event of the passion, he wanted me to be with him more in what was going on inside of him. Many times it was a deep being with each other, without words, while he let me see his interior pain. I felt so close to him and so privileged to be with him. I felt like one of the women who stayed close by him. (Smiles) I even felt myself getting jealous when Veronica went to wipe his face. I wanted to be the one to wipe his face (laughed and continued to share with Dan various moments and experiences).

D7:  Is there any one moment or experience that you and Jesus shared, or way that you were together, that stands out to you, Pam? Or a time you felt closest to him?

P8:   (Pause) Being with him in his inner suffering is when I felt the closest to him. Two times in particular: in the Garden and wiping his face.

D8:   Would you like to tell me about those two times?

P9:   I was standing a couple of feet away from him in the Garden. His head was bent over, and he reached out his hand for me to take it. I went over and held it. It was trembling. I felt his deep fear, yet his desire to do his Father's will. I just kept holding his hand firmly. (They stayed here.)

D9:   That's very moving. How did you feel holding his hand there?

P10:  Well, it was like I wasn't even aware of myself. I just wanted to be with him and support him there. All I could feel was his fear, yet desire, to go through with this. It was so moving for me to be there and feel his inner pain. I wasn't afraid to be there. I just wanted to be with him in the way he needed me. I felt even closer to him when I stepped out of the crowd and went over to wipe his face. I felt totally possessed by him.

D10:  You felt totally possessed by him.

P11:  Yes. I forgot myself completely. I saw his need for me to comfort him, so I went right over. I was so focused on his pain that I forgot my fear of being hurt.

D11:  You forgot your fear of being hurt?

P12:  Yes, I didn't even think about the crowd and the fact that they might hurt me if I go over to Jesus. I was totally unprotected as I stood before him. So he was able to possess all of me.

D12:  How did you feel being so unprotected and possessed by him?

P13:  I felt protected. Gee, I just thought of that. Even though I felt so unprotected I felt protected by him. In letting myself stand before him, so unprotected, I felt very safe and protected as he possessed me.

D13: Even though you were unprotected, you felt very protected and safe as he possessed you.

P14: Yes, as I was possessed by him, no one or nothing could hurt me. All I wanted to do was to wipe his face and relieve his pain—not so much his physical pain, but his inner pain.

D14: What was that like for you to wipe his face and relieve his inner pain?

P15: I felt I was comforting him, and that felt good. He said to me, "You're like a soothing balm."

D15: He said to you, "You're like a soothing balm."

P16: Yes, and I'm just realizing that's what he was for me, too—a soothing balm. I was soothing his inner pain, and he was soothing my inner hurt. I wasn't feeling any specific hurt at the moment. But in letting myself be so totally absorbed in him, he was protecting me and relieving any inner pain I had. (They stayed here.)

D16: How did that feel—that you were a soothing balm to him and he was that for you?

P17: I felt deeply moved to be able to be that for him, and privileged. In being that for him and as I was absorbed in him there, I also sensed that he said to me something like, "You've already been redeemed. I've redeemed your darkness and what I see now is your beauty and goodness. And that's what I want you to see—your beauty and goodness because your darkness has been redeemed and has changed into beauty and goodness." Those were not his exact words, but it was something like that.

D17: He's redeemed your darkness, and what he focuses on now is your beauty and goodness. How did you feel when he said that to you?

P18: I felt like "Aha! Now I see." Things started to make sense. His focus is different than mine, and I was able to believe it. The more I let myself be possessed by him and feel how he sees me right now, the more I could see my own beauty and goodness and grow more comfortable with that.

## Relationship to the *Spiritual Exercises*

Up to this point, Pam had been experiencing First Week dynamics—a deep disorder of low self-esteem and self-annihilation was gradually revealed in prayer and during direction, which was touched by grace. The retreat completed the First Week experience since Jesus had already "redeemed her darkness" and focused on her beauty and goodness. He wanted her to be with him. However, at the beginning of the retreat, Pam adopted more of the familiar First Week stance in her desire to bring her shortcomings and sinfulness to God.

Pam's retreat is a Second Week experience in that she moved into a more intimate and mutual relationship with Jesus. Jesus desires and needs Pam to be with him in his interior pain. He invites her to even deeper intimacy in expressing his need and longing for her presence. Each is a "soothing balm" for the other.

A Third Week dynamic is present in her willingness and ability to step out of the crowd in order to wipe Jesus' face. She wanted to comfort Jesus, even if the crowd seemed threatening. Her desire to be with Jesus was stronger than her fear of being hurt. She was willing to risk pain if necessary in order to encounter Jesus in an unprotected way. She stays with him in his turmoil and holds his hand, as he displays his fear and trembling in the Garden.

Consequently, Pam continued to experience the freedom of the Second Week. She felt free of the rigidity and control that held her back from fully entering into a relationship with Jesus and various life situations. She experienced the "flowing" quality she deeply desired. Her need to control dissipated. She felt unbounded and free to move with the flow of various circumstances in her life.

Second Week elements of Contemplation and the Application of the Senses also apply. The retreat setting and repetition in prayer enabled deeper union—"being possessed and absorbed by him"—to take place. Her interior senses were deeply moved to "taste the infinite fragrance and sweetness of the Divinity" (124).

Many of Hugo Rahner's views relate to Pam's experience, particularly the understanding that the Application of the Senses is a more sublime form of prayer.[4] Further, Rahner's remarks have much in common with Pam's comment of being so deeply possessed and absorbed by the Lord:

> It happens sometimes that the Lord himself moves our souls and forces us, as it were, to this or that particular action by laying our souls wide open. This means that he begins to speak in the very depths of our being, without any clamour of words, he enraptures the soul completely into his love and bestows upon us an awareness of himself, so that, even if we wished, we should be unable to resist.[5]

> And once they [inward senses] are attained the soul beholds Christ, hears him, becomes aware of him through his pleasant fragrance, savours him and embraces him. But this can be grasped only by one who receives this grace of prayer, for this is less a matter of intellectual consideration than of loving experience. Thus at this stage (of prayer) the soul has now won back the interior senses, so that it may behold the supreme beauty, hear the supreme harmony, breathe in the supreme fragrance, savour the supreme sweetness and touch the supreme delight.[6]

Pam's experience echoes Ignatius' experience: "On the way the pilgrim saw a kind of representation of Christ being led away . . . . He was taken through three main streets, and he went without any sadness, but rather with joy and contentment."[7] Even though Pam did not physically experience suffering like Ignatius, she did experience inner turmoil—as well as joy—being with Jesus while he suffered. During prayer she was not fearful of stepping out of the crowd but rather desirous to comfort Jesus in spite of the possibility of being hurt. And, like Ignatius, she saw a vivid representation of Jesus' passion.

"Our Lord insists that we look to the giver, and love him more than his gift, and thus keep him ever before our eyes and in the most intimate thoughts of our heart."[8] Jesus desired that Pam "look to the giver" and be with him intimately rather than focus solely on the gift of what Jesus could do for her—

that is, redeem her sinfulness—especially since he had already done so earlier.[9]

## Subtle Countermovement

Countermovement is expressed as "evil under the appearance of an angel of light" (332). At the beginning of the retreat, Pam, by pursuing her own agenda, lost sight of Jesus' desire for her to accompany him in his suffering. Also, her yearning to bring her darkness and sinfulness to Jesus, a good thing to do, was not what Jesus wanted for her and their relationship and, in fact, moved her further away from Jesus.

Pam's desire to set the agenda for the retreat paralyzed her. The "beginning, middle, and end" of the retreat "distracted" her from Jesus' wishes and her own deeper longing to be with him. Jesus spoke directly to this issue when he told her, "You are already redeemed." This enabled her to believe and feel her redemption. It let the focus rest on her beauty and goodness. Thus, her feelings of unworthiness and self-hatred dissipated.

## Consolation without Previous Cause

Pam experienced Consolation without Previous Cause. She felt "pure receptivity" and "wholly drawn into God's love" when she became totally possessed by Jesus on her retreat. In stepping out of the crowd and walking over to wipe Jesus' face, she totally forgot herself and felt absorbed in him. In being unprotected, she felt protected and could accept her redemption. "Whenever a person comes fully to herself, fully possesses herself, but fully surrenders herself to the loving Mystery of her life calling her beyond herself, she experiences CWPC," writes Harvey D. Egan.[10] Her self-surrender to Jesus was quite different from her instinct to retreat and quite disproportionate to the mediating gesture of reaching out to the Lord. A dramatic shift occurred: she stepped out of the crowd to console Jesus, and Jesus completely absorbed her into himself.

Bob, Pam, and Bill each experienced CWPC uniquely, overwhelmingly, and disproportionately. Pam and Bill experienced this gift in relation to the personal issues they were facing. All experienced a deep felt knowledge of the nature of

God's personal love. Bob experienced God's love as extravagant and unconditional, Bill experientially realized how deeply Jesus wanted him, and Pam discovered both that she was already redeemed and that Jesus focused his attention on her beauty.

## Movement and Countermovement
## Resulting in Freedom and Growth

God's concrete action causes interior reactions of movement and countermovement. The process of these reactions operating together reveals areas of unfreedom. Movement counteracting countermovement results in both inner freedom and relational growth with God and others. The following are concrete manifestations of the positive effects of movement prevailing over countermovement as it applies to Pam's experience.

### Rigidity and Control/Unprotected and Possessed by Jesus

Pam's decision to allow herself to stand before Christ "unprotected" and to be "possessed by him" (a strong movement) counteracted the countermovement of her tendency to be rigid and maintain tight control. By continuing to allow him to possess her after the retreat, she experienced great freedom to "go with the flow" of life situations instead of feeling she had to control or curtail her involvement.

### Focusing on Her Darkness/Already Redeemed

Pam's capacity to accept Jesus' statement, "You have already been redeemed," relieved her anxiety about staying with her darkness and enabled her to become even more deeply absorbed in him. Through Jesus' focusing on her beauty and goodness, she grew more deeply convinced of these personal qualities in herself. Her sense of unworthiness and self-hatred were transformed.

### Pam's Self-hatred/Jesus' Desire for Her to Be with Him

Pam's eventual response to Jesus' desire for companionship frees her from getting "stuck" in her self-hatred tendency that was already redeemed and transformed. By hearing Jesus tell her that she is a "soothing balm," Pam's tendency to pull away because of her feelings of unworthiness, smallness, and "fear of what he might see" dissipated. Further, the fact that they are a soothing balm to each other is also a concrete manifestation of mutual growth in their relationship. When she finally does respond to Jesus' desire to be closer in his suffering, their relationship and the sense of her importance in the relationship changes.

### Keeping Control/Going with the Flow

The dream Pam described during session 7 indicated to her that she was trying to maintain control. Also, her tendency to program times and ways of praying (beginning of direction) happened again during the first three days of the retreat. This subtle unfreedom began to be relinquished by surrendering her agenda and conforming to Jesus' desire.

### Pam's Fear/Jesus Reveals his Fear

In session 6, Pam was afraid to let Jesus hold her hand and look at her. During the retreat, Jesus reached out his hand as he suffered in the Garden. A fearful Jesus showing her how much he needed and trusted her increased her trust.

### Self-consciousness/Self-forgetting

Pam's self-consciousness changed into self-forgetting as she stepped out of the crowd and wiped Jesus' face. This allowed her to let Jesus possess her.

## Conclusion

Pam developed a more intimate relationship with Jesus as she became more attentive to and responsive to his persistent yet gentle love. The more she let go and allowed Jesus to take the lead, the less fearful and less self-absorbed she became. She experienced a variety of interior movements toward and away from him. Jesus used these movements to free her and draw her closer to him. By staying with her consolations and desolations, her fear turned to courage, and her need to control changed to surrender. Her response to Jesus' desire for an intimate relationship made a major difference—an uptight Pam was transformed into a Pam who is alive and free.

# Experiencing God

## Reliving a Movement

Remember a time that you experienced a deep intimacy with Jesus, where there was a mutual give-and-take, a vivid awareness of his presence with you. Savor the richness of the experience, and relive it in your memory, in your imagination, in your heart, and in your mind.

☦ What were the circumstances of the experience? What was Jesus' presence like in the experience?

☦ What were some of your feelings, thoughts, and desires?

☦ What difference did you notice within yourself as a result of this experience?

As you relive the experience, be attentive to God's presence with you now. Share with God any feelings that arise, and listen to God's response.

## Exploring a Countermovement

Remember a time when you experienced fear of growing closer to Jesus, fear of responding to his invitation to grow in an intimate relationship with him.

☦ What were the circumstances?

☦ What was Jesus's presence like? Did you have trouble sensing him in your fear?

☦ What were some of your thoughts and feelings? Do you know the experiential reason—the area of unfreedom—underneath the fear?

☦ How did the desolation get resolved?

✞ What did you learn about yourself and God as a result of this desolating experience?

As you pray about the experience, be attentive to God's presence with you now. Share with God your feelings, and listen to God's response.

## Questions for Reflection and Discussion

1. In what specific ways did Pam grow from the alternation of consolation and desolation? What did she learn about herself? What did she learn about God?

2. How is Pam's Second Week relationship with Jesus different from Laura's First Week relationship? List some qualities and dynamics of each.

3. How is Pam's secret different from Laura's secret?

4. God reveals Self to us in a variety of ways. How is Jesus' self-revelation to Pam different from his self-revelation to Bill?

## For Spiritual Directors

1. What is most striking to you about Dan's approach in session 6? session 8? session 9?

2. Remember a direction experience in which your directee had a vivid and lively sense of Jesus. How did you help your directee stay attentive to Jesus? Does any particular part of the spiritual direction conversation stand out? Were you satisfied with the role you played? Role play this situation.

3. State three significant insights about spiritual direction that you gained or that were reinforced by Pam's experience. State three key insights about the *Spiritual Exercises* and Rules for Discernment.

---|12|---

# Praying with
# Your Experience of God
# and Writing Your
# Own Spiritual Autobiography

The tapestry of religious experience is diverse. As we contemplate our own and other people's lively experiences of God, we notice unique colors and common threads blended together in beauty and richness. God's self-communication and our human response grows even fuller, and the ways in which the Rules for Discernment facilitate that growth become even clearer. Through experiential exploration of the Rules for Discernment, sixteenth-century observations are transformed into contemporary truths, past conclusions evolve into present knowledge, and awareness changes to affirmation as the truths of God's ways and our ways reveal themselves.

As I stated in the introduction, my hope is that, as you read the experiences of Ignatius and others, you will discover not only the sacredness of their experiences but also the richness of your own. I invite you to pray with your own experience of God and to write your own spiritual autobiography. You may choose to concentrate on a particular period, situation, or event in your life, or you may wish to devote yourself to an entire story of God. Through praying and journaling your own experiences of God, the colorful tapestry of your story of God can grow more vivid and beautiful.

The following three aspects of prayer can be used as you spend time with each of the prayer exercises, which are presented after this section.

## Personalizing a Grace

✝ In what area(s) of your heart and life do you most need to experience God's felt presence?

✝ In what area(s) of darkness or unfreedom do you need to experience the light of God's love?

✝ Ask God "for what I want and desire . . . "

## Dialoguing with God

Prayer is affective communication between two persons growing in knowledge, love, and intimacy with each other. This communication can be verbal or nonverbal and may or may not involve images and thoughts. The mutual relating between God and the individual has several functions:

✝ Looking: looking at God and letting God look at you;

✝ Sharing: sharing your interior life and feelings with God and letting God reveal Self to you;

✝ Listening: listening to God and allowing God to listen to you;

✝ Lingering: spending time together so that your mutual looking, sharing, and listening can deepen.

## Lingering with Interior Movements (repetition)

✝ Go back to the moments where you felt an attraction, felt the most alive and engaged. Linger there.

✝ Return to the moments where you experienced love, joy, and peace; fear or disturbance; a felt insight. Linger there. Share your reactions with God and listen.

✞ Continue to be engaged with God in these interior movements toward and away—looking, sharing, listening, lingering.

✞ Let your prayer become a simple "being with" God at the strongest movement of union.

✞ In various ways the prayer exercises can help you to notice, savor, understand, appreciate, and deepen your own experience of and relationship with God. They can also help you develop a deeper understanding of the Rules for Discernment so that they can be of practical use in your own spiritual journey. Use whichever of the exercises that can help your story of God unfold and your relationship with God deepen.

## Deeper Understanding of God's Ways in You

*Grace: a deeper awareness and understanding of God's presence and your movements toward and away from God with regard to a given situation, relationship, event, or decision (past or present).*

Mary in the New Testament "pondered all these things in her heart." She reflected on her concrete experiences by engaging her thoughts, feelings, imagination, and desires. She lingered with her clarity and confusion in order to allow God to reveal more about God-self, herself, and the directions for her life.

✞ As you feel a sense of "we" in prayer, is there a situation, relationship, event, or decision that can help you better understand God's ways in you and your reactions (positive and negative)?

✞ Specifically and concretely, in what ways were you experiencing darkness, desolation, countermovement, and unfreedom?

✞ In what ways were you experiencing light, consolation, movement, and freedom?

✞ Was there a deeper area of unfreedom that surfaced during your experience of consolation and desolation?

✝ What did you learn about God and about yourself through this experience?

## Finding God in Familiar Ways

*Grace: a deeper affective awareness and experience of God's presence in various realities of your life.*

As you get a sense of "we" in prayer (God present with you), let yourself be drawn to a scriptural passage or verse, image of God, aspect of Creation, or place or event in which you often meet God or feel God's presence.

Contemplate this experience by seeing, touching, tasting, smelling, and hearing with your exterior and interior senses.

Linger, savor, and enjoy God's presence. Share any concerns or feelings you might have now, any areas of darkness or unfreedom. Share any positive or negative reactions that arise within you. Be attentive to God's response.

## Discovering God in All Moments of Your Life

*Grace: a deeper recognition of God's presence in all stages and moments of your life.*

Choose a time in your life—such as your childhood, your adolescence, or the past year—and contemplate that period in God's presence with the following questions in mind. Share with God any feelings and insights that surface, and listen to God's response:

✝ In what areas are you experiencing movement toward God or consolation? How are you experiencing this? Can you identify this movement and describe the consolation?

✝ In what areas are you experiencing movement away from God or from desolation? How? Can you name this counter-movement and describe the desolation?

✝ What has been your strongest experience of consolation? What is God like during that consolation?

✝ What has been your strongest experience of desolation? What is God's felt absence like in that desolation? Do you know the reasons underlying the desolation? Have you asked God to reveal them to you?

✠ Have you lingered with your consolations to let them deepen? Have you stayed with your desolations in order to discover their cause? Do you know what prevents you from doing either or both?

✠ Who is the God you are conversing with these days? How would you describe your relationship with God concretely?

✠ Are you noticing differences within yourself? greater self-awareness? greater freedom? life-giving decisions and actions? growth in your relationship with God?

✠ Do any of the Rules for Discernment speak to your experience of God or further your understanding of God's ways in you?

## Attentiveness to God's Affective Presence in Your Prayer

*Grace: a greater attentiveness to God's affective presence and self-revelation in your prayer.*

After a period of prayer, take some time to reflect on the following questions and jot down your responses:

✠ How did you feel during this period of prayer—at the beginning, middle, and end? What was your strongest feeling?

✠ Did you experience an involvement with God? consolation? Can you describe concretely your consolation, such as peace, joy, hope, greater strength, tears of sorrow or a feeling of being loved by God, feeling love for God, or desire for a closer relationship?

✠ Did you experience distance from God? from desolation? Can you describe your desolation, such as agitation, distraction, turmoil of spirit, restlessness, a loss of desire to pray, or a fear to share something important with God?

✠ Who was God for you? What was God's presence like? Can you name three or four qualities that describe God's presence, such as supportive, caring, loving, firm, encouraging, assuring, patient, overwhelming, warm?

✝ Did any insights emerge from your prayer about God, yourself, your life, or a concern or issue about which you were praying?

✝ Did anything that was hidden in your unconscious or subconscious come out into the light of your awareness?

✝ Do you notice any differences in yourself, such as less anxiety, greater openness, deeper freedom, growth in desire, or movement toward a specific action?

✝ Do any of the Rules for Discernment speak to your experience of prayer now or further your understanding of God and God's ways in you?

## Letting Other People's Experiences of God Touch You

*Grace: an ability to notice and understand your own experience of God more deeply by letting others' experiences affect your heart in order to respond more totally to God's unique self-revelation to you.*

Other people's stories of God can inspire us to deepen our own relationship with God. Reread any of the experiences of Ignatius, Fran, Laura, Bob, Bill, or Pam. Take an hour or so to ponder the experiences, both theirs and yours, in order to recognize, understand, and respond more fully to your movements toward and away from God.

### Recognizing (Noticing)

For example, spend time pondering Fran's experience.

✝ What aspects of her experience do you feel most attracted to? Where do you feel some movement toward God within yourself as you ponder?

✝ Where do you feel a negative reaction within yourself? a spontaneous movement away from God? some confusion or doubt?

Share with God your reaction, and be attentive to God's presence as you share.

## Understanding

Reflect on your attractions and negative reactions. Ask God to enlighten the "eyes of your understanding," to "let your eyes be opened."

✟ Do you notice any reason underlying your affective reaction?

✟ Does any new insight or nuanced understanding arise from another person's or your own interior movements?

## Responding

Spend some time pondering your own experience of God during a particular period of time.

✟ What do you notice about your own attractions and negative reactions? your own movements toward and away from God?

✟ Does any aspect of Fran's experience relate to your experience of God?

✟ Does any dimension of her experience provide you with any new or nuanced understanding of your movements toward and away from God?

✟ Do any of the Rules for Discernment add to your understanding, or do they help you respond better to your own experience of God?

Ask for a deepening of your understanding of God's ways in order for you to respond more completely to God's invitation for a closer personal relationship and a deeper interior freedom.

## Gathering the Graces

*Grace: an "intimate knowledge" of the graces and blessings received through praying with your own and others' experiences of God and by experientially exploring the Rules for Discernment.*

Prayerfully read through your journal of the prayer exercises. As you feel a sense of "we" in prayer, become aware of what arises within you. Gather the graces using the following questions:

☦ What have I learned about God?

☦ What have I learned about myself?

☦ What have I learned about God's ways in people? What do I know that I know?

☦ What do I feel?

☦ What do I desire for the future regarding my relationship with God?

☦ Can I symbolize this experience of reading, praying, and journaling?

☦ Do any specific Rules or dynamics of the Rules stand out as particularly helpful for my spiritual journey?

Ask God to help you to continue to notice and respond to God's loving presence in all realities of your life.

Ask God to continue to reveal to you the truths that are within, behind, and underneath the various Rules. Ask God for the gift of a discerning heart.

Sit with the Rules periodically and try to relate them to your experience. Reflect on them, feel them, use aspects of them that relate to your own and other people's experience. Rewrite various Rules in your own words in order to understand their dynamics more experientially and to use them more practically toward your growth of a discerning heart.

## Conclusion

By experiencing God, the presence of God bursts into life within us and overflows into our daily living. The Rules for Discernment are a way to recognize more clearly, understand more deeply, and respond more completely to the loving presence of God as it is revealed uniquely within each of us. Hopefully, through prayerfully reflecting on the rich experiences of God in this book and pondering your own lively experience, a discerning heart can develop and your relationship with God can deepen, so that you can say, along with St. Paul, "In God we live, move, and have our being" (Acts 17:28).

# Part IV

# Education

**Practical Applications for
Spiritual Directors**

---
# 13

## Practical Learning Tools for Spiritual Directors

---

Since 1982 I have been educating spiritual directors in two training programs at the Upper Room Spiritual Center in Neptune, New Jersey. The three-year program emphasizes ongoing spiritual direction while the two-year program focuses on directed retreat spiritual direction. The three major components of the curriculum are: (1) the experience of actually doing spiritual direction; (2) individual and peer group supervision; and (3) theological reflection, which combines both theory and practice. The programs are experiential and deeply rooted in the Ignatian tradition.

A significant way for spiritual directors to learn about interior movements in people is by reflecting on their experience of directing. The Rules provide a context to understand and a language to articulate God's action in individuals and their response to such action. The following four practical learning tools are concrete ways to help spiritual directors reflect on and learn from their directing experiences. The first tool can be used by spiritual directors in both ongoing spiritual direction and directed retreats. The other three are specifically designed for writing case studies. These can be used in educational programs by both beginning and experienced spiritual directors to help deepen their experiential knowledge of the Rules for Discernment.

# Practical Learning Tool #1

## Prayerful Reflection on Spiritual Direction Experience

### Purpose

1. To assist spiritual directors in contemplating and exploring their direction experiences in themselves and in relation to the Rules for Discernment, Ignatius' *Autobiography,* and contemporary writers;

2. To help them understand the various concrete dynamics of spiritual development through reflection of the Rules;

3. To assist them in formulating principles for spiritual direction, based on the Rules and the Annotations, which will help facilitate directees' experience of and relationship with God.

### Approach

The reflective method suggested here is based on a contemplative and evocative approach to spiritual direction. Just as one strives to facilitate individual contemplation of and absorption in God during a spiritual direction session, so too does the director need to contemplate, ponder, and observe other people's experiences of God and then reflect on these experiences after a session.

### Contemplation

Linger with a particular direction experience in God's presence. Look at the experience in its totality, then look at the person and God in the experience. Notice the various movements. Contemplate what is communicated about God and how an individual responds to God's self-communication.

### Description

1. What were the circumstances of the directee's experience of God?

2. What was happening in the person—feelings, thoughts, desires, other interior movements?

3. What was God like?

4. Are there any consequences (change in how a person perceives God) or change in a person (greater self-acceptance) or the way in which a person relates to others or the world?

## Reflection

1. Where did the person experience the most feeling/interior movement? What precisely prompted this feeling (for example, God inviting the person to "come to me")? Is the person moving toward or away from God? Describe the movement, the countermovement.

2. How would you describe the relationship between the person and God, such as difficulty trusting God, intimacy and mutuality, or a call to minister with Jesus?

3. What was your approach as director in this situation?

## Observation in Light of the Rules

1. Does this person's experience remind you of any aspect of the Rules for Discernment?

2. Concretely and specifically, how does this Rule speak to the person's experience?

3. What is happening to this person in light of the particular aspect of the Rule?

4. Does any Rule or Annotation relate to your approach as a spiritual director in this particular situation?

## Further Reflection

Reflect on your contemplation and observations in relation to Ignatius' *Autobiography* and to contemporary writers' perspectives on the Rules.

## Ignatius' *Autobiography*

Does any aspect of Ignatius' experience relate to a particular direction experience and specific Rule?

## Contemporary Writers

Does any perspective or insight from a contemporary writer—Jules J. Toner, for example—shed light on this direction experience or on a specific Rule?

# Practical Learning Tool #2

## Written Reflection on a Spiritual Direction Session

### Verbatim Case Study

Growth as spiritual directors and experiential understanding of the Rules for Discernment requires regular supervision, either on a one-to-one basis or in a group. The focus of supervision lies with the director: that is, what happens within the director—such as interior reactions, blocks, or resistance—while he or she directs. The quality of directing in a particular session is related to the inner awareness of the director. For instance, if directors experience fear or anger in a session, they may move away from the directee's experience of God. Directors' capacity to help directees address their experience of God reflects their ability to be in touch with movements and countermovements within themselves.

To assist spiritual directors' experiential understanding of the Rules, supervisors can help them to reflect on interior movements within the directees and in themselves, as suggested in the Rules. They could explore, for example, how a particular Rule relates to interior movements and then examine how the Rules and Annotations speak to their approach as directors. The following is a verbatim case study and suggested schedule that can be used during supervision and theological reflection sessions:

### Verbatim Case Study

### Background

A brief, up-to-date statement of significant information about the session or sessions.

## Verbatim

Write out a portion of the conversation that reflects the directee's movements and/or countermovements, using one initial to represent the directee's part of the conversation and another initial to represent the director's part. For example:

M1:

D1:

M2:

D2:


## Reactions and Reflections

A. What is happening in you as spiritual director?

1. What was your general feeling during the session?

2. Where in the verbatim conversation do you have the strongest feeling?

3. On what parts of the verbatim conversation would you like to focus? Why?

B. What is happening in the directee?

1. What interior reactions are occurring within the directee? Describe the person's consolation, desolation. Do you notice an overall or pervasive interior movement? Is it toward or away from God?

2. Can you describe the person's relationship with God? Any particular dynamics or rhythm of relationship?

3. Do any of the Rules speak to this person's experience of or relationship with God?

4. Do any of the Rules or Annotations speak to your approach as director in helping people to experience God more fully and relate to God more deeply?


## Tentative Schedule for a Two-hour Session

1. Presentation of case (background and focus):

   15 minutes

2. Supervision—focus on inner reactions of director:

   45 minutes

3. Break:

   10 minutes

4. Reflection on interior movements of directee:

   30 minutes

5. Insights and evaluation:

   20 minutes

## Practical Learning Tool #3

### Theological Reflection on the Overall Experience of a Directee

### Ongoing Case Study

### Purpose

1. To explore empirically various dynamics of the Rules in relation to an ongoing case study. Observing the movements and countermovements in a directee's experience of and relationship with God over a period of time, participants will then reflect on how specific aspects of the Rules and Annotations relate to this experience, relationship, and the approach of the director;

2. To observe underlying issues and patterns in the directee's experience of and relationship with God;

3. To gain more experience being supervised and doing supervision.

### Approach

The ongoing case study is different from the verbatim case study in that it describes a directee's experience of and relationship with God over a period of time rather than during one direction session only. Even so, verbatim excerpts will also be included in this description. This case-study approach provides the opportunity for the presenter and the group to explore the currents and patterns of directees' experiences in relation to the Rules and the Annotations.

## Preparation for Ongoing Case Study

### Preparation Period
Over a period of three to six months observe, contemplate, and linger with a directee's relationship with God.

Contemplate particular experiences of God: look at the circumstances, the person, and God in the experience. Notice what is communicated about God and how the person is responding to God's self-communication.

Contemplate the person's relationship with God; that is, observe the movements toward and away from God. Observe what is happening with God and in the person in these movements and countermovements. Focus on concrete details and interior reactions as well as the overall movement. The following questions may help in your contemplation.

### Contemplation of Experiences of God
1. What are the circumstances of this experience?

2. What is happening in the person, such as feelings, thoughts, desires, and other interior reactions? Describe the consolation and desolation of each experience.

3. What is God like?

4. Are there any consequences or differences in the person, such as greater self-acceptance, freedom, or change in the way the person relates to others or the world?

### Contemplation of Person's Relationship with God
1. What has been the most pervasive movement in the relationship between this person and God (for example, intimacy, initial experience of love, desire to trust)?

2. Describe the person's movement toward God and away from God. Be specific and concrete.

3. At this point, describe the relationship between the person and God.

## Understanding in Light of the Rules

1. Does this person's experience of and relationship with God remind you of any aspects of the Rules? Specifically, how do these points speak to this person's experience and relationship?

2. What is your understanding of what is happening in this person?

3. Regarding the directee's specific experiences of God, does any Rule or Annotation relate to your approach as director?

## Presentation of Ongoing Case Study

### Preparation of Presenter

Write a four- to five-page case study that includes about two pages of verbatim portions describing this person's movement over a three- to six-month period. Describe specific experiences and significant movements toward and away from God. Briefly state your reactions as a director to any of these experiences and movements. Do not make any reference to the Rules in the case.

Be prepared to share connections between this person's experience and the Rules.

Send a typed copy of the case study to each participant one week before the session in order to give the individual time to reflect on it.

### Preparation of Participants

Spend some time contemplating, observing, and reflecting on this case study, keeping in mind the Questions for Contemplation. Afterward, reflect on the person's experience and relationship in light of the Rules, using the same questions.

# Schedule for a Two-and-one-half Hour Session

1. Background:

   10 minutes

   Any further information; questions for clarification.

2. Focus on spiritual director:

   30 minutes

   Presenter will include reactions for the group in order to help them explore specific subjects (for example, impatience when directee resists God).

   Group helps the presenters explore their feelings toward the directee and reactions toward the group.

3. Focus on directee:

   30 minutes

   With questions taken from Contemplation of Person's Relationship with God, the group will now share what they have observed in the directee's experience and the directee's relationship with God.

4. Break:

   10 minutes

5. Observations on directee's experience and the Rules:

   30 minutes

   With questions from Understanding in Light of the Rules, the group will describe the relationship between the directee's experience and the Rules.

6. Observations concerning the approach of the director and the Rules and the Annotations:

   30 minutes

   Participants will share observations concerning the approach of the director and the Rules and the Annotations and offer suggestions for the director at certain moments (such as when directee is vacillating).

7. Evaluation:

   10 minutes

# Practical Learning Tool #4

## Written Reflection on a Directed Retreat Experience

### Directed Retreat Case Study

There are two parts to the preparation of this case study:

1. Prayerful reflection, taking notes, and reading;

2. Writing a three- to four-page case study

The more time you spend with the first half, the more easily and naturally will flow the second half.

### Prayerful Reflection on Retreatants' Experience

In God's presence, spend time contemplating a retreatant's relationship with and experience of God. Ask God for the grace of a discerning mind and heart to notice movements and countermovements in your retreatant and in yourself.

Contemplate each day of the retreat. Linger with particular experiences of God that occurred that day. Look at the circumstances, the person, and God in each experience. Notice what God is communicating and how the person reacts and responds to God's self-communication. Be attentive to what God reveals to the person and how the person reacts and responds to this revelation.

Contemplate the person's relationship with God and the overall experience of the retreat. Observe the movements toward and away from God. Notice what is happening in God and in the person. Focus on concrete details and interior reactions as well as the overall movement.

Contemplate yourself while you are directing and present with the person. Notice where and when you feel attraction or consonant with the person's experience and where and when you feel distance or dissonance. The following questions might help your contemplation:

### Contemplation of Particular Experiences of God

1. What are the circumstances or the context of the experience?

2. Describe the concrete facts of the experience. What is God like?

3. What is happening in the person—feelings, thoughts, desires, and other interior reactions?

4. Are there any specific results or consequences, such as a change in attitude or feeling, greater self-acceptance, and freedom or a change in how the person perceives God and the relationship between God and the person?

## Contemplation of the Person's Relationship with God

1. Describe the person's most pervasive movement toward and away from God, such as:

Movement: initial experience of God's love, revelation of sinfulness or darkness, God's forgiveness, intimacy, growing trust in God, invitation to serve with Jesus, invitation to suffer with Jesus, healing.

Countermovement: struggling to pray and accept God's love, fear of intimacy, unexpressed or repressed anger, feelings of unworthiness.

2. Is there a change, a difference, in the person's relationship with God from the beginning to the end of the retreat? Describe this change.

## Your Experience as a Director

1. In each session, what do you feel most drawn to? most involved in? most moved by? What are you feeling at each of these moments? What is God's presence like?

2. Where and when do you feel distant, least involved, repelled, fearful, tense, anxious, distracted? What specifically are you feeling? Do you notice any "experiential reasons" underlying this feeling? What is God's presence like?

   Share your feelings with God, and be attentive to God's response to you.

## Observations in Light of the *Spiritual Exercises*

1. Does this person's experience of and relationship with God remind you of any aspects or dynamics of the Weeks of the *Spiritual Exercises?* Describe, emphasizing concrete connections.

2. Does this person's experience of God relate to any of the Rules for Discernment? Describe concretely.

3. Do any of the Rules (313–36) or the Annotations (1–20) relate to your approach or interior presence as a director? Describe concretely.

## Writing the Case Study

Compose a three- to four-page case study that includes the following:

### Factual Information
Your name, date, and length of retreat; number of times supervised; and length of supervision sessions.

### Background
Include some brief information about the retreatant, that is, pseudonym, age, occupation, life struggle or issue the person may be facing, and major concerns of the person.

### Retreatant's Experience
1. What dynamic of the Weeks of the *Spiritual Exercises* is operative? Explain your observations.

2. What is the pervasive movement and countermovement that is occurring in the person's experience?

3. Describe one or two particular experiences of God. Be concrete in your description, using direct quotes or brief portions of conversations. State one or two movements and countermovements occurring within the person. Describe one or two concrete relationships between these experiences and the Rules for Discernment.

4. Are there any changes or differences in the person from the beginning to the end of the retreat? any concrete actions the person desires to take after the retreat?

### Director's Experience

1. In relation to the retreatant's experience, what moved you most? when did you feel the deepest movement toward God? Describe your inner experience and feelings.

   Make one or two concrete connections to the Rules for Discernment.

2. In relation to the retreatant's experience, at what point did you feel the strongest resistance within yourself? What were you feeling?

   Make one or two concrete connections to the Rules for Discernment.

3. Describe one or two relationships between your approach as director and the Annotations.

## Conclusion

Contemplating and exploring individual experiences of God can be a significant way for spiritual directors to arrive at a deeper understanding of God's ways in the human heart. Reflecting on these experiences in relation to the Rules for Discernment can deepen spiritual directors' discerning heart and broaden their experiential knowledge of the Rules. These four practical learning tools provide a structure for spiritual directors to grow more attuned to God's action both in their directees and in themselves as directors.

# 14

# Exploring Interior Movements in Two Case Studies

The richness of interior movements grows more vibrant and the dynamics of the Rules for Discernment become more clear as we observe them in people's experiences of God. This chapter describes two case studies, followed by questions for reflection. Spiritual directors can reflect on these on their own or explore them in a peer group setting.

## Case Study #1

### Millie's Experience

*Directions:* In a left-hand column, write "M" for movement and "CM" for countermovement. Reflection questions follow after the two sessions.

*Exploring with a group:* Two of the participants may want to role play the following two sessions in order to experience more fully Millie's interior movements. Then each person can mark the left column accordingly.

### Background

Millie is a novice directee; this is her first eight-day directed retreat. Donna, her director, suggested Psalm 139 for her prayer. (M=Millie; D=Donna)

## Session 1

M1: I was attracted to "He rests his hand upon me." I sense God's hand is resting on my shoulder.

D1: You sense God's hand resting on your shoulder.

M2: Yes, one hand is on my left shoulder, and the other is holding my right arm. It's very peaceful.

D2: It's peaceful. (Pause) Is God in front of you or in back of you?

M3: He's more standing behind me.

D3: He's standing behind you. What is God like there?

M4: (Perplexed look) What do you mean?

D4: I mean do you have any sense of what's going on in God as He stands behind you resting His hands on you?

M5: He's very supportive, like He's holding me up.

D5: God is very supportive, like He's holding you up.

M6: Yes, His hands are supportive, holding me firmly but very gently.

D6: How do you feel as God holds you up firmly and gently?

M7: (Pause) I feel secure and supported. But I'm also a little skeptical—why does God have to hold me up? I'm also noticing a little fear in me as we are talking—is God going to ask something difficult of me during this retreat? (They explore these feelings further.)

D7: I encourage you, Millie, to linger with God's hands resting on your shoulder and arm, and let yourself feel his support and gentle touch. Also, share your skepticism and fear, and see how God responds.

M8: (Smiles) The psalm says, "He knows me inside and out." Do I need to tell God what He already knows?

D8: (Smiles) People always wonder about that. Yes, God does know you inside and out. But, as in any significant relationship in which someone knows what we're feeling without our saying it, it frees us to verbalize our feelings and also helps the relationship to grow. Sharing our feelings with God can help us to get even more in touch with them and open us more deeply to God. Does this make sense?

M9:  Yes, it does. I never thought of that before.

# Session 2

M1:  The Lord resting His hands on my shoulder and arm continued to be very important in my prayer again today. They continued to be very supportive.

D1:  They continued to be very supportive.

M2:  Yes, and I shared with God my anxieties about what His hands supporting me might mean.

D2:  What was that like for you—sharing your anxieties?

M3:  I felt funny saying it to God at first. But after awhile it just seemed like those anxieties were gone. I don't even know when they left me. But I just became more aware of God's hands resting on me, and I just happened to notice my fears were gone.

D3:  How did you feel when you noticed your fears were gone?

M4:  I was surprised. And I felt freer. (They lingered here.)

D4:  As you became more aware of God's hands resting on you, did anything more happen?

M5:  God whispered in my ear, "I know you inside and out." He kept whispering that over and over again, "I know you inside and out."

D5:  What was God like as he whispered, "I know you inside and out"?

M6:  Very gentle. God also said He wanted the inside of me to be a place for Him. I don't know what kind of place yet. He was showing me that all I have to do is be present to Him, and He will do the rest. His hands and heart will do the rest. All I have to do is let Him. That feels really good.

D6: It makes you feel really good. Can you say more about that "good" feeling?

M7: I feel happy, content, fulfilled.

D7: Happy, content, and fulfilled.

M8: Yes, it makes me feel "fearfully wonderfully made" inside and out. (Pause) And in my later prayer time God kept whispering over and over again in my ear, "I love you inside and out."

D8: Wow! He loves you inside and out. What was God's presence like there as He whispered that to you?

M9: God was very close. His whisper was so intimate. And I truly felt "fearfully wonderfully made." At first I felt stuck at that verse, real uneasy. I couldn't accept that because of my overweight problem. Now I feel that I am, "fearfully wonderfully made." I feel encouraged to do something about my weight.

D9: You feel encouraged to do something about your weight?

M10: Yes, I've been putting it off for awhile. But my sensing how God sees me as wonderfully made moves me to want to do something about my weight after the retreat. I feel an excitement about it now, whereas I often feel discouraged so I don't bother doing anything.

(The director helps Millie to articulate her feelings. By the end of the retreat, her desire and excitement grow into a concrete plan of action—to lose weight. She continues to experience God's loving presence in various concrete ways during the retreat.)

## Contemplation of Experiences of God

1. What are the circumstances of this experience?

2. What is happening in the person—feelings, thoughts, desires, other interior reactions? Describe the consoling and desolating movements.

3. What is God like?

4. What are the consequences and differences in Millie as a result of this experience?

## Understanding in Light of the Rules and Annotations

1. Does Millie's experience of and relationship with God remind you of any aspects or dynamics of the Rules? Specifically, how do these aspects or dynamics speak to Millie's experience?

2. How would you describe the spiritual director's approach? Why does the spiritual director focus on God's presence in specific ways? (See D3.) Does any Rule for Discernment or Annotation relate to the director's approach?

# Case Study #2

## Doug's Experience

*Directions:* In a left-hand column, write "M" for movement and "CM" for countermovement. Read the case study through once. After reading it a second time, see if you notice any patterns in the rhythm of movement and countermovement and any connections between them.

*Exploring with a group:* Two of the participants may want to role play verbatim excerpts, and a third person may wish to read the narrative. Each person should then mark the left-hand column accordingly. Paragraphs are numbered in order to make references to them easier during the discussion.

## Background

Doug, forty-two years old, came to Marge for weekly spiritual direction for eight months. About eight years ago, he had a very deep experience of God's powerful and warm love in which, "God picked me up and held me, and has not let me go ever since." He describes his relationship with God as "deep, quiet, and consistent. Jesus and I are like partners."

1. During the first several months of direction, Doug's prayer centered around Psalm 139. God invited him to greater

intimacy: "If I go East or West I cannot run from your Spirit." His response was a deep desire: "I don't want to run from it; I want intimacy with God." His desire for deeper intimacy with God and others continued to grow.

2. Doug had been attending counseling sessions for several months—which were discontinued when he moved to another state—before beginning direction. He had just begun to deal with two areas associated with his mother: repressed sexuality and repressed anger. Further, his relationships with people, particularly women, were moving in a positive direction. He was finally able, for example, to share deeper feelings with a few women friends.

3. A significant breakthrough occurred after two months of weekly spiritual direction: Doug cried for the first time in twenty-seven years. He was by himself. A letter from a close friend precipitated his tears. He felt deep love for her and a few other friends. He cried for about five hours. He felt God was very close to him during that time. God was glad he was crying, glad that he could let his feelings be alive.

4. This experience was significant for several reasons. Doug allowed his feelings of love to move outward rather than inward. He explained that usually something in his unconscious would smother strong feelings of love toward another person. He was growing in his ability to feel his vulnerability and fragility and could let himself stay with it. He brought more feeling into his prayer.

5. For the next month his prayer was rather subdued. Doug was under much pressure at work. He was drawn to the story of Elijah (1 Kings 19). As God gave Elijah "jugs of bread and water in the desert," Doug sensed God revealing small ways in which he was supporting him. This gave Doug encouragement to keep going. Also, a line from Deuteronomy continued to stay with him: "I am doing new things in you." He was aware that the "new things" related to openly displaying his feelings by crying, letting himself be vulnerable with his spiritual director, and allowing God to invite him to a deeper intimacy. He was waiting for new

things to happen. During this "waiting" period a few memories of hurtful encounters between his mother and himself surfaced. Marge and Doug explored these in depth, and Marge encouraged him to share his feelings with God.

6. On Christmas Eve, Doug attended a liturgy in a home in which children were present. He described the liturgy as "messy." The next morning, as he was contemplating Jesus, Mary, and Joseph in the stable, he began to think about the liturgy, and he had a very deep and moving experience of God. God said to him: "That's where I am." In that family he found the intimacy of the Holy Family, with all the "messiness" that goes with intimacy.

> I experienced the incarnation with that family and messy liturgy on Christmas Eve. That's where God was for me. That family was like the Holy Family. So on Christmas morning I felt like I came home. I felt such deep peace. It was all so simple and intimate. It felt like my experience of the last few months came together in my prayer that morning. Everything was united. The intimacy God has been inviting me to I experienced with that family and the Holy Family.

7. For approximately six weeks following that experience, Doug's prayer was very "scattered and unfocused. I begin to pray, and then I start thinking about work. I can't keep my mind on what I'm praying about." He felt anxious and worried about his inability to keep focused, so Marge encouraged him to share those feelings with God. He said, "God is relaxed about it, not as excited about it as I am. It's almost like he's saying: 'Don't worry about it.'" God's relaxed presence helped Doug feel less anxious.

8. During this time, even though his prayer was distracted, Doug was attracted to various events in Mark's Gospel. The one that broke through his "unfocused" period of prayer was the story of the paralyzed man. For several weeks he stayed with the image of Jesus healing the paralyzed man. Just as Jesus healed the man on a deeper level, so too Doug felt Jesus healing him at that same level. One manifestation of this healing was the release of some sexual

struggles ("Jesus is peeling off layers"). In one session, Doug spoke about changes he noticed in himself:

D1:  In praying over the paralyzed man again the other day, I realized I'm different.

M1:  You're different. Are you able to say what you're noticing about yourself?

D2:  I'm not as restless and anxious. I've always been a deeply anxious person. There's a deep calmness in me now. I notice in groups that I take more risks, and I'm more willing to confront something directly. And I'm becoming more comfortable with my sexuality. I'm letting myself feel my vulnerability and fragileness and can stay with feelings of love toward another.

9. For several weeks after, Doug experienced strong counter-movement in his weakest area: feelings in life and prayer ("where the enemy finds us weakest and most in need for our eternal salvation, there he attacks us and aims at taking us" [327]). It had been an area where, he felt, he had been making some progress. Doug was stuck. The counter-movement began the middle of March, around the time of his birthday. Feeling tired, irritable, and distracted in prayer, he sensed his struggle had something to do with his approaching birthday. Although they explored this for several weeks (he knows something happened on one of his birthdays, but he can't remember) and he took his feelings to prayer, still no movement or clarity occurred.

10. Doug experienced slight movement before Easter while praying over the story of Lazarus. Struck by Jesus weeping because of his love for Lazarus, Doug asked Jesus to help him feel in a similar way. Doug realized he did not focus much on what Jesus felt but rather moved too quickly onto his own desire to feel. He expressed regret over this and had a desire to focus more on Jesus and the relationship.

11. Doug was deeply disappointed that nothing occurred inside him during Holy Week. Marge encouraged him to share these feelings with God. They stayed with one prayer time.

D1: I feel cold. I have no desire to pray. I didn't even want to stay with the disappointment, and I didn't even feel that this week.

M1: You feel cold. Can you say more about that?

D2: I just feel very lethargic. I just don't care about prayer. Even this healing thing I'm losing interest in. I feel like just putting it off until I get home. (Doug was returning to another state in six weeks.)

M2: So you feel lethargic and like you don't care about prayer and the healing that's been happening.

D3: Yeah, I'd pray for about a minute, then my mind would wander. And I didn't feel like bringing it back. I tried to pray the Emmaus walk and stayed with it for almost an hour. I attempted to pray affectively, trying to tell God my disappointment and "recognize" Him, but nothing would happen. It was a real struggle to stay there.

M3: How did you feel as you struggled so hard? (After some effort, he answered.)

D4: Defeated. I felt defeated.

M4: Defeated?

D5: Yes, I felt like there has been no progress, whatever progress is (that is, more progress in his ability to feel). My feelings are closed down again. I don't even feel the disappointment. I feel like there's a web around me that's pulling me backwards. (He felt that he was "caught," "couldn't get out," and "regressing." After staying there awhile, they returned to the topic of defeat.)

M5: When you prayed Sunday, did you notice any feeling underneath your defeated feeling?

D6: I was frustrated. I suppose there's anger there too, but I didn't feel it. I felt like "Why bother? I'm not getting anywhere anyway." (Here Marge tried very hard to get to the source of the anger, which she sensed strongly, but was unsuccessful.)

M6:  Were you able to stay with your defeated and frustrated feelings? And tell God about them as you felt them?

D7:  No, not really. These feelings were very faint. And I didn't really know they were there until now.

M7:  Are you feeling them again now as we're talking?

D8:  No, I don't really feel anything. I'm closing off my feelings, whatever that is in me that does that. (They stayed with this, his expectations from God, his disappointment, which he has shut off too.)

M8:  You hoped God would peel off another layer at Easter.

D9:  (Pause) I just remembered as you said that—every once in a while lately an image of myself being wounded comes to me.

M9:  Can you say more about that image?

D10: (Pause) As you ask that, a dream I had last night pops into my mind. I think I'll tell you about it. I was in a house. It was dark. It got light all of a sudden. It was 7:10 in the morning. My mother was upstairs, moving around, getting ready to come down. I wanted to get out of the house before she came down. There was an oblong chocolate cake on the table, cut evenly. I wanted to take a piece from the middle and get out. (They explored this dream for the rest of the sessions.)

12. During the last several sessions, as they stayed with Doug's feeling of being "wounded," more memories began to surface regarding his mother, especially a recent one. He talked about a diatribe of anger his mother dumped on him, in which "she wrote me and my whole life off in about five minutes." He was deeply hurt and finally realized he was angry too. Doug tried bringing his feelings to prayer but did not feel them strongly enough for any significant movement to occur. Since there were only a few sessions remaining before he moved to another state, he realized he was putting his strong emotions on hold.

## Contemplation of Experiences of God

1. What is happening to Doug—his thoughts, his desires, his other interior reactions? Describe the consoling and desolating movements.

2. What is God like for Doug?

3. What are the consequences and differences in Doug as a result of his experiences of God?

4. What is the relationship between God and Doug like at this point?

## Understanding in Light of the Rules and Annotations

1. Does Doug's experience of and relationship with God remind you of any particular Rules or dynamics of the Rules? Specifically, how do these aspects or dynamics speak to Doug's experience?

2. How would you describe the spiritual director's approach, particularly in the verbatim portion in paragraph 11? Does any Rule for Discernment or Annotation relate?

# Conclusion

By reflecting on direction experiences, such as those of Millie and Doug, spiritual directors can gain a deeper felt knowledge (*sentir*) of interior movements. By praying with their own and others' experiences of directing, directors can grow in a deeper understanding of God's ways in people and savor the richness of spiritual experiences. This knowledge, understanding, and savoring helps their hearts to become discerning hearts.

---
| 15 |
---

# Implications and Questions

In this book, I have focused primarily on individual experiences of God and interior movements in relation to the Rules for Discernment. Further implications and questions for the ministry of spiritual direction can be experientially explored, of course. Chapter 15 will examine some of the implications suggested by the book as well as pose some questions for further experiential research related to the practical use of the Rules for Discernment.

## Implications for the Ministry of Spiritual Direction

Various implications arise from an experiential study of the Rules for Discernment.

The same dynamics of movement and countermovement are experienced in ongoing spiritual direction as well as during directed retreats, although these dynamics often intensify during a retreat because the whole person is focused on the relationship with God. The suggestions Ignatius gives for spiritual directors in the Rules and the Annotations are as applicable for ongoing spiritual direction as they are for retreat direction. Therefore, spiritual directors in various settings can benefit from reflection on the dynamics of the Rules and Annotations.

The Rules and Annotations are a condensed form of discernment and direction. Ignatius presents his experiential insights in a precise way. These insights are, he states, "rules for understanding to some extent the different movements" (313), yet he did not envision his compilation to be the final word on discernment. Therefore, we need to observe whether there are more dynamics related to discernment than Ignatius articulates. In our contemporary approach to theology, we specifically need to ask: are there more observations about discernment that can help us relate to God more deeply and live life more fully? Spiritual direction can be one of the best ways to develop a deeper understanding of discernment because its primary content is religious experience.

An experiential approach using case studies can be an excellent way of conducting theological reflection related to various ministries in the Church, such as spiritual direction, pastoral counseling, leadership training, or prayer group development. This approach gives people an opportunity to reflect on their experience concretely as well as offers a practical grounding in foundational theology. Therefore, it would be advantageous for those involved in parish teams, spiritual direction training, and adult education to use various types of case studies for supervision and theological reflection.

Supervision is essential for people in ministry. Spiritual directors and other ministers encounter challenging situations and serious struggles daily. Supervision is an important way for individuals to receive insight into the struggle and to gain a sense of direction. Therefore, spiritual direction and other ministry teams would benefit greatly from having ongoing supervison as an essential aspect of their ministry.

Little has been written on the practical use of the Rules and Annotations in spiritual direction. For this reason, experienced spiritual directors would provide a great service to novice directors by publishing their experiential insights.

Training programs can help spiritual directors understand more fully the religious experience of their directees through reflecting on the dynamics of the *Spiritual Exercises* and the Rules for Discernment.

## Questions for Further Experiential Exploration

Because the Rules for Discernment have such a richness, breadth, and depth to them, pastoral ministers in the Church can find great value by examining their dynamics and exploring their concrete applications in various areas of spiritual development and human growth. Possibly my experiential research can be a basis for inductive exploration of contemporary experience. The following are questions for further study.

The dynamics of the Rules for Discernment apply in all types of experiences of God. I have focused primarily on kataphatic and immanent experiences. What do movement and countermovement look like in apophatic experiences? How are the Rules operative in more transcendent experiences of God? What are further nuances of the dynamics of the Rules?

Groups as well as individuals can experience these dynamics. How do consolation and desolation apply in groups that pray, work, and live together, such as parish teams, leadership groups of religous congregations, families, or religious communities? What are the effects and ramifications of consolation and desolation on these groups? For example, when the group process is characterized by desolation, how does that affect the way members relate to one another and their ability to work together?

Authentic spiritual development occurs holistically. Relationship with God affects our entire self and human growth process. How do the dynamics of the Rules relate to ongoing human development? For instance, do people in their twenties experience countermovement differently than do individuals in their forties who are undergoing a midlife crisis? Do relationships exist between experiencing God as described in the First and Second Week Rules and experiencing God as explained in the theories of human growth, such as Carol Gilligan and Lawrence Kohlberg's view of moral development or James Fowler's theory of faith development? Does liberation from an underlying disorder through movement and countermovement affect the way one makes moral decisions?

Movement and countermovement are alive in the spiritual director's as well as in the directee's experience. Although frequently mentioned throughout the book, I did not specifically focus on reactions within the director. How do the Rules for Discernment concretely relate to the director's own interior movements while directing? For example, what effect does a directee's intense experience of consolation or desolation have on the director? When a director experiences counter-movement in a session, how do Ignatius' suggestions about dealing with desolation (318–321) apply? In what ways does a director experience subtle and obvious countermovement?

Movement and countermovement can occur in the supervisors of spiritual directors as they are actually doing supervision. How do the Rules for Discernment apply to the supervisor's interior reactions while supervising?

Men and women may uniquely experience dynamics of movement and countermovement regarding their sexuality. Considering Jung's view of the feminine and masculine dimensions of our personality, are there any similarities and differences between these dimensions and the dynamics of the Rules? For instance, looking at "what to do in desolation" (318–321), do some ways of dealing with desolation happen more naturally from our "anima" side than from our "animus" side? Considering the various ways desolation can be experienced (317), is the feminine dimension of our psyche affected more acutely in any of these ways?

People can experience various nuances of movement and countermovement during times of crisis and emotional trauma. How are movement and countermovement experienced as serious emotional traumas surface through our felt relationship with God in prayer? As painful memories of sexual abuse emerge during prayer, how can the Rules help? How are consolation and desolation experienced in persons suffering from depression, and how can the dynamics of the Rules help to free people of this depression? How do movement and countermovement apply to homosexuals coming to terms with their sexual orientation?

People with severe personality disorders can experience movement and countermovement while relating to God, even though a dimension of their personalities may be severely crippled. How does the experience of movement and countermovement relate to personality disorders, such as obsessive compulsion or passive aggression? When people have trouble relating to God in a felt way (that is, they cannot be attentive to God or share with God their feelings) due to obsessive-compulsive behavior—such as alcoholism or overeating—how might the Rules for Discernment concretely help to free them from this compulsion?

Cultural factors affect the way individuals relate to God. How does our cultural experience influence how we experience God? For instance, how would someone working among the destitute in the inner city experience countermovement as opposed to a person serving the wealthy in an affluent suburban parish? What are some subtle ways that people experience countermovement, and how can they move against these subtleties?

## Conclusion

As I come to the end of the book, I view my exploration of the Rules for Discernment as only a beginning—a beginning in which the Rules can reveal their richness in the lived experiences of contemporary people. Studying any of the above questions could be a challenging adventure and a stimulating way to broaden our understanding of discernment. My hope is that further reflection of the Rules will assist many people to develop a discerning heart that is rooted in God's unlimited self-communication.

# Conclusion

The development of a discerning heart takes place because of God's gracious self-giving and our commitment to our own spiritual growth. It is a life-giving experience, opening us to the dynamic life of God and helping us to see what leads to death. It is an incarnational experience, taking place in the specific circumstances of our life and the concrete movements of our heart. Growing in the art and skill of discernment is a life-time endeavor. As we journey with God through the years, our awareness of interior movements becomes more constant, pervasive, subtle. We develop a habit of paying attention to and responding to God's quiet whisperings. We humbly allow our loving God to transform our inner darkness, even when that transformation is discomforting. We discover the painful joy of being intimate with God. We experience the mysterious delight of finding God in all things.

By reading this book, I hope that the skeletal structure of the Rules for Discernment became enfleshed for you so that you can continue to use the Rules for the ongoing growth of your own discerning heart. Through entering into the experiences of Ignatius and contemporary people, I pray that the colorful tapestry of your own experience of God became even more vibrant. By praying with the prayer experiences, I hope that you discovered God in a more personal and intimate way and that you became more keenly aware of your own interior movements. On your ongoing journey of discernment, I pray that you can allow God to enlighten your darkness and shine in your heart so that people can see God through you, as is brought out so beautifully in this prayer by St. John Newman:

Dear Jesus, help me to spread your fragrance everywhere I go. Flood my soul with your spirit and life. Penetrate my being so that all my life may only be a radiance of you.

Shine through me, and so be in me that every person I come in contact with may feel your presence in my soul. Let them look and see no longer me, but only Jesus.

Stay with me, and then I shall begin to shine as you shine, so to be a light to others. The light, O Jesus, will be all from you; none of it will be mine. It will be you shining on others through me.

Let me thus praise you in the way you love best, by shining on those around me.

The words of this prayer dynamically reflect the goal of a discerning heart: to allow God's loving presence to so flood the inner and outer realities of our life that others can see only God shining through us.

# Appendix

## 313. Rules for Discernment of St. Ignatius of Loyola

### Rules for the Discernment of Spirits*

### Week 1

*Rules for understanding to some extent the different movements produced in the soul and for recognizing those that are good to admit them, and those that are bad, to reject them. These rules are more suited to the first week.*

314.1. In the case of those who go from one mortal sin to another, the enemy is ordinarily accustomed to propose apparent pleasures. He fills their imagination with sensual delights and gratifications, the more readily to keep them in their vices and increase the number of their sins.

With such persons the good spirit uses a method which is the reverse of the above. Making use of the light of reason, he will rouse the sting of conscience and fill them with remorse.

315.2. In the case of those who go on earnestly striving to cleanse their souls from sin and who seek to rise in the service of God our Lord to greater perfection, the method pursued is the opposite of that mentioned in the first rule.

Then it is characteristic of the evil spirit to harass with anxiety, to afflict with sadness, to raise obstacles backed by fallacious reasonings that disturb the soul. Thus he seeks to prevent the soul from advancing.

It is characteristic of the good spirit, however, to give courage and strength, consolations, tears, inspirations, and peace. This He does by making all easy, by removing all obstacles so that the soul goes forward in doing good.

---

*Source: Louis J. Puhl, S.J., *The Spiritual Exercises of St. Ignatius* (Chicago: Loyola University Press, 1951), 141–50.

316.3. *Spiritual Consolation.* I call it consolation when an interior movement is aroused in the soul, by which it is inflamed with love of its Creator and Lord, and as a consequence, can love no creature on the face of the earth for its own sake, but only in the Creator of them all. It is likewise consolation when one sheds tears that move to the love of God, whether it be because of sorrow for sins, or because of the sufferings of Christ our Lord, or for any other reason that is immediately directed to the praise and service of God. Finally, I call consolation every increase of faith, hope and love, and all interior joy that invites and attracts to what is heavenly and to the salvation of one's soul by filling it with peace and quiet in its Creator and Lord.

317.4. *Spiritual Desolation.* I call it desolation what is entirely the opposite of what is described in the third rule, as darkness of soul, turmoil of spirit, inclination to what is low and earthly, restlessness rising from many disturbances and temptations which lead to want of faith, want of hope, want of love. The soul is wholly slothful, tepid, sad, and separated, as it were, from its Creator and Lord. For just as consolation is the opposite of desolation, so the thoughts that spring from consolation are the opposite of those that spring from desolation.

318.5. In time of desolation we should never make any change, but remain firm and constant in the resolution and decision which guided us the day before the desolation, or in the decision to which we adhered in the preceding consolation. For just as in consolation the good spirit guides and counsels us, so in desolation the evil spirit guides and counsels. Following his counsels we can never find the way to a right decision.

319.6. Though in desolation we must never change our former resolutions, it will be very advantageous to intensify our activity against the desolation. We can insist more upon prayer, upon meditation, and on much examination of ourselves. We can make an effort in a suitable way to do some penance.

320.7. When one is in desolation, he should be mindful that God has left him to his natural powers to resist the different agitations and temptations of the enemy in order to try him. He can resist with the help of God, which always remains, though he may not clearly perceive it. For though God has taken from him the abundance of fervor and overflowing love and the intensity of His favors, nevertheless, he has sufficient grace for eternal salvation.

321.8. When one is in desolation, he should strive to persevere in patience. This reacts against the vexations that have overtaken him. Let him consider, too, that consolation will soon return, and in the meantime, he must diligently use the means against desolation which have been given in the sixth rule.

322.9. The principal reasons why we suffer from desolation are three:

The first is because we have been tepid and slothful or negligent in our exercises of piety, and so through our own fault spiritual consolation has been taken away from us.

The second reason is because God wishes to try us, to see how much we are worth, and how much we will advance in His service and praise when left without the generous reward of consolations and signal favors.

The third reason is because God wishes to give us a true knowledge and understanding of ourselves, so that we may have an intimate perception of the fact that it is not within our power to acquire and attain great devotion, intense love, tears, or any other spiritual consolation; but that all this is the gift and grace of God our Lord. God does not wish us to build on the property of another, to rise up in spirit in a certain pride and vainglory and attribute to ourselves the devotion and other effects of spiritual consolation.

323.10. When one enjoys consolation, let him consider how he will conduct himself during the time of ensuing desolation, and store up a supply of strength as defense against that day.

324.11. He who enjoys consolation should take care to humble himself and lower himself as much as possible. Let him recall how little he is able to do in time of desolation, when he is left without such grace or consolation.

On the other hand, one who suffers desolation should remember that by making use of the sufficient grace offered him, he can do much to withstand all his enemies. Let him find his strength in his Creator and Lord.

325.12. The enemy conducts himself as a woman. He is a weakling before a show of strength, and a tyrant if he has his will. It is characteristic of a woman in a quarrel with a man to lose courage and take to flight if the man shows that he is determined and fearless. However, if the man loses courage and begins to flee, the anger, vindictiveness, and rage of the woman surge up and know no bounds. In the same way, the enemy becomes weak, loses courage, and turns to flight with his seductions as soon as one leading a spiritual life faces his temptations boldly and does exactly the opposite of what he suggests. However, if one begins to be afraid and lose courage in temptations, no wild animal on earth can be more fierce than the enemy of our human nature. He will carry out his perverse intentions with consummate malice.

326.13. Our enemy may also be compared in his manner of acting to a false lover. He seeks to remain hidden and does not want to be discovered. If such a lover speaks with evil intention to the daughter of a good father, or to the wife of a good husband, and seeks to seduce them, he wants his words and solicitations kept secret. He is greatly displeased if his evil suggestions and depraved intentions are revealed by the daughter to her father, or by the wife to her husband. Then he readily sees he will not succeed in what he has begun. In the same way, when the enemy of our human nature tempts a just soul with his wiles and seductions, he earnestly desires that they be received secretly and kept secret. But if one manifests them to a confessor, or to some other spiritual person who understands his deceits and malicious designs, the evil one is very much vexed. For he knows that he cannot succeed in his evil undertaking once his evident deceits have been revealed.

327.14. The conduct of our enemy may also be compared to the tactics of a leader intent upon seizing and plundering a position he desires. A commander and leader of an army will encamp, explore the fortifications and defenses of the stronghold, and attack at the weakest point. In the same way, the enemy of our human nature investigates from every side all our virtues, theological, cardinal, and moral. Where he finds the defenses of eternal salvation weakest and most deficient, there he attacks and tries to take us by storm.

## 328. Rules for Discernment of Spirits

### Week 2

*Further rules for understanding the different movements produced in the soul. They serve for a more accurate discernment of spirits and are more suitable for the second week.*

329.1.  It is characteristic of God and His Angels, when they act upon the soul, to give true happiness and spiritual joy and to banish all the sadness and disturbances which are caused by the enemy. It is characteristic of the evil one to fight against such happiness and consolation by proposing fallacious reasonings, subtleties, and continual deceptions.

330.2.  God alone can give consolation to the soul without any previous cause. It belongs solely to the Creator to come into a soul, to leave it, to act upon it, to draw it wholly to the love of His Divine Majesty. I said without previous cause, that is, without any preceding perception or knowledge of any subject by which a soul might be led to such a consolation through its own acts of intellect and will.

331.3.  If a cause precedes, both the good angel and the evil spirit can give consolation to a soul, but for a quite different purpose. The good angel consoles for the progress of the soul, that it may advance and rise to what is more perfect. The evil spirit consoles for purposes that are the contrary and that afterwards he might draw the soul to his own perverse intentions and wickedness.

332.4.  It is a mark of the evil spirit to assume the appearance of an angel of light. He begins by suggesting thoughts that are suited to a devout soul and ends by suggesting his own. For example, he will suggest holy and pious thoughts that are wholly in conformity with the sanctity of the soul. Afterwards, he will endeavor little by little to end by drawing the soul into his hidden snares and designs.

333.5.  We must carefully observe the whole course of our thoughts. If the beginning and middle and end of the course of thoughts are wholly good and directed to what is entirely right, it is a sign that they are from the good angel. But the course of thoughts suggested to us may terminate in something evil, or distracting, or less good than the soul had formerly proposed to do. Again, it may end in what weakens the soul, or disquiets it; or by destroying the peace, tranquility, and quiet which it had before, it may cause disturbance to the soul. These things are a clear sign that the thoughts are proceeding from the evil spirit, the enemy of our progress and eternal salvation.

334.6.  When the enemy of our human nature has been detected and recognized by the trail of evil marking his course and by the wicked end to which he leads us, it will be profitable for one who has been tempted to review immediately the whole course of the temptation. Let him consider the series of good thoughts, how they arose, how the evil one gradually attempted to make him step down from the state of spiritual delight and joy in which he was, till finally he drew him to his wicked designs. The purpose of this review is that once such an experience has been understood and carefully observed, we may guard ourselves for the future against the customary deceits of the enemy.

335.7.  In souls that are progressing to greater perfection, the action of the good angel is delicate, gentle, delightful. It may be compared to a drop of water penetrating a sponge.

The action of the evil spirit upon such souls is violent, noisy, and disturbing. It may be compared to a drop of water falling upon a stone.

In souls that are going from bad to worse, the action of the spirits mentioned above is just the reverse. The reason for this is to be sought in the opposition or similarity of these souls to the different kinds of spirits. When the disposition is contrary to that of the spirits, they enter with noise and commotion that are easily perceived. When the disposition is similar to that of the spirits, they enter silently, as one coming into his own house when the doors are open.

336.8.  When consolation is without previous cause, as was said, there can be no deception in it, since it can proceed from God our Lord only. But a spiritual person who has received such a consolation must consider it very attentively and must cautiously distinguish the actual time of the consolation from the period which follows it. At such a time the soul is still fervent and favored with the grace and aftereffects of the consolation which has passed. In this second period the soul frequently forms various resolutions and plans which are not granted directly by God our Lord. They may come from our own reasoning on the relations of our concepts and on the consequences of our judgments, or they may come from the good or evil spirit. Hence, they must be carefully examined before they are given full approval and put into execution.

# Notes

## Introduction

[1] The *Spiritual Exercises* were written by St. Ignatius of Loyola during the sixteenth century. There have been many translations since then.

I will make references to the *Spiritual Exercises* throughout the book, so its specific contents will unfold as I proceed. However, a general description of this classic work of spirituality is in order. The *Spiritual Exercises* offers prayer exercises to help people grow in their relationship with God, it describes various dynamics that take place interiorly as people relate with God affectively, and it provides clear guidelines for decision making in a prayerful context.

[2] The Rules are found in the *Spiritual Exercises of St. Ignatius,* paragraphs 313–36. I use two translations: David L. Fleming, *The Spiritual Exercises of St. Ignatius: A Literal Translation and a Contemporary Reading* (St. Louis, Mo.: Institute of Jesuit Sources, 1978) and Louis J. Puhl, S.J., trans., *The Spiritual Exercises of St. Ignatius* (Chicago: Loyola University Press, 1951).

The term *rules* can have a rigid connotation that implies that one must obey these rules in order to discern. By Rules, Ignatius means "observations" or "descriptions" of what happens in people when they experience God. Jules J. Toner remarks:

> That content (referring to Rules) is . . . simply a description or explanation of spiritual experience, or a statement of norms for judging such experience. When directives are given, they are like all else in the *Spiritual Exercises,* flexible and adaptable to each individual person and situation. See Jules J. Toner, S.J., *A Commentary on Saint Ignatius' Rules for the Discernment of Spirits* (St. Louis, Mo.: Institute of Jesuit Sources, 1982), 9.

Since most people familiar with the Rules understand them in this latter meaning of "observations" or "norms," I use Ignatius' own term throughout the book.

[3] In addition to examining the Rules for Discernment, I also explore the Annotations or Introductory Observations found in

the *Spiritual Exercises of St. Ignatius,* paragraphs 1–20. The Annotations are notes for spiritual directors to assist directees grow in a personal relationship with God. They also suggest ways in which the director can use the Rules to facilitate individual experiences of prayer.

⁴ Louis J. Puhl, *Spiritual Exercises,* 332.

⁵ Ibid., 317, 319–22.

⁶ The following are a few of the many examples of the theological, textual, and contextual approaches to the Rules. Although stating that his book is a "practical theology," Jules J. Toner mostly examines the meaning of the Rules in relation to Christian tradition, in the context of other aspects of the *Spiritual Exercises,* and in relation to the text of the Rules themselves (Toner, *Commentary on Saint Ignatius' Rules for the Discernment of Spirits,* 20). Implicitly he may be writing from his experience of being a spiritual director, but he makes little explicit reference to direction experiences.

Harvey D. Egan, S.J., explores some aspects of the Rules from a foundational perspective and in the environment of the *Spiritual Exercises.* See Harvey D. Egan, S.J., *The Spiritual Exercises and Ignatian Mystical Horizon* (St. Louis, Mo.: Institute of Jesuit Sources, 1976).

John Sheets writes a theology of discernment of Spirits, emphasizing the role of the Holy Spirit from different perspectives, such as eschatological Spirit or Spirit of Truth. See John Sheets, "Profile of the Spirit: A Theology of Discernment of Spirits," *Review for Religious* 30, no. 3 (May 1971): 363–76.

⁷ Two examples are Chris Aridas, *Discernment: Seeking God in Every Situation* (New York: Living Flame Press, 1981) and John Carroll Futrell, S.J., "Ignatian Discernment," *Studies in the Spirituality of Jesuits* II, no. 2 (April 1970).

⁸ There are many examples of this in Ignatius' *Autobiography.* I refer to some of these in this book. See Joseph F. O'Callaghan, trans., *The Autobiography of St. Ignatius of Loyola* (New York: Harper and Row, 1974) and William J. Young, S.J., trans., *St. Ignatius' Own Story* (Chicago: Loyola University Press, 1980). Also, aspects of Ignatius' numerous letters reflect the dynamics of the Rules.

⁹ Louis J. Puhl, *Spiritual Exercises,* 316, 330.

¹⁰ Ibid., 313.

## Chapter 1

[1] William J. Young, *St. Ignatius' Own Story*, 3–4.

[2] Ibid., 4.

[3] Ibid., 69.

[4] Ibid., 7–11. I left out some of the less pertinent circumstantial facts, as not to make the story too long. The boldfacing is my emphasis. I do so to highlight some key inner aspects of Ignatius' experience.

[5] Karl Rahner, S.J. and Paul Imhof, S.J., *Ignatius of Loyola* (New York: Collins, 1978), 49.

[6] Ignatius' personal relationship with God evolved in the environment of his life experience. A severe physical illness, recuperating in bed, and reading about God were the life circumstances that God used to draw Ignatius into an inner spiritual journey. Ignatius already was a person of religious practices, as he prayed to the saints and went to confession. However, his heart, mind, and behavior were permeated with the things of the world and not with the realities of God. In telling his story, Ignatius often indicates that it was through God's assistance that he was physically healed and spiritually changed. Although not yet having an explicit sense of God in his twenty-sixth year, Ignatius did experience God implicitly, affectively, gradually, and quietly working within him. The differences in his felt reactions revealed that something significant was happening to him interiorly.

So too the *Spiritual Exercises* are grounded in life experience. For instance, in the Annotations, Ignatius states that the *Spiritual Exercises* must be adapted according to individual differences of spiritual readiness, age, education, talent, and life circumstances (4, 9, 18, 19). The Five Exercises of the First Week continuously remind individuals of their past and present life experience and the effect that sin has upon it. In the Contemplations of the Second, Third, and Fourth Weeks, Ignatius encourages us to place ourselves in scriptural events so that our life experience can be connected to and affected by Jesus' experience of life on earth. The grounding of the *Spiritual Exercises* in our lives, then, has its origin in Ignatius' conversion experience that takes place in the context of his life circumstances.

[7] William J. Young, *St. Ignatius' Own Story*, 4.

[8] Ignatius' encouragement of the use of repetition has its beginnings in his conversion experience. *Repetition* for Ignatius means

that "we should pay attention to and dwell upon those points in which we have experienced greater consolation or desolation or greater spiritual appreciation" (Puhl; 62, 118). In consolation, repetition is a way to savor, relish, and deepen God's action in our hearts and lives. In desolation, it is a way to examine thoughts and feelings that are hiding an inordinate attachment that prevents us from following Jesus more completely.

Repetition spontaneously occurred while Ignatius lay in bed, pausing and thinking about things he had read, dwelling on something for hours at a time, and experiencing various thoughts and affections as a result of this lingering. Ignatius suggests this type of prayer throughout the *Spiritual Exercises* as a way to allow interior movements to occur and to open the self to greater awareness and freedom.

⁹ During the conversion experience, Ignatius' total humanity was affected. "Thoughts" refers not only to understanding with his mind ("he acquired no little light from this reading") but also indicates the use of his imagination ("the succession of diverse thoughts . . . took hold of his imagination to such an extent"), the affections of his heart ("took possession of his heart"; "thinking . . . was filled with delight, left dry and dissatisfied"), his desires ("desires of imitating the saints"), and his behavior ("great need to do penance, undertake disciplines and abstinence"). Ignatius' total humanness was affected by this experience.

In turn, the *Spiritual Exercises* affect our total humanness. Suggested ways of praying can unify the various dimensions of our humanity. The First Exercise encourages us to use the three powers of the soul—"memory to recall . . . , understanding to think over the matter in more detail . . . , and the will to rouse more deeply the emotions" (50, 51). The Grace and Colloquy are related to desire while the Contemplation of the Second, Third, and Fourth Weeks suggests the use of the imagination, our exterior and interior senses, and a change in behavior.

¹⁰ In the atmosphere of interior motions, Ignatius experienced heart-changing and life-changing effects. Choices and actions already began to flow from undergoing and realizing different affective reactions. For instance, while people were living in his household, he devoted his time to the things of God that "brought profit to their souls." He did more spiritual reading and wrote down things that moved him. He grew in a strong desire to serve God, and he considered certain life-styles that would enable him to live a life of perpetual penance. Thus, the Ways of Election in the *Spiritual Exercises* were already operative in his experience.

Luis González de Camara declares: "The forms of election in particular, he told me, came from that variety of movement of spirits and thoughts which he experienced at Loyola, while he was still convalescing from his shattered leg." (William J. Young, *St. Ignatius' Own Story*, 69).

[11] Louis J. Puhl, *Spiritual Exercises*, 313.

[12] Jules J. Toner, *Commentary on Rules*, 22. Toner writes: "In various Ignatian writings, *sentir* indicates cognition savored so repeatedly that it becomes a framework of reference instinctively or affectively used to guide one's thinking, deciding, and acting."

[13] John Futrell, "Ignatian Discernment," *Studies in the Spirituality of Jesuits*, II, no. 2 (April 1970), 56–57.

[14] Jules J. Toner, *Commentary on Rules*, 49–70. Toner uses the phrase "spiritually regressing" to describe people who are in a 314 stance and "spiritually maturing" for those in a 315 posture.

## Chapter 2

[1] William J. Young, *St. Ignatius' Own Story*, 13–14.

[2] Ibid., 14.

[3] Ibid.

[4] Ibid.

[5] Ibid., 14–15.

[6] Ibid., 17.

[7] Ibid., 17–18.

[8] Ibid., 18.

[9] Ibid.

[10] Ibid.

[11] Ibid.

[12] Ibid., 18–19.

[13] Ibid., 19–21.

## Chapter 3

[1] William J. Young, *St. Ignatius' Own Story*, 22.

[2] Ibid., 18–19.

[3] Ibid., 22–24.

[4] Ibid., 17–24.

[5] Harvey D. Egan, S.J., in *The New Dictionary of Catholic Spirituality* (Collegeville, Minn.: The Liturgical Press, 1993), 522–23.

[6] Ibid., 21.

[7] Ibid., 39–40.

[8] Ibid., 57.

## Chapter 4

[1] Jean Laclercq, O.S.B., *The Love of Learning and the Desire for God* (New York: Fordham University Press, 1974), 7:

> A canticle of this kind (Canticle of Canticles), fervor alone can teach; it can be learned only through experience. Those who have experienced it will recognize this. Those who have not experienced it, may they burn with desire not so much "to know" as "to experience."

[2] Ibid., 41.

[3] David L. Fleming, *Spiritual Exercises,* 15.

[4] Mark 5:25–34, *The New American Bible* (New York: Thomas Nelson. Inc., 1971).

[5] Bernard of Clairvaux, *On the Song of Songs,* Vol. IV (Kalamazoo, Mich.: Cistercian Publications, 1976), 91.

[6] David L. Fleming, *Spiritual Exercises,* 3.

[7] Ibid., 120–25.

[8] Bernard of Clairvaux, *On the Song of Songs,* Vol. IV, 91.

[9] Ibid., 91–92.

[10] Joseph F. O'Callaghan, *Autobiography of St. Ignatius,* 24.

[11] Ibid.

[12] Ibid., 30.

[13] Ibid., 33.

[14] Ibid.

[15] Ibid., 34.

[16] Julian of Norwich, *Showings,* Edmund Colledge and James Walsh, trans. (New York: Paulist Press, 1978), 139–40.

[17] For a good explanation of human desires in relation to God, see E. Edwark Kinerk, S.J., "Eliciting Great Desires: Their Place in the Spirituality of the Society of Jesus," *Studies in the Spirituality of Jesuits* XVI, no. 5 (November 1984).

[18] Leonardo Boff, *Liberating Grace* (New York: Orbis Books), 44.

[19] Jean Laclercq, *The Love of Learning and the Desire for God,* 40.

[20] Ibid., 85.

[21] David L. Fleming, *Spiritual Exercises,* 5.

[22] Harvey D. Egan refers to the grace of the Four Weeks—"what I want and desire"—as the "backbone of the Exercises":

> The clear, simple and explicitly conscious desire of what one really wants, especially when this flows from the salvific effects of each meditation, purifies the exercitant of his inordinate affections by awakening him to the deepest desires of his true self (*Ignatian Mystical Horizon,* 74–75).

[23] Ephesians 3:18, *The New American Bible.*

[24] See "The So-called Letter to Diognetus" in *Early Christian Fathers* 1, trans. and ed. Cyril C. Richardson (Philadelphia: Westminister Press, 1953), sec. 10, 221–22. This letter declares:

> For God has loved people. He has created the world for them. He has subjected to them everything that exists on earth. He has given them reason and intelligence . . . He has formed them in His image. He has sent them His own Son. He has promised them the kingdom of heaven . . .

[25] Isaiah 43:4, *The New American Bible.*

[26] David L. Fleming, *Spiritual Exercises,* 1. We engage in spiritual exercises "as ways of preparing and disposing the soul to rid itself of all the disordered tendencies, and after it is rid, to seek and find the Divine Will as to the management of one's life for the salvation of the soul."

[27] Jean Laclercq, *The Love of Learning and the Desire for God*, 38, quoting from St. Gregory the Great in *Moralia*, 32, I. See also, *Spiritual Exercises*: ". . . the good spirit uses the opposite method, pricking them and biting their consciences through the process of reason" (David L. Fleming, 314).

[28] Jean Laclercq, *The Love of Learning and the Desire for God*, 40, 42, quoting from St. Gregory the Great on Ezekiel.

[29] Bernard of Clairveaux, *On the Song of Songs*, Vol. IV, 91.

[30] Louis J. Puhl, *Spiritual Exercises*, 48, 55, 65.

[31] Louis J. Puhl, *Spiritual Exercises*, 104.

[32] Ibid. In several places in the *Spiritual Exercises*, Ignatius speaks about God "laboring" for us, and God and ourselves "laboring" together. Three examples follow: "This is to consider how God works and labors for me in all creatures upon the face of the earth, that is, He conducts Himself as one who labors" (Louis J. Puhl, *Spiritual Exercises*, 236); "Therefore, whoever wishes to join with me in this enterprise . . . must work with me by day, . . . that as he has had a share in the toil with me, afterwards, he may share in the victory with me" (Puhl, *Spiritual Exercises*, 93); and ". . . Whoever wishes to join me in this enterprise must be willing to labor with me . . . " (Puhl, *Spiritual Exercises*, 95).

[33] "The So-called Letter to Diognetus" in Cyril C. Richardson, *Early Christian Fathers*, 221–22. Ignatius' own experience of God instilled in him a desire to serve God in specific ways; for example, he cites an instance when he gave his clothes to a poor man (Joseph F. O'Callaghan, *The Autobiography of St. Ignatius of Loyola*, 32).

[34] Louis J. Puhl, *Spiritual Exercises*, 193, 203. Our suffering with Jesus is an essential aspect of the Third Week (190–209). Our willingness to suffer with Jesus is also referred to in the third degree of humility:

> . . . in order to imitate and be in reality more like Christ our Lord, I desire and choose poverty with Christ poor, rather than riches, insults with Christ loaded with them, rather than honors; I desire to be accounted as worthless and a fool for Christ, rather than to be esteemed as wise and prudent in this world. So Christ was treated before me (Louis J. Puhl, *Spiritual Exercises*, 167).

See William J. Connolly, S.J., "Experiences of Darkness in Directed Retreats," *Review for Religious* 33 (1974): 609–615. Connolly clearly develops the difference in the experience of darkness during the First Week and Third Week of the *Spiritual Exercises*.

[35] Louis J. Puhl, *Spiritual Exercises*, 21. See also 218–29, for a full description of the Fourth Week.

[36] Thomas N. Hart, *The Art of Christian Listening* (New York: Paulist Press, 1980), 27–28.

[37] Contemplation to Attain the Love of God is a synthesizing exercise that helps the retreatant to find God in all aspects of reality (Louis J. Puhl, *Spiritual Exercises*, 230–37).

[38] Leonardo Boff, *Liberating Grace*, 40.

[39] St. Irenaeus, "Against the Heretics" in Cyril C. Richardson, *Early Christian Fathers*, 343–97.

## Chapter 5

[1] See William A. Barry and William J. Connolly, *The Practice of Spiritual Direction* (New York: Seabury Press, 1982), 8. In my practice of spiritual direction, I take a contemplative approach as described throughout the book. The following excerpt from Barry and Connolly is a description of such an approach:

> We define Christian spiritual direction, then as help given by one Christian to another which enables that person to pay attention to God's personal communication to him or her, to respond to this personally communicating God, to grow in intimacy with this God, and live out the consequences of the relationship. The focus of this type of spiritual direction is on experience, not ideas, and specifically on religious experience . . . Religious experience is to spiritual direction what foodstuff is to cooking. Without foodstuff there can be no cooking. Without religious experience there can be no spiritual direction.

[2] For a more complete description of the spiritual direction relationship and atmosphere, see Maureen Conroy, *Growing in Love and Freedom: Personal Experiences of Counseling and Spiritual Direction* (Denville, N.J.: Dimension Books, 1987).

[3] Alan Jones, *Exploring Spiritual Direction: An Essay on Christian Friendship* (New York: Seabury Press, 1982), 39.

[4] See Maureen Conroy, "A Life-Giving Presence: An Analogy between Spiritual Direction and Midwifery," *Sisters Today* (June 1989), 607–14. In this article, I describe in detail how a spiritual director is like a midwife.

[5] James J. Gill, S.J., M.D., "Empathy Is at the Heart of Love," *Human Development* 3, no. 3 (Fall 1982): 31.

[6] Thomas N. Hart, *The Art of Christian Listening,* 18.

[7] Ibid.

[8] Transference occurs when a directee reacts to the director based on an experience or image derived from one's childhood. Countertransference is when a director overreacts to a directee because of a childhood experience. For a description of how transference and countertransference can be operative in a spiritual direction relationship, see William A. Barry and William J. Connolly, *The Practice of Spiritual Direction,* 155–74. For a description of resistance in spiritual direction, see 80–100.

[9] Barry and Connolly, *The Practice of Spiritual Direction,* 76.

[10] Joseph F. O'Callaghan, *The Autobiography of St. Ignatius of Loyola,* 23–24.

[11] David L. Fleming, *Spiritual Exercises,* 4.

[12] Ibid., 11.

[13] Ibid., 8.

[14] Ibid., 9.

[15] Louis J. Puhl, *Spiritual Exercises,* 62; see also, 118.

[16] David L. Fleming, *Spiritual Exercises,* 2.

[17] Ibid.

[18] Ibid., 15.

[19] In the various verbatim excerpts I use examples that clearly demonstrate directors being concretely evocative in their responses. However, as the directee *internalizes* this "evocative approach," frequently all the director needs to do is to provide an "evocative presence." That is, as directees grow in their ability to notice and talk about God's presence and their interior reactions,

directors do not need to *explicitly* evoke as much. For instance, directees may describe in depth the fullness of their felt reaction to God's acceptance ("I felt joyful, at one with God, loved, free . . . ") for a half hour without the director saying a word, but it is the director who provides a caring and interested presence that enables the directee to be "self-evocative."

[20] Ignatius refers to this reciprocity in the Contemplation to Gain Love:

> . . . love consists in a mutual sharing of goods. For example, a lover gives and shares with the beloved something of his personal gifts or some possession which he has or is able to give; so, too, the beloved shares with the beloved . . . (David L. Fleming, *Spiritual Exercises*), 231.

[21] Ibid., 7.

## Chapter 6

[1] See the following article for examples of prayer experiences rooted in the kataphatic mode: Maureen Conroy, R.S.M., "A Dwelling Place: Images and Our Experience of God," *Studies in Formative Spirituality* VI, no. 1 (February 1985): 11–27.

[2] William A. Barry and William J. Connolly, *The Practice of Spiritual Direction*, 99. Barry and Connolly are the first ones to use the terms *movement* and *countermovement* to describe progression toward God and resistance to God and prayer.

## Chapter 8

[1] Harvey D. Egan, *Ignatian Mystical Horizon*, 76.

[2] Ibid.

[3] Jules J. Toner, *Commentary on Rules*, 138.

[4] Ibid.

[5] Ibid.

[6] Ibid.

## Chapter 9

[1] Harvey D. Egan, *Ignatian Mystical Horizon*, 55.

[2] Herve Coathalem, S.J., *Ignatian Insights* (Taichung, Taiwan: Kuangchi Press, 1971), 270–71. Coathalem writes: "Ignatius treats here of a spiritual consolation of a very high form, and rare in occurrence . . . " I agree with Egan rather than Coathalem. It is Coathalem who views CWPC as a rare phenomenon.

[3] Karl Rahner in Harvey D. Egan, *Ignatian Mystical Horizon,* 32.

[4] Letter to Sister Teresa Rejadell in William J. Young, S.J., trans., *Letters of St. Ignatius of Loyola* (Chicago: Loyola University Press, 1959), 21–22.

[5] Harvey D. Egan, *Ignatian Mystical Horizon,* 31.

[6] Ibid.

[7] Ibid., 35.

[8] Ibid.

[9] Ibid., 57.

[10] Ibid.

[11] Ibid., 61.

[12] Ibid., 51.

[13] Ibid., 40.

[14] Ibid., 57.

[15] Ibid., 49.

[16] Ibid., 32–33.

[17] Ibid., 31.

## Chapter 10

[1] Jules J. Toner, *Commentary on Rules,* 104–5.

## Chapter 11

[1] Hugo Rahner, *Ignatius the Theologian* (New York: Herder and Herder, 1968), 196.

[2] Joseph F. O'Callaghan, *Autobiography of St. Ignatius of Loyola,* 38.

[3] Ibid., 47.

[4] Hugo Rahner, *Ignatius the Theologian,* 190–211.

5 Ibid., 197. Rahner is quoting a letter from Ignatius. *Monumenta Ignatiana*, I, 1, 105: 18 July 1536.

6 Ibid., 202. Rahner is quoting St. Bonaventure from *Itinerarium mentis im Deum*, chap. 4.

7 Joseph F. O'Callaghan, *Autobiography of St. Ignatius of Loyola*, 55.

8 William J. Young, *St. Ignatius' Own Story*, 75.

9 This relates to God's desire to give of Self as described in the Contemplation to Attain the Love of God:

> I will ponder with great affection how much God our Lord has done for me, how much He has given me of what He possesses, and finally, how much, as far as He can, the same Lord desires to give Himself to me . . . (Louis J. Puhl, *Spiritual Exercises*, 234).

10 Harvey D. Egan, *Ignatian Mystical Horizon*, 56 (my change to feminine pronoun).

# Bibliography

Aridas, Chris. *Discernment: Seeking God in Every Situation*. New York: Living Flame Press, 1981.

Barry, William A., and Connolly, William J. *The Practice of Spiritual Direction*. New York: Seabury Press, 1982.

Bernard of Clairvaux. *On the Song of Songs*, Vol IV. Kalamazoo, Mich.: Cistercian Publications, 1976.

Boff, Leonardo. *Liberating Grace*. New York: Orbis Books, 1979.

Coathalem, Herve, S.J. *Ignatian Insights*. Taichung, Taiwan: Kuangchi Press, 1971.

Connolly, William J., S.J. "Experiences of Darkness in Directed Retreats." *Review for Religious* 33, (1974).

Conroy, Maureen, R.S.M. "A Dwelling Place: Images and Our Experience of God." *Studies in Formative Spirituality* VI, no. 1 (February 1985): 11–27.

———. *Growing in Love and Freedom: Personal Experiences of Counseling and Spiritual Direction*. Denville, N.J.: Dimension Books, 1987.

———. "A Life-Giving Presence: An Analogy Between Spiritual Direction and Midwifery," *Sisters Today* (June 1989).

Egan, Harvey D., S.J. *The Spiritual Exercises and Ignatian Mystical Horizon*. St. Louis, Mo.: Institute of Jesuit Sources, 1976.

———. "Ignatian Spirituality." *The New Dictionary of Catholic Spirituality*. Collegeville, Minn.: The Liturgical Press, 1993.

Fleming, David L. *The Spiritual Exercises of St. Ignatius: A Literal Translation and a Contemporary Reading*. St. Louis, Mo.: Institute of Jesuit Sources, 1978.

Futrell, John Carroll, S.J. "Ignatian Discernment." *Studies in the Spirituality of Jesuits* II, no. 3 (May 1971).

Gill, James J., S.J., M.D. "Empathy Is at the Heart of Love." *Human Development* 3, no. 3 (Fall 1982).

Hart, Thomas N. *The Art of Christian Listening.* New York: Paulist Press, 1980.

Jones, Alan. *Exploring Spiritual Direction: An Essay on Christian Friendship.* New York: Seabury Press, 1982.

Julian of Norwich. *Showings.* Edmund Colledge and James Walsh, trans. New York: Paulist Press, 1978.

Kinerk, Edward, S.J. "Eliciting Great Desires: Their Place in the Spirituality of the Society of Jesus." *Studies in the Spirituality of Jesuits* XVI, no. 5 (November 1984).

Laclercq, Jean, O.S.B. *The Love of Learning and the Desire for God.* New York: Fordham University Press, 1974.

O'Callaghan, Joseph F., trans. *The Autobiography of St. Ignatius of Loyola.* New York: Harper and Row, 1974.

Puhl, Louis J., S.J., trans. *The Spiritual Exercises of St. Ignatius.* Chicago: Loyola University Press, 1951.

Rahner, Hugo, S.J. *Ignatius the Theologian.* New York: Herder and Herder, 1968.

Rahner, Karl, S.J., and Imhof, Paul, S.J. *Ignatius of Loyola.* New York: Collins, 1978.

Richardson, Cyril C., trans. and ed. "The So-called Letter to Diognetus." *Early Christian Fathers* I. Philadelphia: Westminister Press, 1953.

Sheets, John. "Profile of the Spirit: A Theology of Discernment of Spirits." *Review for Religious* 30, no. 3 (May 1971).

*The New American Bible.* New York: Thomas Nelson, Inc., 1971.

Toner, Jules J., S.J. *A Commentary on Saint Ignatius' Rules for the Discernment of Spirits.* St. Louis, Mo.: Institute of Jesuit Sources, 1982.

Young, William J., S.J., trans. *Letters of St. Ignatius of Loyola.* Chicago: Loyola University Press, 1959.

————. trans. *St. Ignatius' Own Story.* Chicago: Loyola University Press, 1980.

# Index